T0344080

THE BEST
NEW
TEN-MINUTE
PLAYS
2021

THE BEST NEW TEN-MINUTE PLAYS 2021

Edited and with an Introduction by
Lawrence Harbison

With a Comprehensive List of
Ten-Minute Play Producers

APPLAUSE
THEATRE & CINEMA BOOKS
Guilford, Connecticut

APPLAUSE
THEATRE & CINEMA BOOKS

An imprint of Globe Pequot, the trade division of
The Rowman & Littlefield Publishing Group, Inc.
4501 Forbes Blvd., Ste. 200
Lanham, MD 20706
ApplauseBooks.com

Distributed by NATIONAL BOOK NETWORK

British Library Cataloguing in Publication Information available

Library of Congress Cataloging-in-Publication Data

Names: Harbison, Lawrence, editor.
Title: The best new ten-minute plays, 2021 / edited with an introduction by
    Lawrence Harbison.
Description: Guilford, Connecticut : Applause, 2021.
Identifiers: LCCN 2021021974 (print) | LCCN 2021021975 (ebook) | ISBN
    9781493060450 (paperback) | ISBN 9781493060467 (epub)
Subjects: LCSH: One-act plays, American. | American drama—21st century. |
    LCGFT: One-act plays.
Classification: LCC PS627.O53 B38 2021 (print) | LCC PS627.O53 (ebook) |
    DDC 812/.04108—dc23
LC record available at https://lccn.loc.gov/2021021974
LC ebook record available at https://lccn.loc.gov/2021021975

♾™ The paper used in this publication meets the minimum requirements of American National Standard for Information Sciences—Permanence of Paper for Printed
Library Materials, ANSI/NISO Z39.48-1992

Contents

Introduction

In this volume, you will find thirty terrific new ten-minute plays. They are written in a variety of styles. Some are realistic plays; some are not. Some are comic (laughs); some are dramatic (no laughs). The ten-minute play form lends itself well to experimentation in style. A playwright can have fun with a device that couldn't be sustained as well in a longer play. Several of these plays employ such a device.

In years past, playwrights who were just starting out wrote one-act plays of thirty to forty minutes in duration. One thinks of writers such as Eugene O'Neill, A. R. Gurney, Lanford Wilson, John Guare, and several others. Now, new playwrights tend to work in the ten-minute play genre, largely because there are so many production opportunities. When I was senior editor for Samuel French, it occurred to me that there might be a market for these very short plays, which Actors Theatre of Louisville (ATL) had been commissioning for several years for use by their Apprentice Company. I made a deal with Jon Jory and Michael Bigelow Dixon of ATL, who assisted me in compiling an anthology of these plays, which sold so well that Samuel French went on to publish several more anthologies of ten-minute plays from Actors Theatre. For the first time, ten-minute plays were published and widely available, and they started getting produced. There are now many ten-minute play festivals every year, not only in the United States but all over the world. I have included a comprehensive list of theaters that do ten-minute plays, which I hope playwrights will find useful.

What makes a good ten-minute play? Well, first and foremost I have to like it. Isn't that what we mean when we call a play, a film, or a novel "good?" We mean that it effectively portrays the world *as I see it*, written in a style that interests *me*. Beyond this, a good ten-minute play has to have the same elements that *any* good play must have: a strong conflict, interesting, well-drawn characters, and compelling subject matter. It also has to have a clear beginning, middle, and end. In other words, it's a full-length play that runs about ten minutes. Some of the plays that are submitted to me each year are scenes, not complete plays; well-written scenes in many cases, but scenes nonetheless. They left me wanting more. I chose plays that are complete in and of themselves, which I believe will excite those of you who produce ten-minute plays; because if a play isn't produced, it's the proverbial sound of a tree falling in the forest far away.

This year, for the first time, Applause is the licensor for all the plays in this book. In order to acquire performance rights, on the title page of each play you will find a link to our licensing web page.

This year, there are new plays by masters of the ten-minute play form whose work has appeared in previous volumes in this series, such as Don Nigro, Jenny Lyn Bader, Jennifer O'Grady, and David MacGregor; but there are also many plays by wonderful playwrights who may be new to you, such as Hallie Palladino, Nandita Shenoy, Laurie Allen, John Bavoso, Gabrielle Fox, Connie Bennett, and Mildred Inez Lewis.

I hope you enjoy these plays. I sure did!

Lawrence Harbison

THE ARCHITECTURE OF DESIRE

by Brian Leahy Doyle

The Architecture of Desire was produced as part of The Secret Theatre's One Act Play Festival 2019. It was directed by Artie Rose and featured original music by Michael Dilthey. It was first performed on July 14, 2019, with subsequent performances on July 24, August 1, August 9, and August 17. Jessica Fornear was the production stage manager.

Cast List:
LINDSAY/OLGA/WOMAN #1: Justyna Kostek
CAMERON/THE WRITER: Max Wingert
DR. STANLEY OLIVER NUSSBAUM: Artie Rose
DR. HEATHER DUPRIS NUSSBAUM/WOMAN #2: Melene Sosi

Brian Leahy Doyle earned his MFA in theatre, with emphases in directing and dramaturgy, from the University of Utah, where he served as the first resident dramaturge of the Pioneer Theatre Company. Professional directing credits: Whole Theatre, Cincinnati Theatre Festival, Louisville's Classics in Context, Irish Arts Center, Riverside Shakespeare, the Open Eye, the 92nd Street Y/Makor, and the New York premiere of Pulitzer Prize-winning composer Aaron Jay Kernitz's *The Four Seasons of Futurist Cuisine* at Weill Recital Hall at Carnegie Hall. His book, *Encore! The Renaissance of Wisconsin Opera Houses*, published by the Wisconsin Historical Society Press, focuses upon the renovation and restoration of historic theaters in Wisconsin and has received the Theatre Historical Society of America's Outstanding Book of the Year Award, among other honors. His first full-length play, *Greetings from Fitzwalkerstan*, with music by Michael Dilthey, was produced at the Broom Street Theatre in Madison, Wisconsin, in January–February 2015. Produced by John Camera and directed by Wayne Maugans, Brian's second full-length play, *The Chancers!*, was given a staged reading at The Players in Manhattan in June 2016. Brian has also written the libretto to an opera, *The Weeping Woman*, also in collaboration with Michael Dilthey, which was performed at MASS MoCA in North Adams, Massachusetts, in August 2019. In November 2019, his third full-length play, *Light from the Pleiades*, was given a reading at The Players. He currently teaches at Mercy College.

CHARACTERS

LINDSAY, mid to late 20s or early 30s, an actress, ingénue type, pretty with a dramatic intensity when called for. In the opening scene she plays OLGA, the pampered, precocious, self-absorbed daughter of a Ukrainian oligarch. She will later play WOMAN #1.

CAMERON, mid to late 20s or early 30s, an actor, handsome, young leading man type. In the opening scene he plays JEAN-CLAUDE, a French-Basque academic who is struggling to complete a monograph on French novelist Marcel Proust. He will later play THE WRITER.

DR. STANLEY OLIVER NUSSBAUM, mid to late 30s or early 40s, a couples' sex therapist of dubious integrity, nerdy, and ingratiating.

DR. HEATHER DuPRIS NUSSBAM, late 30s, attractive and sensual, perhaps taller than her husband. She will later play WOMAN #2.

SETTING

A bare stage.

TIME

The present.

• • •

The stage is in total darkness. Then, gradually illuminated in a tight spot down stage right, we see OLGA, *her face contorted in agony.*

OLGA: Proust! Proust!! PROUST!!! I cannot endure another mention of twentieth-century French novelist Marcel Proust!

(*She emits an earwax-clearing primal scream. As the scream reaches its decrescendo, the lights come to full and reveal* JEAN-CLAUDE, *who is sitting on a trendy-looking couch and typing into a trendy-looking laptop computer, which sits on a trendy-looking table. As the dialogue will reveal, he is attempting to write a monograph on French novelist Marcel Proust. Beside* OLGA *is a fashionable carry-on rolling luggage, with a fashionable purse resting on top of the luggage. Both* OLGA *and* JEAN-CLAUDE *are dressed in identical, stylish, form-fitting outfits that reveal the lean, body fat-free physiques of people who are unfamiliar with such simple tasks as boiling an egg.*)

JEAN-CLAUDE: Olga, shut up, you stupid Russian bitch! Can you not see how I am trying to complete my monograph on the twentieth-century French novelist Marcel Proust?!

OLGA: I am not Russian! I am Ukrainian!

JEAN-CLAUDE: (*As he is typing.*) Same difference!

OLGA: Hah! Some genius intellectual you are! That's a tautology, Jean-Claude! You French-Spanish bastard!

JEAN-CLAUDE: It's an oxymoron, you Slavic moron! And besides, you well know that my mother's family is Basque, not Spanish! Once and for all, be quiet—or you will become for me a "remembrance of things past"!

OLGA: (*A look of frozen horror on her face.*) Are you threatening me?!

(JEAN-CLAUDE *sniffs, gives her a Gallic shrug of indifference, perhaps sips from a cup of coffee on the table, and resumes typing.* OLGA *becomes gradually more and more hysterical.*)

You *are* threatening me. How can you treat me with such callous, apathetic, impassive indifference after all I have given you—trips to Nice, this 4,500-square foot loft apartment in Soho, and a Roger Dubuis' Excalibur Spider watch with engraved strap and rubber inlays from certified Pirelli-winning tires that is also adorned with legendary tread motifs reproducing a profile of a Pirelli Cinturato intermediate tire, expertly manufactured in Switzerland from durable black titanium, fitted with an 820SQ caliber movement that everyone can see is hard at work through a skeleton dial and exhibition case, which I bought for your last birthday with money my *tata* gave me from laundering money through Deutsche Bank and the Trump Organization! How can you treat me so? Well? Well?!

JEAN-CLAUDE: (*Deep into his writing process.*) What's a synonym for "intransigent?"

(OLGA *suddenly goes berserk, screaming and muttering in gibberish Ukrainian. Without warning, she lunges at* JEAN-CLAUDE, *who pulls out a knife in order to defend himself. She freezes for a moment and then cautiously backs away from him. Brandishing the knife, he approaches her, a murderous glint in his eyes. Suddenly, she pulls a small revolver from out of her purse, an equally murderous glint in her eyes. They freeze in place, each with a look that could kill.*)

(*Lights dim center stage, and a spot comes up downstage left to reveal* NUSSBAUM. *He wears a white lab coat, black horn-rimmed glasses, and perhaps a bad comb-over or comparably bad haircut. He speaks in the stilted manner of someone reading cue cards for an infomercial. He holds a book by his side.*)

NUSSBAUM: Hi! I'm Dr. Stanley Oliver Nussbaum, noted couples' sex therapist. Friends, do you find yourself bringing a knife to a gunfight with your spouse or significant other when struggling to complete your monograph on twentieth-century French novelist Marcel Proust—or maybe that dissertation abstract on the mating rituals of the Agami heron, a Neotropical species of bird located in the following countries—Mexico, Guatemala, Belize, El Salvador, Honduras, Nicaragua, Costa Rica, Panama, Colombia, Ecuador, French Guiana, Suriname, Venezuela, Peru, Bolivia, *and* Brazil? Well, no more feeling lost once you purchase my book (*holding up his book*), *The Architecture of Desire*! For only $29.95 (tax, shipping, and handling not included), you'll learn my secrets on how to preserve and grow a loving relationship while completing that annotated bibliography! But wait there's more! (*He flips the book to reveal an 800 number.*)

Call the number appearing on your screen right now and sign up you and your loved one for one of my weekend couples' getaways where you'll learn even more healthy tips on how to integrate a burgeoning academic career with a sensuous, sensual relationship! Want to learn more? I'll bet you do! But, first, let's give our actors, Lindsay and Cameron, a rousing hand for their superb acting job as Olga and Jean-Claude!

(*He applauds, encouraging the audience to join him in the applause.* LINDSAY *and* CAMERON *break out of their freeze.* CAMERON *gestures grandly to* LINDSAY, *who performs a deep curtsy to the audience. Rising from her curtsy, she humbly acknowledges the audience, her hands crossing her upper chest, like a prima ballerina who's given the performance of a lifetime. Then* LINDSAY *gestures to* CAMERON, *who bows with dignity and grace, and when he rises from his bow, he holds her hands, gazes deeply into her eyes, and kisses her hands.*)

Weren't they just marvelous, or as you young people like to say, "really dope"? Okay, you kids "be chill" and get ready for our next presentation!

(LINDSAY *and* CAMERON *exit into the wings.* NUSSBAUM *returns to addressing the audience.*)

Before I go any further, ladies and gentlemen, I'd like to introduce my special someone, the person who got me through my dissertation—*The Domestication of the Volatile Emissions Produced by Male Queensland Fruit Flies During Sexual Advertisement*—the *sine* in my *qua non*, my lovely wife, the one and only Dr. Heather DuPris Nussbaum!

(HEATHER *enters onstage. While likewise wearing a lab coat and horn-rimmed glasses,* HEATHER *is clearly a beautiful, vivacious, sensuous, and voluptuous woman. Her hair is pulled back in a ponytail. She gazes at the audience, frequently. Her voice has a breathy, throaty quality. In short, she's a total knockout!*)

HEATHER: Hello darling! (*She kisses him passionately, perhaps holding him in a dip, and coming out of the kiss he staggers and stands limply for a moment. To the audience:*)

Hello everyone! What a pleasure it is to be here tonight and introduce you all to *The Architecture of Desire*! Act now and for only $1,799.95 paid in six monthly installments we will sign you and your loved one up for our Architecture of Desire Weekend Getaway in beautiful, sunny Kissimmee, Florida!

NUSSBAUM: Tax and handling fees not included! That's right, Heather! Sign up today, folks, and join us at the Kissimmee Ramada Inn for the Architecture of Desire Weekend Getaway! The salad bar is simply stellar!

HEATHER: My darlings, forget about tantric sex, nudist beaches, and gazing at sunsets in Sedona! The Architecture of Desire Weekend Getaway is the only tried and true couples' therapy that will unlock your writing of that monograph, that dissertation, or even—dare I say it!—that great American novel lying dormant in your subconscious. Or even that trendy, hip, insouciant ten-minute one-act play that will keep an audience of millennials so engaged that they won't dare look at their cell phones or deign to text!!! Darling, should we demonstrate?

NUSSBAUM: Yes, Heather, I think that Lindsay and Cameron should be ready! Sit back, folks, you're in for a treat!

(*He exits, followed by* HEATHER, *who gazes at the audience and then winks before exiting. Lights go to black.*)

(*Ethereal music should cover this transition. On a table exactly center is an open laptop computer. Stage left of the laptop there is a legal pad, preferably yellow, and a pen. Stage right of the laptop there is a white coffee cup resting on a white saucer. As the lights come up, we see the man's face caught in the glow of the laptop's monitor. It is an intelligent face, deep in concentration, perhaps frowning. He wears glasses. His lips moving, he is reading to himself what he has just written. He frowns. As the lights come to full, the man and the table are lit in a circle of light that extends out approximately five feet in all directions. The man, CAMERON as THE WRITER, stretches, yawns, and reaches for the coffee cup, which is empty. He frowns, thinks, and then types. LINDSAY as WOMAN #1 enters stage right, bearing a coffee pot and approaching the table cautiously. She wears glasses, her hair pulled back in a ponytail.*)

LINDSAY/WOMAN #1: More coffee, darling?

CAMERON/THE WRITER: (*Still typing.*) Please.

(*She pours.*)

CAMERON/THE WRITER: Thanks.

LINDSAY: How's it coming?

CAMERON: (*Still typing.*) Coming along.

LINDSAY: Need some company?

CAMERON: Uh, sure.

LINDSAY: You're sure?

CAMERON: Sure, yes, I'm sure.
(*Another pause. He continues typing.*)

LINDSAY: It must be very exciting to be at the beginning of creating something, a work of art, giving voice to ideas, characters, plumbing the depths of your psyche, the contours of your imagination, engendering the genesis of a world unto itself.

CAMERON: (*Still typing.*) Can be.

LINDSAY: Where do you get your inspiration? Do you have a muse? If you want (*An intake of breath . . . tremulously.*), I can be your muse . . .

(*He pauses in his typing, turns his head to look at her. In one graceful motion she sits in the chair stage right of the table. They both lean in toward each other, gazing deeply into each other's eyes. She removes his glasses. He removes her glasses. They breathe each other in.*)

CAMERON: (*Seductively.*) That could be very exciting, invigorating, stimulating . . .

LINDSAY: I think so, too!

CAMERON: Okay.

LINDSAY: Okay . . . Then I'll let you get back to engendering the genesis of a world unto itself.

(LINDSAY *smiles, puts her glasses back on, stands, begins to exit stage right. He follows her with his eyes. She stops, pivots, and smiles seductively, winks, before exiting.* CAMERON *returns his focus to his laptop, thinks, ponders, resumes, typing and finishes after a moment. A pause. To himself.*)

CAMERON: " . . . engendering the genesis of a world unto itself." Hmm, not bad.
(*He resumes typing, incorporating the phrase into his manuscript. Then stretches again, yawns, rolls his shoulders, removes his glasses, rubs his eyes. From stage left,* HEATHER *enters, crosses to behind him. She also wears glasses, her hair also pulled back in a ponytail.*)

HEATHER/WOMAN #2: You look tired, exhausted, worn out, undone by life's travesties and your creative process . . .

CAMERON: Yes. I am.

HEATHER: Back rub?

CAMERON: Please.

HEATHER: You're sure?

CAMERON: Sure, yes, I'm sure.

(HEATHER *stands behind him. She begins to massage and knead his neck and shoulders. He leans his head back against her torso.*)

CAMERON: Oh, yes . . . yes . . .

HEATHER: You're so tense—your neck and shoulders, all knots.

CAMERON: The weight of creation hangs heavy on my shoulders.

HEATHER: (*Chuckles.*) Funny, so funny . . . How's the writing coming along?

CAMERON: (*Closing the laptop.*) Good. It's coming along good—well. Coming along *well.*

HEATHER: (*Ever so slightly miffed.*) You don't want me to see it?

CAMERON: It's not ready to be seen yet.

HEATHER: You're awfully edgy lately. (*Sitting in chair stage left of table.*) You're drinking way too much coffee.

CAMERON: I know, I know. Deadlines looming, burning the midnight oil, candle at both ends, no rest for the weary.

HEATHER: I hope none of those clichés end up in this *roman a clef.*

CAMERON: No, no, all original stuff herein.

HEATHER: Good, because you shouldn't trivialize your ideas.

CAMERON: Agreed.

HEATHER: Because I couldn't *be* with you, wouldn't *want* to be with you otherwise (*Leaning into him*), and I *want* to be with you . . . *otherwise* . . . days and nights, *particularly* nights . . . *otherwise-wise* . . .

CAMERON: (*Removing his glasses, with a wink.*) I'll strive to find my own true, authentic voice.

HEATHER: (*Removing her glasses, flirting.*) You do that. Or else . . .

(*They gaze into each other's eyes for a beat. Then she leans into him for a kiss only to pull away at the last second. Then she stands, puts on her glasses, and walks stage left, stops, pivots, and then winks.*)

HEATHER: Much can be profited from the architecture of desire.

(*She exits. He does a slow take to the audience, a smile of recognition, opens the laptop, a flurry of typing.*)

CAMERON: (*Finishing his typing, smiling.*) ". . . the architecture of desire." . . . Not bad.

(NUSSBAUM *is downstage left.*)

NUSSBAUM: (*In a stage whisper.*) You see how we fit in the title of the book and our weekend getaway package? It's called "branding."

(*His line should interrupt* LINDSAY'*s next entrance.* CAMERON *looks irritated.*)

Oops! Sorry, sorry—keep going!

(CAMERON *indicates for* LINDSAY *to reenter, which she does.* CAMERON *types furiously.*)

LINDSAY: You really want me to be your muse, yes?

CAMERON: Yes, yes. With all my heart and soul, with my every fiber of my being!

LINDSAY: Oh, I feel such joy and sense of purpose! I am in ecstasy!

(*As she exits,* HEATHER *reenters.*)

HEATHER: You really want to be with me . . . *otherwise-wise*, yes?

CAMERON: Yes, yes. With all my heart and soul, with every fiber of my being!

HEATHER: Oh, I feel such joy and sense of purpose! I am in ecstasy!

(*As she exits,* LINDSAY *reenters with the coffee pot.*)

LINDSAY: More coffee?

CAMERON: (*Typing furiously now, the ideas flowing from his mind to his fingers.*) No, no!

(HEATHER *reenters. Perhaps she is wheeling in a massage table or has various lotions, etc.*)

HEATHER: Deep tissue massage?

CAMERON: (*Still typing furiously now, the ideas flowing from his mind to his fingers, he looks as though he may combust.*) No, no!

HEATHER and LINDSAY: Who is this woman?!

(CAMERON *is typing even more furiously, unable to respond to the questions he is being asked.*)

HEATHER and LINDSAY: I said, who is this woman?! Why is she here?

LINDSAY: I thought I was your muse!

HEATHER: I thought you wanted me *otherwise-wise*!

(LINDSAY *and* HEATHER *simultaneously remove their glasses and undo their ponytails in dramatic fashion. They square off against each other, circling each other, ready to pounce and attack. Suddenly we hear tango music. The two women circle each other in a series of tango-like steps. Then* CAMERON, *who has been furiously typing throughout this previous action, jumps up and dances with first one woman and then the other woman, and then all three of them dance together.*)

LINDSAY: Oh, such rapture!

HEATHER: Oh, such unrestrained bliss!

CAMERON: Oh, such ecstasy! I am convulsed in transports of joy! Wait, that's it!

(*He breaks out of the dance. The tango music continues at a lower volume. He returns to his laptop, the women following him, one on either side as he types furiously, their eyes aglow as they read over his shoulder. Everyone is breathing heavily.*)

HEATHER: Holy *deus ex machina*!

LINDSAY: (*Aroused.*) Oh, I feel like I'm negotiating the forested chasm!

HEATHER: (*Equally aroused.*) I could laugh out loud and disturb the cat!

LINDSAY, HEATHER, and CAMERON: (*In an orgasmic release.*) *La petite mort*!

CAMERON: (*With French accent.*) Fine!

(*Lights fade out center stage and come up on* NUSSBAUM *down left, applauding.*)

NUSSBAUM: I'll see *you* in Kissimmee! The Architecture of Desire!

(*Lights fade, tango music to full.*)

END OF PLAY

ATTACHMENT DISORDER

by Hallie Palladino

Attachment Disorder received its world premiere on October 21, 2019, with the NoMads Art Collective Sparks Festival at the Jackalope Frontier in Chicago. The Producing Artistic Council were Bethany Arrington, Ben Claus, Scott Jackoway, Marjorie Muller, and Danielle B. Szabo, with Taran Snodgress as stage manager. The director was Kelly Levander. The cast was as follows:

RENÉE: Janki Mody
DINA: /BOSS: Brianne Duncan Fiore
NATURAL MOM: Havalah Grace
EURO MOM: Amanda Marcheschi
ATTACHMENT MOM: Lynnette Li

Attachment Disorder received a benefit reading May 4, 2018, at Outpost Rep in Lubbock, Texas, produced by Jesse Jou and directed by Katie Hahn. The cast was as follows:

RENÉE: Melissa Miller
DINA: /BOSS: Hillary Boyd
MOTHER 1: Winter Davis
MOTHER 2: C. Alex Webster
MOTHER 3: Lydia McBee Reed

Hallie Palladino's recent plays include *Operation Marshmallow Fluff* (Broken Nose Theatre's Bechdel Fest presented by Steppenwolf LookOut Series),

Attachment Disorder (Nomads Art Collective), *The Persuadables* (Prop Thtr Church of the New Play), *Derailed* (O'Neill Semi-Finalist; Seven Devils Semi-Finalist; Broken Bells Reading Series), *Infatuation* (Ojai Playwrights Conference; Chicago New Works Festival; Dandelion Theater Reservoir Series), *Missed Connections* (Wayward Sisters, Idle Muse Theater's Athena Festival; Pride Films and Plays LezPlay Festival), *The Hanukkah Story* (Three Cat Productions "Holiday Radio Show 1943"), and *Sunrise: Ardmore Beach* (Something Marvelous Festival). Her upcoming play *Skeptics* is being developed by The New Colony. Hallie is a member of The Dramatists Guild.

CHARACTERS

RENÉE, a new mother carrying a rag doll in a baby carrier.
CHORUS OF MOTHERS, three mothers carrying rag dolls in baby carriers.
DINA, Renée's friend. Also plays Boss.

PLACE

America.

TIME

Now.

• • •

RENÉE *at Target staring at a wall of sunscreen.* CHORUS OF MOTHERS *with baby-carriers stream by.*

RENÉE: (*Reading labels. Talking to her baby.*) Hmm . . . both of these sunscreens are non-toxic. But only this one is phylate-free.

EURO MOM: (*Without stopping.*) Not that one.

RENÉE: Oh. (*She picks up another product.*)

ATTACHMENT MOM: Stay away from that stuff.

RENÉE: Sorry?

NATURAL MOM: Here. This one is cheaper and Oxybenzone free.

EURO MOM: (*Approaching.*) Don't let her buy that.

NATURAL MOM: Why not?

EURO MOM: It's Octinoxate based.

RENÉE: What?

EURO MOM: Octinoxate. Known hormone disrupter. Causes thyroid problems.

NATURAL MOM: No, no, no. It's Oxybenzone that causes thyroid problems.

ATTACHMENT MOM: Actually, they're both hormone disrupters. Oxybenzone is the one that acts like estrogen and causes endometriosis. Octinoxate causes hyperactivity.

NATURAL MOM: Oh no. I've been using Octinoxate for years. Do you think that could be the reason Oregano misbehaves so much when it's sunny?

ATTACHMENT MOM: Who's to say.

RENÉE: Oregano?

NATURAL MOM: I like to name my children after herbs and spices. This one's little Tarragon.

RENÉE: Aww. Mine are named after Heirloom Tomatoes. This one's Brandywine.

NATURAL MOM: Really?

RENÉE: No.

NATURAL MOM: Bitch. I was only trying to help.

RENÉE: (*To Euro Mom.*) What sunscreen do you prefer?

EURO MOM: Me? Nothing they sell here. I special order mine from Sweden.

RENÉE: How much does that cost?

EURO MOM: Around eighteen dollars.

RENÉE: A bottle?

EURO MOM: I wish, no. An ounce. Plus international shipping.

RENÉE: Whoa.

EURO MOM: Why do you think the Swedish are so far ahead of us?

RENÉE: Are they?

EURO MOM: Isn't your baby worth it? You're worth it, yes you are, Brandywine. You don't want your mommy to poison you, no, no, no you don't . . .

RENÉE: Her name's Nora, actually.

NATURAL MOM: Of course, with her complexion she probably doesn't need sunscreen at all.

RENÉE: Except UV rays and skin cancer don't discriminate so . . .

ATTACHMENT MOM: Your mommy's right Princess. She wants to protect you because you're her sweet little royal Princess. Aren't you? Aren't you?

RENÉE: Please don't call my daughter princess.

ATTACHMENT MOM: But all little girls are princesses, aren't they? Pretty little Disney princesses. Goodness, you're only a tiny little newborn. How old are you Sleeping Beauty?

RENÉE: Her name is Nora. And she's ten days old.

ATTACHMENT MOM: Don't you know never to use sunscreen under six months? Leeches straight into the bloodstream. Might as well bathe her in toxic waste. It's all poison anyway.

RENÉE: But it's sunny.

ATTACHMENT MOM: (*Tossing her a sunhat.*) Get a hat.

> (RENÉE *at home breastfeeding. Baby has fallen asleep attached. She strains to reach her phone.*)

RENÉE: Almost . . . got it . . .
> (*Success. She attempts to scroll email without moving her arms. Doorbell. Baby starts to cry.*)

RENÉE: Goddamn it. Sorry, sweetie, sorry, not you.

> (DINA *enters. Surveys the scene disapprovingly.*)

DINA: Renée, I've come to rescue you.

RENÉE: Oh, Dina, thank God. I could really use help with all this laundry.

DINA: No not from laundry. From yourself. From this.

RENÉE: My apartment?

DINA: No. From the Patriarchal Institution of Motherhood. As defined by Adrienne Rich in her seminal text, *Of Woman Born*. Well seminal probably isn't the right word, maybe ovual. Ovual text. Remember? We read it in college.

> (*Baby is still crying.* RENÉE *reattaches her.*)

RENÉE: Sorry, following conversation, isn't. Can't quite. What?

DINA: Don't worry. I came prepared. (*She produces a stack of books.*)

RENÉE: *The Motherhood Trap, The Mother-Blame Paradox, Lactation: Tool of the Patriarchy.* Thanks, I guess. But did you bring any food? All I've got are these frozen pot stickers, but I'm too sleepy to cook them. I've just been letting them get melty. Eating from the bag.

DINA: That's disgusting.

RENÉE: I know. They might have raw chicken. Label reading. Can't. Tiny letters so swimmy. Do you have any doughnuts? I could really go for a Boston cream.

DINA: Not the pot stickers. The breastfeeding. Privilege of an elite class. Classist!

RENÉE: What?

DINA: Plus, perpetuating gender roles. Participating in the subjugation of women.

RENÉE: But my daughter is . . .

DINA: What?

RENÉE: Hungry.

DINA: Read these.

> (*Mama and Baby Yoga. The moms unroll mats and start breastfeeding in the lotus position.* RENÉE *rushes in with a car seat, frazzled. Baby*

screaming. Everyone watches her juggle her mat, car seat, and giant diaper bag. ATTACHMENT MOM *beckons.*)

ATTACHMENT MOM: Here, let me help you get settled.

RENÉE: Thanks.

ATTACHMENT MOM: (*Soothing tone, sweet as pie.*) She's probably just traumatized because you keep her in that car seat.

RENÉE: What?

ATTACHMENT MOM: Don't you know that's gonna flatten out her head? She'll have to go around in one of those helmets. The helmets they put on neglected babies.

RENÉE: Excuse me.

ATTACHMENT MOM: You should really be wearing her at all times.

RENÉE: But I drove here.

ATTACHMENT MOM: Like Buddha says, all our choices have consequences.

RENÉE: I don't, actually—is that even—true?

(*The Office. The Chorus of Mothers don blazers. They stuff their "babies" in briefcases.*)

ATTACHMENT MOM: Better Lean In or you'll be mommy-tracked.

NATURAL MOM: Hope you pumped enough breast milk—It'll help you lose the baby weight.

EURO MOM: Swedish mothers don't gain weight because of socialism and oily fish.

BOSS: Well, look who's finally back. Hope you had fun on your vacation.

RENÉE: I was—having a baby.

BOSS: Yeah, the first thirty-two hours. It's been ten weeks.

RENÉE: Three actually. Just three.

BOSS: Meanwhile things here have gone to shit.

RENÉE: Yes. You emailed me about that. Every. Single. Day.

BOSS: Hope you aren't gonna bore us all with constant talk of little Zora.

RENÉE: Nora.

BOSS: I prefer Zora.

RENÉE: But her name is actually Nora.

BOSS: See there you go—droning on about your baby already. Bad for the progress of women in our business.

RENÉE: How?

BOSS: Appearances, Renée, appearances. I raised four babies. Never mentioned it once. Kept it all completely hidden. Not like you women today with your breast-pumps and your three months of maternity leave.

RENÉE: Three weeks. Unpaid.

(*Target again.* RENÉE *reading baby food labels.*)

Beets, Greek Yogurt and Dandelion Greens or Acai, Purple Carrot and Fava Bean?

NATURAL MOM: Careful. Those aren't non-GMO fava beans.

EURO MOM: In Sweden they don't have baby food. Their babies eat mackerel and nettle soup. That's why they're kicking our ass in the STEM fields.

ATTACHMENT MOM: Is she even old enough for solids? Food before six months leaches straight to the bloodstream. It's all poison anyway.

(NORA *starts to cry.* DINA *enters.*)

DINA: There you are, Renée. Have you read those books? Or are you too busy participating in this sickening orgy of bourgeois over-consumption. Gracious, does that baby ever shut up.

RENÉE: Wow, Dina. Could you be any less supportive?

DINA: Someone's touchy. You don't have postpartum depression, do you?

ATTACHMENT MOM: You know, you could've prevented that by eating the placenta.

EURO MOM: In Sweden they call placenta moderkaka.

NATURAL MOM: If you keep letting your baby cry like that, she's gonna get brain damage.

RENÉE: Okay. You are a horrible person. And that is a horrible thing to say!

ATTACHMENT MOM: Stay calm, Renée. Buddha says maternal rage causes Attachment Disorder.

RENÉE: No he doesn't! You're all just trying to make me feel bad with your teabag spirituality and your culturally appropriative tone policing. And you, why don't you just move to Sweden already. Because here in what's left of the United States, I'm just trying to raise my daughter. And yes, I have a long list of fears for the kids of her generation but genetically modified fava beans aren't even close to making that list. And, Dina, of course I have postpartum depression. My nipples feel like they've been run across a belt-sander and I haven't slept in five months. And no, it's not because I didn't eat the placenta. I did eat it! I had it freeze dried and encapsulated and swallowed every crumb. But did it help me? No! Not with work, or laundry or the wage gap or the lack of affordable childcare. You should all be ashamed. Come on Nora, let's go.

EURO MOM: Wait. Sometimes . . . I let my children eat Funyuns.

NATURAL MOM: Sometimes, I snort Oregano's crushed up Adderall.

ATTACHMENT MOM: Sometimes I fantasize about quietly smothering all the yoga mothers during Savasana. Then I feel guilty for not eating the placenta and lying about it.

DINA: I binge shop at Container Store and Pinterest about it while watching Hoarders.

RENÉE: See. Was that so hard? Now who's in the mood for a doughnut?

ALL: "Yes, please." "God, yes." "That would be awesome."

(*They exit with their arms around each other.*)

END OF PLAY

THE BEACH

by Laura Hirschberg

Original Production Information:
Producing organization: The Workshop Theater
Date of performance: October 19, 2019

Original Cast:
CAPTAIN HUGO DUNBAR: JaQwan J. Kelly
DR. LUNA FOSTER: Maggie Horan

Director: Laura Hirschberg

Laura Hirschberg is a New York City-based playwright/director/stage manager. Her plays, including *Verona Walls, Fire Thief,* and *Heart Of Oak* have been developed, workshopped, and produced by Harvard University, The WorkShop Theater, The Looking Glass Theatre, 3V Theatre, Caps Lock Theater, the Frigid Festival, Everyday Inferno, Rising Sun Performance Company, and the 9BC Performance Series. Monologues from Laura's plays have been published by Smith & Kraus and Applause Theatre and Cinema Books. Her plays to date have featured titans, Shakespearean characters, cowboys, superheroes, lady pirates, and the occasional talking whale. They also explore family, friendship, loyalty, and love. And in one case, Big Foot. Visit New Play Exchange (newplayexchange.org) to explore more of Laura's work. For more information about Laura's latest projects, please visit www.laurahirschberg.com.

CHARACTERS

CAPTAIN HUGO DUNBAR, early 20s. A test pilot for Virtual Reality research, recently stationed on Orion following his accelerated completion of the secondary training program.

DR. LUNA FOSTER, mid to late 20s. Virtual Reality architect and researcher. Supervisor of Lab 47B.

SETTING

Virtual Reality Lab 47B, Space Station Orion.

• • •

HUGO *is lying on the floor with his hands pressed into the ground and his eyes closed. He is wearing tactile sensor pads, attached at the palms and fingertips.* LUNA *is working at her module on the other side of a partition that is transparent for her* (and the audience) *and opaque for* HUGO.

LUNA: What about now?

HUGO: Sand.

LUNA: Mr. Dunbar, if you're not going to take this seriously . . .

HUGO: OK, OK. Volcanic sand.

LUNA: Yes.

HUGO: You haven't got the smell right yet.

LUNA: Excuse me?

HUGO: The feel is spot on. But if you wanna sell it, you're gonna have to lose that factory-fresh aroma.

LUNA: Mr. Dunbar, the olfactory . . .

HUGO: Give it some salt, is what I'm saying.

LUNA: Mr. . . .

HUGO: It's Captain Dunbar. Actually. When you graduate the secondary program, they promote you to captain.

LUNA: Apologies.

HUGO: Haven't been a mister since I started at the academy. Took me a year to get used to people calling me Lieutenant.

LUNA: If we could get back to . . .

HUGO: Mr. Dunbar is kinda cute though. Could be a nickname, just between us.

LUNA: You've made your point, I think.

HUGO: Have I, Ms. Foster?

LUNA: Doctor.

HUGO: Right. Apologies.

LUNA: Are we going to have a problem?

HUGO: No ma'am.

LUNA: You've been giving me static for three days, Captain. And I've got people banging down the lab doors to run these tests if you'd rather be elsewhere.

HUGO: Nowhere else I'd rather be.

LUNA: Good. (*She brings up a new protocol at her console.*) And now?

HUGO: Grass. Freshly mowed. Slightly dewy. (*Beat.*) But there *is* something. Chalk.

LUNA: What?

HUGO: There's a chalky residue.

LUNA: Hang on. (*She checks her code.*) No. I'm not seeing it.

HUGO: Maybe not, but it's there.

LUNA: We should check the receiver.

HUGO: There's nothing wrong with my gear. I've seen this kind of thing before. The system gets clogged up with old layers. Sometimes they co-express. You still have that cliff face protocol up somewhere? Running in the background?

LUNA: Just the daily auto-checks. That protocol would've been up for maybe two seconds. Deep background.

HUGO: Shut it down.

LUNA: (*Sighs.*) Try it. Can't hurt.
(*She shuts down the auto-checks.*)

LUNA: Going to zero space.

HUGO: Copy zero space.

(LUNA *shuts down the system and restarts.* HUGO *is momentarily in empty space, feeling and seeing nothing. System restarts.*)

HUGO: Nice.

LUNA: No more chalk?

HUGO: None.

LUNA: Good catch, Dunbar. I've never seen that bug before.

HUGO: It's easy to overlook if you're not in the flight suit. (*Beat.*) Not knocking the architect, just saying. It's different.

LUNA: I've worn the suit.

HUGO: (*Sits up.*) Yeah?

LUNA: You can get through architecture certification without it, but that always seemed ridiculous to me. We're designing for the suits. I mean, yes, we soften things up and pad the sharp edges before they get to the users, but the essential experience—without all the distractions—is the flight suit. I could see the Environment in the code, but it was theoretical. I needed to feel it on my skin, walk around in it, to actually understand.

HUGO: How'd it go? Your test drive.

LUNA: I threw up.

(HUGO *laughs.*)

LUNA: The vertigo was unreal.

HUGO: Ever gone in as a customer? No sharp edges. And I'm sure there's some nice, flat meadow you could try for a couple of hours.

LUNA: Not since I was a kid.

HUGO: Come on.

LUNA: Never saw an Environment that seemed worth the price of admission.

HUGO: Not even one of yours?

LUNA: Well. Mine. Mine *are* very good. But I see what I need to see in the code. And the station is very beautiful.

HUGO: If you like stainless steel.

LUNA: It's very clean.

HUGO: (*Smiles.*) Yeah.

LUNA: Suit up.

> (HUGO *begins to put on the rest of his VR suit—optic patches attached at the temples, and a modified space suit.*)

LUNA: Are you a user?

HUGO: Me?

LUNA: You obviously don't think much of stainless steel. Not subject to vertigo, sea-sickness, agoraphobia . . . The perfect customer. Which Environment's your favorite? (*Beat*) Don't say Peterson's Versailles. Everyone loves Versailles.

HUGO: It's not Versailles.

LUNA: Good. Because the Hall of Mirrors is barely more than a cut-and-paste job, but you cover everything with gold and people don't notice the compromises in the design.

HUGO: Never seen it. (*Beat.*) Garden of the Gods.

LUNA: Say that again?

HUGO: No contest really. Best Environment I've ever seen.

LUNA: You're making fun of me.

HUGO: I'm not.

LUNA: (*Skeptical.*) My first Environment. Really?

HUGO: My first too. It was released right after my eighteenth birthday. So, you must've been . . .

LUNA: I was twenty.

HUGO: Prodigy, right?

LUNA: That was your first?

HUGO: My folks couldn't afford the rentals. Didn't see the point in saving up for one. Always said "It couldn't compare to the real thing." (*He has finished putting on and starting up the suit.*)
Flight suit ready to engage.

LUNA: Stand by engage. (*She flips switches as she runs down her checklist.*) Pressure system activated.

HUGO: Check.

LUNA: Olfactory sensors go.

HUGO: Check.

LUNA: Optics go.

HUGO: Check.

LUNA: Somatosensory gloves engage.

HUGO: Engaged. So where to? (*Beat. No response.*) Dr. Foster?

LUNA: Couldn't compare to the real thing.

HUGO: What?

LUNA: Did you grow up planet-side?

HUGO: My parents did. When I came along, our quadrant was too close to the population quota. So, it was goodbye Pacific Northwest, hello Station Andromeda. (*Beat.*) You'd like it there. Very clean.

LUNA: Doesn't seem to have done you any harm.

HUGO: Thanks, Doc. I'm flattered.

LUNA: You know what I mean. You don't see a lot of earthers in the Academy.

HUGO: Well. If you've got the real sky and land right in front of you, I guess it's hard to see the appeal of playing pretend.

(*Beat.*)

LUNA: Speaking of which . . .

HUGO: Yeah. Where are we headed?

LUNA: Back to the beach.

(HUGO *readjusts the vest of his suit and optic patches.*)

HUGO: Yeah?

LUNA: We're incorporating the sea today. If you're ready.

HUGO: That's a quick turnaround.

LUNA: There's a high demand. Stand by for zero space.

HUGO: Standing by.

(LUNA *flips a switch and* HUGO *is again in the void.*)

LUNA: Environment loading. Stand by for touchdown.

HUGO: Ready.
(*The Environment activates and* HUGO *is experiencing the sights, sounds, and feeling of an Atlantic beach. He's impressed.*)
Night!

LUNA: Observant.

HUGO: Any reason for . . . ?

LUNA: Keeps the temperature down. Inspires heightened optic and olfactory responses.

HUGO: And you're showing off a little.

LUNA: You were a bit of a jerk those first three days. Hard to please. Thought this might shut you up.

(HUGO *nods. He looks around, taking in the sky. Beat. Beat.*)

LUNA: Worked like a charm.

HUGO: Gives the Garden of the Gods a run for its money. Ready for initial data collection?

LUNA: Go ahead.

HUGO: Suit reads lab temperature at 70 degrees Fahrenheit. Perceived temperature 62. Cool evening. A little brisk for a swim.

LUNA: We'll adjust before getting your feet wet.

HUGO: Appreciated. (*He crouches down to pick up perceived wet sand.*) Sand texture consistent with mid-Atlantic. Fine, semi-coarse grain. Packs well. I could do a sand castle if you'd program in a pail.

LUNA: Accessories cost extra.

HUGO: What's the point of getting through the Academy if you don't get the free perks?

LUNA: Contribute to the ongoing effort to facilitate extraplanetary life through the creation and development of livable virtual environments. Do your family proud.

HUGO: Wow. Did you swallow the recruiting pamphlet?

LUNA: Photographic memory.

HUGO: Ah. So. Are you one of those?

LUNA: What?

HUGO: Parent-pleasers? Doing your family proud.

LUNA: Aren't you?

HUGO: (*Smiles slightly.*) Check my file. (*He starts to test the ground—pacing, running, jumping, checking readings on his suit as he goes along.*)

LUNA: What do you mean?

HUGO: Top sheet. (*He continues testing. Luna checks the top sheet of Hugo's file and finds . . .*)

LUNA: Parents deceased. I'm sorry.

(*Beat.*)

HUGO: Gravity's good. You compensated for the inconsistency we found. It's good. Sand has just enough give.

LUNA: (*Slight hesitation.*) Excellent. (*She makes a note.*) You should be getting some stimuli in the somatosensory system.

HUGO: Yes. (*He stops moving.*) Light wind coming from the . . . (*He holds up a finger, checks his suit's compass.*) Northwest. There's that salt I was looking for. You were holding out on me. (*Beat. He listens.*) The sound's a bit off.

LUNA: I haven't activated the sea yet.

HUGO: Yeah. But the win . . .

LUNA: Are you ready for full activation?

HUGO: No. I don't wanna rush the . . .

LUNA: It's fine. If you want to calibrate the auditory inputs for wind, they're embedded in the sea code, so . . .

HUGO: Hang on.

LUNA: It's not a problem.

HUGO: Just—wait a second, OK?

LUNA: I'm getting some elevated readings from your biometrics, Dunbar. Are you all right?

(*Pause. No response.* HUGO *is taking slow, deep breaths.*)

Captain Dunbar? (*Beat.*) Hugo?

HUGO: Yeah. Good to go. Standing by for full activation.

LUNA: Wait a minute.

HUGO: Is there a problem?

LUNA: You want to tell me what that was?

HUGO: It's nothing.

LUNA: Well, I'm not an idiot and you're plugged into a computer, so really there are several ways to refute that claim. Did you just have a panic attack?

HUGO: No.

LUNA: Stand by to abort . . .

HUGO: It's not necessary. It was—it was maybe the beginning of a panic attack.

LUNA: Your file doesn't indicate any history of . . .

HUGO: It doesn't happen often.

LUNA: It shouldn't happen at all. If you're unfit . . .

HUGO: I'm *not* unfit. (*Beat.*) Can I get some sunlight in here? Please?

(LUNA *shakes her head, then enters a command into her console.* HUGO *perceives noon sunlight.*)

HUGO: Thanks. (*Checks his suit monitor.*) My pulse is just a little elevated. Respiration's fine. Let's go.

LUNA: It might have slipped your mind, with all our discussion of your rank. But this is my lab. We'll continue when I am ready to continue. I'm not interested in collecting useless data. I need a test pilot whose levels are all within control range. Do you qualify?

HUGO: Don't be ridiculous. Yes. Of course I qualify.
(*Beat.*)

LUNA: Is it the sea?

(*Beat.* HUGO *sits.*)

HUGO: Y'know, my family only won the visitation lottery once. I was twelve. We could go anywhere. Twenty-four hours planet-side. I begged my folks to go to the beach. Have you ever seen one? The real thing?

LUNA: No. Just video.

HUGO: Mom and Dad told me about it. Like a bedtime story. Long as I can remember, they'd tell me about the mountains, forests. And the sea. And it all sounded impossible, or at least unlikely. Like, I'd seen the videos too, but they could all be computer generated by geniuses like you, so . . . It's not like I thought my folks were liars. I just . . . the imagination only takes you so far. And the ocean . . . I just couldn't wrap my head around it. The size of it. I got a little obsessed. I'd dream about it. So, when we got the chance, it was obvious. Where we had to go. They set us down at the edge of America. We drove over miles of sand. And then, there it was. The Pacific. (*Beat.*) I was overwhelmed. Couldn't breathe. It was too big. I mean. I grew up on a station. Look out a window, any window, and you see the infinite. The ocean is nothing compared to that . . . vastness. Any kid knows that. I knew that. But I couldn't take it in. That sky. The horizon. My parents thought I was having a fit. Which, I guess, I was. See, the thing about space is . . . there's so much nothing. Right? Goes on forever, but it's full of . . . emptiness. I looked at the sea and, I dunno, it was the most . . . substantial thing I'd ever seen. There was so much there. After twelve years of looking out the window at nothing, I guess my mind just wasn't prepared. And then suddenly, I was running into the waves. Fully dressed. My parents chasing after me. I'm a great swimmer now. Swim a mile a day when work allows. Academy requires it if you want to graduate with full honors. When I was twelve, I knew enough to close my mouth when the first wave hit me. And I went down. Hard. The Pacific is, uh, undeniable. Dad had me in his arms before the second wave hit and he was solid. Immovable. Mom came running up and grabbed onto both of us and when the third wave hit, she laughed. And then we were all laughing. Three fully dressed, soaked to the bone idiots, laughing at the ocean.

(*Beat.*)

LUNA: Why'd you do it?

HUGO: Hmm?

LUNA: Why'd you run in?

HUGO: I don't know. Maybe I needed to feel it to believe it?

LUNA: You're lucky you didn't drown.

HUGO: Wasn't luck. I had them. And because of me . . .
    (*Beat. He shakes his head.*)

LUNA: What?

HUGO: Because of me they had to give it up.
    (*He stands.*)
I mean, I knew that. I knew that before. But all of it—earth, mountains, the sea—it was all just an idea before the visitation. After the beach, it was a solid, infinite, immense fact. What they gave up for me. What they gave to me.

(*Beat.*)

LUNA: You knew what you'd be working on, coming here.

(HUGO *nods.*)

LUNA: If you'd prefer work on one of the larger forest Environments, or a city . . .

HUGO: No.

LUNA: They're recreating Milan over on Station Calliope.

HUGO: Dr. Foster, I'm not trying to . . .

LUNA: Or if you prefer to stay local, Lab 28 is doing some great work on arctic Environments. They're just down the hall.

HUGO: Do you want me to leave?

LUNA: I'm not particularly interested in running an incredibly expensive highly elaborate therapy session for one. If you're looking for a way to . . . conquer a phobia or make peace with . . . There are other ocean Environments already up and running. I'm sure any of those architects would jump at the chance to have a test pilot of your skill on their upgrade team.

HUGO: Look, I'm sorry I was kind of a pain the first few days, but . . .

LUNA: I don't care about that.

HUGO: I want to stay here.

LUNA: You're not mentally fit. This is the largest endeavor of this kind ever attempted. It's highly complex and exceedingly dangerous at this stage.

HUGO: I know that.

LUNA: Are you aware of how quickly you could do yourself serious damage if you panic during the full exercise of this protocol? Sudden vasoconstriction, oxygen deprivation . . .

HUGO: I'm not gonna give myself a stroke.

LUNA: And there's the obvious potential for psychological harm.

HUGO: I'm willing to take the risk.

LUNA: That's nice and very dashing or courageous or whatever effect you're trying to achieve. But again, this isn't your lab. I'm responsible for you and for this Environment, and I won't compromise in my care for either.

HUGO: I understand.

LUNA: Good.

HUGO: And I was going for a combination of brave and self-sacrificing.

LUNA: Noted.

HUGO: Standing by for full activation.

LUNA: Captain Dunbar . . .

HUGO: I knew what I'd be working on, coming here.

LUNA: Then it was irresponsible . . .

HUGO: You're the reason I went to the Academy.

LUNA: Garden of the Gods? Really?

HUGO: It was a gift. Not too expensive. I guess they discounted it 'cause you were still in school and no one was making any guarantees about the quality.

LUNA: Thanks.

HUGO: I went in there skeptical. I'd been planet-side. Considered myself an expert. Knew an Environment couldn't compare to the real thing. It activated and . . .

(*He shakes his head and smiles.*) The air was thin and dry. You had these tiny lizards skittering over every surface. And those red rocks against the blue sky. I could feel the grit come off the sandstone and form a thin layer on my fingertips. It was sunny—I guess you know that. It's always sunny. And the stones held the heat. From the sunlight. It was perfect. I believed it. And I thought, if most of us can't have the earth, we'd be lucky to have this. And test pilots get to ride for free.

LUNA: You entered one of the most prestigious and selective training programs in the system . . . for free Environment access?

HUGO: There may have also been a few aptitude tests that I aced. Seemed like a good fit.

LUNA: And fate just happened to land you at my lab door?

HUGO: No. I planted myself there. I've seen some of those other ocean Environments. Pale imitations. Good enough for some. I wanted the real thing.

LUNA: Did you come here to torture yourself?

HUGO: That's not what I'm doing.

LUNA: Your cardiogram from a few minutes ago says different. The idea of the ocean—the real ocean—makes you miserable. Anxious. If this

Environment is as good as you're hoping it'll be, all you're doing is hurting yourself. And screwing up my data. I can't have you panic and . . .

HUGO: That wasn't panic.

LUNA: You admitted—you said it was the beginning of a panic attack.

HUGO: I didn't know what else to call it. Or . . . I didn't want to sound cheesy.

LUNA: If it wasn't panic, what was it?

HUGO: Hope?

(LUNA *sighs.*)

HUGO: I told you. Cheesy. But it was like . . . the feeling you get when you've wanted something for so long and you're finally gonna get it. You'll blink and the next time you open your eyes it'll be there. And there's all this hope and expectation, but there's also this stab of fear. Because what if it's not enough? What if it's exactly what you wanted and it turns out you wanted the wrong thing?

(*Beat.*)

LUNA: OK.

HUGO: OK?

LUNA: Promise me you're not going to freak out.

HUGO: I solemnly swear I'm done freaking out.

LUNA: You swim a mile a day?

HUGO: Freestyle.

LUNA: You want to see the ocean again?

HUGO: Yes. Please.

LUNA: Stand by for full activation.

HUGO: (*Closes his eyes.*) Standing by.

(LUNA *enters the activation code. She flips a switch and* HUGO *hears, smells, and feels the ocean at his feet. He opens his eyes. He takes a deep breath.*)

(*Blackout.*)

END OF PLAY

BLADES

by Margo Hammond

Original Production:
Producing organization: Artistic New Directions (AND)
Director of production of "Blades": Margo Hammond

Original Cast:
THE ONE: Jacob Silburn
THE OTHER: Ruby Hankey

Dates: February 28–March 8, 2020

Margo Hammond's plays have been produced in London, England; Milan, Italy; New York City, and at various theaters across the United States. *Mistress Marlene* and *Mae the Magnificent* have been published in Smith & Kraus' *Best Ten-Minute Plays of 2015/2019*, respectively. Luna Stage (West Orange, New Jersey) recently included *Mae* in their 7th Annual New Moon Short Play Festival. Her full-length play *Let Maisy Rest in Peace* was presented at Barter Theatre's 2019 Appalachian Festival of Plays and Playwrights. Other plays have been done in New York City at 78th St. Theater Lab, Soho Playhouse, Theater 54, CAP21, Little Church Around the Corner, Directors Company, and at the Workshop Theater. Her play *Look Me in the Eyes* was produced in Colorado Springs, Colorado, at Six Women Playwright's Festival and in San Diego, California, at North Park Playwright Festival. She was first place recipient of the 2016 Jerry Kaufman Award for Excellence in Playwriting. She is an Actors Studio PDU member, Dramatist Guild member, and AEA, SAG/AFTRA. For more about Margo, see www.margohammond.com.

CHARACTERS

THE ONE, comfortable, content (any age, any gender).
THE OTHER, uncomfortable, discontented (any age, any gender).

TIME

Now.

SETTING

Bare stage, an imaginary world, a sidewalk near a plush lawn (suburb or city).

• • •

THE ONE *and* THE OTHER *are separated by several feet, their* heads hanging limp. They do not notice each other, at first. Both are in their own experience. THE ONE *sighs and raises his/her head.* HE/SHE *smiles and arches toward the sky.*

THE ONE: Ahhhhh!

   (THE OTHER *grunts and slowly raises her/his head.*)

THE OTHER: Ugg. Ahgg.

   (THE ONE *takes a deep breath, happy.*)

THE ONE: Nice.

   (THE OTHER *seems uncomfortable, cramped.*)

THE OTHER: Ow. (*Sniffs the air.*) Huh?

THE ONE: Hello.

THE OTHER: What?

THE ONE: I said hello.

THE OTHER: Who?

THE ONE: Over here.

   (THE ONE *looks.*)

THE OTHER: Hi.

THE ONE: Nice day.

THE OTHER: It is?

THE ONE: The sun. The air?

THE OTHER: I'm stuck over here, man!

THE ONE: Well, I'm stuck here but . . . it's nice. I like it.

THE OTHER: Eeee, gee, gee, gee, gee, gee. (*Or some strange plant sound.*)

THE ONE: You okay?

THE OTHER: *No.* (*Squirming.*) *Eeeeeg.*

THE ONE: You're not from here.

THE OTHER: *Huh?*

THE ONE: (*Speaking very slowly.*) You-are-not-from-around-here.

THE OTHER: I . . . I just flew in.

THE ONE: Ah, from away.

(THE OTHER *ducks, as if dodging something.*)

THE OTHER: Hey, what? What is that?

THE ONE: Looks like a cigarette butt.

THE OTHER: Hell.

THE ONE: People throw them all the time. Watch out!

(*Something hits* THE OTHER.)

THE OTHER: Hey! Where the . . . what?

THE ONE: Now that's a cup. Nasty little things. Styrofoam? They say it lasts forever. They're made of benzine, dioxins; yeah, all that stuff washes into the ground.

THE OTHER: The water does taste funny.

THE ONE: Like Chlorine?

THE OTHER: Yes!

THE ONE: That's common. The water is better over here.

THE OTHER: It is?

THE ONE: Yeah, our water tastes pretty good actually.

THE OTHER: Lucky you.

THE ONE: Yup!

THE OTHER: It looks lush over there too.

THE ONE: It is. Yes.

THE OTHER: I'm cramped.

THE ONE: Hmm.

THE OTHER: Where am I anyway?

THE ONE: (*Matter-of-factly.*) You're in a crack.

THE OTHER: What?

THE ONE: In the sidewalk. A crack in the sidewalk.

THE OTHER: Oh.

THE ONE: Yeah.

THE OTHER: What is this stuff?

THE ONE: Concrete? Mostly sand, I guess? And maybe a few heavy metals mixed in.

THE OTHER: Heavy metals?

THE ONE: Yeah, maybe a little lead or chromium, maybe aluminum? Maybe?

THE OTHER: That doesn't sound good.

THE ONE: Well.

THE OTHER: It's uncomfortable.

THE ONE: Watch it!

(THE OTHER *gets slimed.*)

THE OTHER: What?! Oh my God, was that?

THE ONE: Spit.

THE OTHER: *Huh?*

THE ONE: Somebody spit on you.

THE OTHER: YUK!

THE ONE: I know.

THE OTHER: Damn.

THE ONE: That happens.

THE OTHER: Why aren't they spitting on you?

THE ONE: Well.

THE OTHER: What?

THE ONE: This is a designated area. See the sign? "No Spitting, No Littering."

THE OTHER: I wanna be over there.

THE ONE: No.

THE OTHER: Why?

THE ONE: We're all alike over here. We're all one kind.

THE OTHER: Whaddaya mean?

THE ONE: Our kind, we fit perfectly in these conditions.

THE OTHER: Like what conditions?

THE ONE: Well, for one, we require little water.

THE OTHER: Yeah?

THE ONE: We're low maintenance.

THE OTHER: So am I.

THE ONE: Yeah but we can withstand a lot of activity and we survive short periods of drought.

THE OTHER: I can tolerate drought.

THE ONE: Well.

THE OTHER: And I can grow in sand or clay, alkaline or acid.

THE ONE: Impressive.

THE OTHER: That's right.

THE ONE: But you're different. You look different.

THE OTHER: So?

THE ONE: It wouldn't work out.

THE OTHER: I get along with others very well.

THE ONE: I'm sure you do but this lawn requires the same *kind* of grass. We all look good together, in a bunch.

THE OTHER: I can look good.

THE ONE: We are all Bermuda grass, perfect for a lawn.

THE OTHER: Maybe you could use a little variety. It's healthy.

THE ONE: No.

> (THE OTHER *curls one leg up, stretches it out and rotates his/her foot like a roto-rooter in* THE ONE'S *direction.*)

THE ONE: Stop it!

THE OTHER: I'm coming.

THE ONE: No. You don't belong!

> (*Something hits* THE OTHER *in the head.*)

THE OTHER: OUCH! Damn it. That's a plastic bottle. It's dangerous over here. I'm coming over.

THE ONE: No, stop.

THE OTHER: I'm coming. (THE OTHER *stretches, scooches, slaps leg into Sumo stance and pops up right next to* THE ONE.) Ha, ha. There. Here I am!

THE ONE: You do not belong here!

THE OTHER: I'm here.

THE ONE: The people won't like it.

THE OTHER: People?

THE ONE: (*Pointing upward.*) Them!

THE OTHER: Ha, what do they know? They can look at all that plastic trash and cigarettes, but they can't stand looking at a lawn with different kinds of grass?

THE ONE: Correct.

THE OTHER: You're saying they're okay with Tobacco, BEN: zene, Dioxins, Chlorine, and Plastics but they can't look at me?

THE ONE: You're considered a weed to them.

THE OTHER: I am not! I'm a respected species.

THE ONE: Crabgrass is a weed.

THE OTHER: NO.

THE ONE: They spray carcinogens on your kind to get rid of you. Now move over.

THE OTHER: (circling hips in a grinding motion) I've already taken root.

THE ONE: How dare you!

THE OTHER: *I'm movin in*!

THE ONE: You're crowding me.

THE OTHER: You'll get used to it.

THE ONE: Damn!

    (*Distant sound.*)

THE OTHER: What?

THE ONE: Hear that?

THE OTHER: Yeah. Geez. What is it?

THE ONE: They call it *a lawn mower*.

THE OTHER: A what?

THE ONE: WATCH OUT!

>   (*Sound of loud lawn mower passing over.* THE ONE *and* THE OTHER *abruptly lean sideways.*)

THE ONE and THE OTHER: AHHHHHHH!!!
>   (*Abrupt blackout as loud sound continues.*)

END OF PLAY

BOOK OF LIFE

by Judy Klass

Original Production:
November 9 through November 24, 2019, SkyPilot Theatre One-Act Festival: Future Shock
Series B in Los Angeles

Directed by Arden Haywood Smalls

Cast:
DIANA: Ayla ROSE: Barreau
LIBRARIAN: Albert Garnica

Seven of **Judy Klass**' full-length plays have been produced. One, *Cell*, was nominated for an Edgar Award and is published by Samuel French. Another mystery, *Country Fried Murder*, won the Shawnee Playhouse S.O.P.S. competition in the full-length category and was produced there, in Pennsylvania, in 2019. Her full-length comedy *Stop Me If You've Heard This One* won the Dorothy Silver Award. It came in second place in Chaffin's Barn Theatre's Clash of the Playwrights Competition in Nashville, and was produced there in 2019. Thirty-five of Judy's one-act plays have been produced. Three are published, each as a stand-alone script, by Brooklyn Publishers. Her play *Untethered* won the William Faulkner Literary Competition in the One Act Play category in 2019. Her play *Timeshare* came in first place in the Tallahassee Writer Association's Seven Hills contest 2019–2020 in the Ten-Minute Play category. In 2019, *Book of Life* was a winner and had a reading with Theatrikos Theatre in Flagstaff in the Northern Arizona Playwriting Showcase, was a finalist with the Old Library Theatre in Fair Lawn, New Jersey, and when it was produced by SkyPilot Theatre in Los Angeles in Future Shock, their Second Annual One-Act Festival, it won the Audience Award.

CHARACTERS

DIANA, female, 30s through 50s, socially awkward, nervous.
LIBRARIAN, casting is open in terms of gender, late 20s through 70s, warm and reassuring.

SETTING

A public library.

TIME

The not-so-distant future.

• • •

DIANA *enters the library and looks around. The* LIBRARIAN *comes over to greet her.*

LIBRARIAN: Yes, may I help you?

DIANA: Yes. I'm looking for something in the young adult section.

LIBRARIAN: Certainly. Was this for a teen you know?

DIANA: It's for myself.

LIBRARIAN: I see. And is there an era when you'd like this volume to be set?

DIANA: The years when I was growing up. I'd like it to happen when I was in my teens.

LIBRARIAN: Of course. I hear that a lot. Could you let me know what years those were?

DIANA: My age is right on my Identity Card.

> (*She hands the card to the* LIBRARIAN, *who studies it.*)

LIBRARIAN: Diana Davis. May I call you Diana?

DIANA: Sure.

LIBRARIAN: We accept community ID cards as library cards now. I don't think we've had you in here before.

DIANA: No, I only moved to this sector a few months ago. And—usually, I prefer to buy experiences. Own them myself, in case I want to relive them . . .

LIBRARIAN: Many do. But I think you'll be pleasantly surprised by the selection here, right in the neighborhood library. A whole range of experiences, some not commonly found in lifetime experience stores—and all in excellent condition.

DIANA: No—bugs? No viruses that could infect . . .

LIBRARIAN: Your own equipment? Absolutely not. We check the volumes and clean them thoroughly, before returning them to our shelves.

DIANA: Well, that's what I've heard. I mean, I know this is a pretty exclusive community; I was lucky when a housing unit opened up here that I could afford . . .

LIBRARIAN: That's just it. Our community library is of the highest caliber. Just like our community gym and recreation center, and our park, with actual trees and animals—

DIANA: Yeah, I visited it, it's *amazing*, sixty square feet of park, with twelve actual trees, and a pond . . . There were just too many people there, and, like, kids running around and shouting. But yes, I know I'm lucky to be here . . .

LIBRARIAN: You may find this library to be—quite a wonderful resource. You can experience every kind of adolescence imaginable. And if you find a volume you've enjoyed living, you can always take it out again.

DIANA: That sounds great. I know I could have signed up online and arranged for a volume to be delivered:—but I really wanted to talk to someone face to face. I've got all these questions.

LIBRARIAN: Of course.

DIANA: Are you the main Librarian here? Or are you a hologram?

LIBRARIAN: I'm real.

DIANA: 'Cause you're as reassuring as a hologram. You interact in a smooth, comforting way.

LIBRARIAN: Thank you. On weekends, I usually receive help from a hologram assistant program, when a lot of children come with their parents. The children want to try on some grown-up careers, and meet extinct animals, and wander through a forest—that sort of thing.

DIANA: Is that safe?

LIBRARIAN: Yes, the experiences we let them live are carefully test-driven, and quite educational. But on a rainy afternoon like this, I have plenty of time to help you. We might find the ideal life, one you didn't know was possible. What kind of adolescence would you like to have?

DIANA: Well. A girl. Not too different from me. But more creative. You know? An artist, or someone who plays guitar . . .

LIBRARIAN: Popular?

DIANA: Oh. Not ditsy-cheerleader-popular. She doesn't have to be, like, a homecoming queen. But *some* kids think she's really, really cool.

LIBRARIAN: Nerdy kids?

DIANA: No, not just the nerds. Kids who'd like to be . . . like . . . artistic and different, but they're not that creative, or they're afraid to stand out . . . just regular kids. Like I was.

LIBRARIAN: Does this girl do well in school?

DIANA: You know . . . It's not her top priority. She's good at English. She writes poems. Deep poems that impress her teacher. But you can cut Spanish class and gym class out.

LIBRARIAN: The program will allow you to edit out certain kinds of experiences.

DIANA: Yeah, sometimes I have trouble working those controls. I frankly think the design could be more user-friendly, at least in most volumes I've tried.

LIBRARIAN: Mmm. I'd be glad to help you with that—again, one of the benefits of having a Librarian assist you.

DIANA: Well, I appreciate that. This has been a low-stress interaction for me, so far.

LIBRARIAN: I'm glad. Now, in terms of the volume you want to check out—do you have ideas about the home life of this girl?

DIANA: Nice parents. A mom that's more like a friend to her, you know? The mom isn't obsessed with watching shows and VR, and living other lives. She's not always zoned out on happiness pills. This mom wants to actually spend time with me. With the girl. And the dad is . . . a little gruff, maybe, but also funny and nice. A proud father. He listens to the songs I write. Or looks at the pictures I paint, or whatever.

(*The* LIBRARIAN *takes notes on a phone or tablet.*)

LIBRARIAN: I see. Siblings?

DIANA: Naah. Maybe a sister.

LIBRARIAN: Older or younger?

DIANA: I dunno. Maybe a twin? Actually, scratch the sister. Give her a best friend. Who thinks she's, like, a hero, and wants to be like her.

LIBRARIAN: Pets?

DIANA: I don't think so. No. But give her, like, a big backyard. With trees and a garden. And animals and bugs in it.

LIBRARIAN: But—you said . . .

DIANA: Yeah, I know, I said I want it to be set in the same years I was growing up. And I do, in terms of the clothes and the slang and the shows and the hit songs and celebrities. You know? But can't it be *enhanced* reality? Can't she have a big backyard with, like, leafy plants, and, and butterflies, and praying mantises, and, like, things that burrow in the ground, like beavers—

LIBRARIAN: Is this by a stream?

DIANA: Well—whatever used to dig holes. Moles, or raccoons, or . . .

LIBRARIAN: Rabbits, perhaps?

DIANA: Sure, rabbits. That sounds great. And birds in the trees, building birds' nests. I mean, you *do* have that kind of enhanced reality life experiences here, right? Because they *are* available in volumes I can order from commercial stores.

LIBRARIAN: Yes, we do have them. I'm simply trying to gauge—how close to reality you want this experience to be. You don't want the girl to have magical powers, do you?

DIANA: No. She's just, like, really deep. Poetic. Fearless.

LIBRARIAN: I understand. Should she have a significant other?

DIANA: Oh. I don't know. I'd rather find out. Like, maybe there are some cute guys, or one guy, and he's kind of deep and brooding also, and he can tell how deep she is, and he's shy at first. But don't tell me what happens. I'd rather just experience it. You know?

LIBRARIAN: I believe I do. There are several volumes that I think will be excellent matches. I'll pull them and you can preview them in the next room: try the girls on for size, as it were. They all have partially adjustable settings—

DIANA: But if I edit it—if I add in certain kinds of people and animals, or change the way the girl looks—it won't be all CGI and fakey and lame, will it?

LIBRARIAN: I haven't heard any complaints about that.

DIANA: Okay. So, how long can I have it?

LIBRARIAN: Well, we recommend checking out one volume at a time. And you can renew it online every two weeks, for up to six weeks. Do you commute to a job?

DIANA: No. I create specialized ambiance music, for scenarios that people act out with sex bots—I write the music on my desktop. So, I'm in my unit, plugged into my port most of the time. I find it stressful to—be around people a lot. I get my meals delivered.

LIBRARIAN: Community members like you who set their own schedules, and have many secluded hours, often get the most out of this sort of experience.

DIANA: And how long does it last?

LIBRARIAN: Potentially, you can live months of this teenager's life, with sleep and the boring and unpleasant parts left out.

DIANA: That would be so cool! 'Cause when I buy life experience—I can't afford more than, like, a few days, tops. And so, I wind up reliving them, with little changes, till I'm sick of 'em.

LIBRARIAN: Then, that's another reason, Diana, why I think you'll find this experience to be a revelation. Don't be surprised if living this teenager's life becomes a second skin to you. And don't be surprised if you become one of this library's best customers.

DIANA: Yeah.

> (*The* LIBRARIAN *starts to exit the stage, to find volumes in the next room, but* DIANA *grabs hold of the* LIBRARIAN's *arm.*)

It's just . . .

LIBRARIAN: What? Please tell me, I'd like to help you put aside all of your concerns.

DIANA: I'm sorry to be so freaked out about this . . . You're absolutely, one hundred percent sure it's safe? No digital bugs infecting my home system— 'cause I've been having health problems as it is.

LIBRARIAN: I promise.

DIANA: And nobody else able to see, later, what I did when I was living this kid's life? It's private?

LIBRARIAN: Diana, I guarantee you that it's as safe and as sanitary as if you borrowed one of the sex bots from the community recreation center and took it home with you. When you brought it back, it would be sterilized from top to bottom, and its memory drive would be completely wiped. Keep in mind, there are some very important people who live in this community. They use these facilities also. They wouldn't stand for anything less.

DIANA: Okay.

LIBRARIAN: I can have our written pledges sent to you at home . . .

DIANA: No, I already read the guarantees online.

LIBRARIAN: Good. Is there anything else before we go browsing in the young adult section for lives?

DIANA: Yeah. It's . . . I don't want this girl to be lonely. You know? Like, so what, she's not the queen of popularity. She's so confident, she's not afraid of being alone sometimes . . . But still. I want her to have a network of people she can talk to. Like, parents, and friends, and maybe ultimately a good guy . . . I want her to feel like she *belongs*, like other people really care about her. She has empathy for them, and they totally get where she's coming from.

And she can do fine in social situations, whenever they come up: talk, give advice, pick up on, like, cues—she's *connected* to other people.

LIBRARIAN: I know exactly what you mean. Community, caring. That's high on the wish list for many residents who use this library, and it's a key element in most of the volumes in our collection.

DIANA: Another thing—this girl shouldn't be all wussy and passive, you know? She has courage! She doesn't just stand on the sidelines of life watching, absorbing stuff, being entertained. She's a doer! She makes things happen. She dives in, she's heroic, she's a person of action!

LIBRARIAN: I promise. We'll find the right volume, and this girl will be all of those things. It was brave of you to come here and interact with me, live, and in person—and now you'll be rewarded by experiencing everything that this daring, artistic, well-loved girl says and does.

DIANA: Then, excellent, I'm totally into it!

LIBRARIAN: Ready to browse? Ready to try some volumes on?

DIANA: Show me some teen lives, and I bet I'll know who I want to be, as soon as I am her—in the first five minutes, I'll look in the mirror, and I'll know!

(*They head offstage together.*)

(*Lights down.*)

END OF PLAY

BULLET ALWAYS WINS

by Erik Christian Hanson

Bullet Always Wins was produced by the Actors' Theatre Grand Rapids in June 2019, as part of their "Living on the Edge" Festival. It was directed by Tony Peraino. (Slight changes have been made to the original script based on multiple productions.) The cast was as follows:

TEACHER: Anna Swanson
BULLET: Aaron Skorka

Erik Christian Hanson earned his MFA in dramatic writing from NYU's Tisch School of the Arts and was the recipient of an "Outstanding Writing for the Screen" certificate from the Goldberg Department. During his time at NYU, he was a literary intern at The New Group. His work has been published by Smith & Kraus and Applause Books in eight play anthologies. More than thirty-five of his plays have been developed and produced in Alaska, California, Connecticut, Indiana, Maryland, Massachusetts, Michigan, Missouri, Nebraska, New York, Ohio, Oregon, South Carolina, Virginia, and Washington. They include: *Property of Africa, Whoa Means No* (Boston Theater Marathon), *Same Only Different* (Great Plains Theatre Conference), *Polish the Turd* (Last Frontier Theatre Conference), *Celebration* (Selection, WILL: iam Inge New Play Lab), *The Jane Austen Expressway* (MadLab Theatre), and *Blue Lagoonin' It* (Selection, Midwest Dramatists Center Conference). He has been a finalist for Nantucket Film Festival's Screenwriters Colony, Lark Playwrights' Week, EST's Marathon of One-Act Plays and the Sewanee Writers' Conference; he has been a semifinalist for the O'Neill Conference, Theater Masters' National MFA Playwrights Festival, and Theatre

503's International Playwriting Award. As an educator, Hanson has taught undergraduate and graduate-level courses for the past decade at Sacred Heart University.

CHARACTERS

TEACHER, any age, female, any race.
BULLET, any age, any gender, any race.

SETTING

A room with no furniture and minimal lighting.

TIME

A few days after yet another school shooting.

AUTHOR'S NOTE

Teacher is rambling due to her mental state. She never acknowledges the presence of Bullet.

• • •

Lights up. A dark room. A TEACHER stares off into space. A BULLET, shiny and lethal, sits in the corner.

TEACHER: The bullet missed my face by a hair.

BULLET: I was closer than that.

TEACHER: I can still hear the ringing.

(*A prolonged ringing sound comes from* BULLET's *direction.*)

BULLET: That was me, sorry. (*He laughs.*)

TEACHER: Why can't I get it out of my head?!

BULLET: It is my intention to haunt you.

TEACHER: I . . .

BULLET: And every other breathing person.

TEACHER: I . . .

BULLET: Spit it out.

TEACHER: I don't think I should set foot inside a school again.

BULLET: I second that notion.

TEACHER: I can't set foot inside a school again.

BULLET: That was my goal.

TEACHER: But I have to.

BULLET: You are not ready.

TEACHER: I cannot let this win.

BULLET: I always win.

TEACHER: My coworkers . . .

BULLET: Plenty of them are dead.

TEACHER: . . . would want me . . .

BULLET: I got nine of them.

TEACHER: . . . the students would want . . .

BULLET: And sixteen of those little buggers.

TEACHER: . . . me . . .

BULLET: They would want you to quit.

TEACHER: I need to be strong.

BULLET: Strong is overrated.

TEACHER: I need to . . .

BULLET: Quit.

TEACHER: I . . .

BULLET: QUIT.

TEACHER: I . . .

BULLET: Three of your coworkers did.

TEACHER: . . . need to be a symbol of . . .

BULLET: They left the field of education for good.

TEACHER: . . . strength.

BULLET: What strength exists in that choice?

TEACHER: I . . .

BULLET: Because of me, the school is bringing in extra counselors and therapy dogs.

TEACHER: This is what teachers do.

BULLET: Teachers are going to leave their profession in droves.

TEACHER: Teachers keep going amidst all odds.

BULLET: Perhaps, but most teachers now live with the daily fear that I provide. All schools will be shut down after my work is done.

TEACHER: I have to join a group that says, "No, this will not continue."

BULLET: (*Amused.*) Is there a group out there that says that?

TEACHER: This cannot continue.

BULLET: Oh, but it will.

TEACHER: We can't let it.

BULLET: You and others are no match.

TEACHER: We . . .

BULLET: Should retire.

TEACHER: . . . must find ways to . . .

BULLET: There are no ways. There is only surrender.

TEACHER: . . . protect our children's futures.

BULLET: They have no futures.

TEACHER: That is all that matters.

BULLET: Self-preservation is what matters, honey.

TEACHER: They are all that matter.

BULLET: They are not worth your sacrifice.

TEACHER: They . . .

BULLET: Mean nothing.

TEACHER: . . . are . . .

BULLET: Ants in the overall scheme of things.

TEACHER: I have to do something!

BULLET: You have to do something? You must do something? I'll tell you what to do. You do this: buy a plane ticket in three days. My next shooting will occur 1,211 miles from here. Do your best to stop it. (*Laughs.*) If you fail, do not fret because the shooting after that will be 379 miles from here. Are you willing to travel to stop me? Are you that committed to this cause? Short of that, you should take early retirement and reserve a stool at the local bar. Current *happy hour* prices are mind-blowing.

TEACHER: I will be strong . . .

BULLET: Waste of your energy.

TEACHER: I will take a more active role in the lives of my students . . .

BULLET: Waste of your time.

TEACHER: I will . . .

BULLET: Go through life thinking you can change a force as strong as I am, but you will be proven wrong in the end and you know it. Deep down, you know it.

TEACHER: I . . .

BULLET: Know it.

TEACHER: I don't know!

BULLET: You do know.

TEACHER: What can I do?

BULLET: Nothing.

TEACHER: What should I do?

BULLET: Ab-solutely nothing.

TEACHER: Why?

BULLET: Because I always win and you always lose.

TEACHER: The world isn't fair.

BULLET: Duh.

TEACHER: The world . . .

BULLET: Is a series of stories made up of people's daily suffering.

TEACHER: . . . needs a makeover.

BULLET: I am in the process of giving it said makeover. Want to hear how many I will take at the next shooting?

TEACHER: The second amendment . . .

BULLET: Is a thing of freaking beauty.

TEACHER: . . . needs . . .

BULLET: Spoiler alert: it will never be modified.

TEACHER: . . . to be amended . . .

BULLET: The powers that be will never allow it.

TEACHER: . . . the psychiatric field needs . . .

BULLET: Even with better and more timely evaluations, I will be victorious. Have you seen what these counselors do with the kids?

TEACHER: They'll . . .

BULLET: Talk about emotions. Tell the little kiddos not to get stuck on their emotions, play a social-slash-board game, and then send them back to class with a sticker.

TEACHER: But counselors are not the problem.

BULLET: They're part of it.

TEACHER: It has to change. Everything needs to change.

BULLET: Be a part of the so-called change all you like, the results will be the same.

TEACHER: I am going to lead that change.

BULLET: Lead away.

TEACHER: I am that change.

BULLET: All righty . . .

TEACHER: I hope I am that change.

BULLET: You won't be, but it's fun to dream.

TEACHER: Maybe this has all been a dream.

BULLET: I am sorry to report that it is all quite real, and that it is going to get much worse from here on out. More tears. More bloodshed. More confusion. More chaos. More rage.

TEACHER: A dream that I will emerge from and . . .

BULLET: You may have emerged, but you have entered a nightmare, dear. There are no exit doors for this one because I tossed out all the keys.

TEACHER: I can . . . conquer this.

BULLET: Humans don't defeat bullets.

TEACHER: I . . .

BULLET: . . . will earn an "A" for trying.

TEACHER: . . . can do this. I will do this.

BULLET: I wish you luck. Truly. The best of luck.
> (*He snorts.* TEACHER *scans her surroundings, hoping a positive answer will come.*)

> (*Lights dim.*)

> (*Blackout.*)

END OF PLAY

BUT WHO'S COUNTING?

by Connie Bennett

But Who's Counting? was produced by Oregon Contemporary Theatre, Eugene, Oregon, on March 20–29, 2020, as part of the Northwest Ten Festival: Oh, Boise! Directed by Ellen Gillooly-Kress.

Cast:
JAX: BEN: Minnis
MISSY: Mary McCoy
NIX: James Holechek

Connie Bennett is a Eugene, Oregon, based playwright, and is a member of the Dramatists Guild, the Playwrights' Center, and the International Centre for Women Playwrights. Connie participated in the first two years of the William Inge Festival Play Lab. She has written annually for 365 Women A Year: a playwriting project. She contributed to the collective script, *Playwrights Say Never Again to School Shootings*. In 2018, a staged reading of Connie's full-length version of *Amanda Transcending* was performed as part of the National Endowment for the Arts NEA Big Read: a community celebration of Joy Harjo's "How We Became Human" at the Eugene Public Library and the Oregon Contemporary Theatre; this script will be workshopped during the summer of 2021 by Theatre33. Connie's *Gray Reflections* was a finalist in the Actors Theatre of Louisville 2010 National Ten-Minute Play Contest and her full-length play, *Hungry Hearts* (based on the novel by Francine Prose), was a finalist at the National Yiddish Theatre–Folksbiene in New York. Also at Oregon Contemporary Theatre, she's coproduced the annual "Northwest Ten! Festival" since 2009 and, since 2015, the SWAN Day Readings of new works by Oregon women.

CHARACTERS

JAX, a Sasquatch.
MISSY, a census worker. Young, petite, female.
NIX, a Sasquatch, JAX's partner.

SETTING

A pleasant living room, home of NIX and JAX.

TIME

Early evening, April 2020.

• • •

In the darkness, a doorbell rings. Lights up on a pleasant living room. As the bell rings again, JAX, *a Sasquatch, enters to answer the door. Simultaneously,* NIX, *another Sasquatch, unlocks the door from the outside, holding it open for* MISSY, *who is armed with a briefcase and badge. It is an awkward, three-way mess in the doorway.*

JAX: (*To* NIX.) So you finally decided to show up . . .

    (NIX *gestures incomprehensibly to* JAX *about* MISSY's *presence*)

JAX: What, you forgot your ke—? (*Noticing* MISSY, JAX *breaks off.*)

MISSY: Good evening, uh, sir? I'm Missy Dorland with the Census.

NIX: Good evening.

MISSY: (*Holding up her ID badge.*) Uh, yes, good evening to you both. I'm with the Census Bureau. May I come . . .

JAX: With the . . . ?

MISSY: May I come in? I'm, um, I'm with the Census . . . just, uh, just following up on an incomplete self-reported, um . . . forms.

JAX: Wait, um, wait. "The Census?" "Incomplete forms . . . ?"

MISSY: Or sometimes it's just random, you know, statistical. Maybe your forms were absolutely perfect—complete—and you just got the lucky draw to be the long form interview. You know, the in-person follow-up? I'm not actually totally sure, I'm new. This is my very first interview.

NIX: (*To* JAX, *sotto voce*) I'm not sure I trust her.

MISSY: (*Taking out an iPad or clipboard.*) So, anyway, let me just pull up the data, see what we have . . .

JAX: (*To* NIX, *sotto voce.*) Look who's talking. Where were you last night?

MISSY: Actually, the only, uh, all that shows for this address—122B? Right?—is that it's a rental, um, a duplex?

NIX: (*To* JAX.) Did you send in any forms?

MISSY: Nothing about the actual residents.

JAX: (*To* NIX.) I don't remember any forms.

MISSY: So, uh, let's start with, well, have you lived here very long?

NIX: (*To* JAX.) Well, I sure didn't see any forms.

MISSY: Look, you can forget about the forms, I'll just collect your data now.

NIX: (*To* JAX.) You're the one who's always tossing mail!

JAX: (*To* NIX.) Just junk mail! Publisher's Clearing House and more requests from some charity we already . . .

NIX: (*To* JAX.) And form letters? Like from the government!?

MISSY: You're actually living here, right? Not just visiting or . . .

JAX: (*To* NIX.) Some of those donation requests pretend to be surveys, you know!

MISSY: And it's just the two of you?

NIX: Yes!

MISSY: Children? Snowbirds? Um, another roommate? I mean, does anyone else "live and sleep here most of the time?"

JAX: Most of the time? (*To* NIX.) Maybe she should just be interviewing me!

MISSY: (*To* NIX.) You live somewhere else? I mean, more than here?

NIX: You can count me. (*To* JAX.) Why would you say that?

MISSY: We're not supposed to count temporary visitors, they're counted at their . . .

JAX: (*to Nix*) You took the cactus.

MISSY: So, uh, who's head of household?

NIX: (*To* JAX.) You're overwatering the cactus.

MISSY: (*Checking her instructions.*) Okay, here we are . . . (*Reading.*) pick one of the adults . . .

JAX: (*To* NIX.) You have to take care of, of things, if you neglect them, they die.

MISSY: *To* NIX.) Can you tell me your full name?

NIX: Nix

MISSY: I'd really appreciate it if you would . . . um, cooperate? Mr, uh, Ms, uh . . . ?

JAX: His name's Nix.

NIX: Nix. N—I—X.

MISSY: And, your surname? Or, um, is this your—uh, which name is this? Um, "Nix?"

NIX: Nix is my full name.

MISSY: Oh, dear. Let me check the guidelines on . . . um, you're sure you don't have a . . . ? Well of course you're sure. And your age?

NIX: I can't answer that.

MISSY: But this is the, the Census, you have to answer. To not answer is against the law.

JAX: I think we would qualify for the personal belief exemption.

MISSY: My training didn't—Er, well, (*To* JAX.) your name?

JAX: Jax. J.A.X. Only name, no first, last, whatever. Like Prince.

MISSY: And, uh, Jax, you were born in . . . what year?

NIX: I think we've spent enough time on . . .

MISSY: Just a few more questions!

NIX: Here's your briefcase.

MISSY: Please! I don't want you to get into trouble. For that matter, I don't want to get into trouble. But seriously, it's against the law to not answer the Census questions. There's a $100 fine.

JAX: Nix, uh, maybe we just answer . . . ?

MISSY: And you two are, uh, roommates? Oops, let's do this one at a time. Um, Nix, what's your current marital status?

NIX: What are my choices?

MISSY: Married, Unmarried Partner, Widowed, Divorced, Separated, or Never Married.

JAX: (*Jumping in.*) Unmarried Partner.

NIX: (*Overlapping, but clearly heard.*) Married.

MISSY: One at a time, there's several questions about—

JAX: (*To* NIX.) Marri . . . ? Oh, Nix!

MISSY: Um, Jax, do you have an Opposite-Sex-Married Husband/Wife/ Spouse or a Same-Sex-Married—wait, I knew I would screw this up!

NIX: (*To* JAX.) I know I've been hard to . . . .

MISSY: I am such a . . . Why didn't I just take that cashier job at Safeway?

JAX: (*To* NIX.) It depends how you define it.

MISSY: Maybe we'll come back to that one . . . ?

NIX: (*To* JAX.) Don't worry, the cactus is just fine.

MISSY: Okay, next question. "What is this person's race?"

NIX: Sasquatch.

MISSY: Wow! Really?!? I've never—I'm from California . . .

JAX: (*To* NIX.) That's just your Canadian bias showing, Nix . . .

MISSY: This is so exciting!

JAX: (*Continuing.*) . . . the proper Pacific Northwestern term is Bigfoot!

MISSY: (*Checking instructions.*) Got it! I find the right box and then fill in the blank about origin! See, their example is you mark the box for "White" and then you write in "German" or "Irish" or . . . whatever . . .

NIX: So, tell us the boxes.

JAX: Yeah, what are our choices?

MISSY: Well, White, of course. I mean, like I already said. "Black or African American." American Indian or Alaska Native . . .

NIX: Keep going.

MISSY: There's a bunch, uh . . . Chinese, Vietnamese, Filipino, Korean, Asian Indian, Japanese, Other Asian, uh, like um, Pakistani, Cambodian, Hmong—

NIX: Maybe Other Asian? I love Thai food, would that count?

MISSY: You aren't taking this seriously! It's important! Federal dollars and congressional seats hang in . . .

JAX: (*To* NIX.) Are you sure there's no Yeti strain in your . . . ?

NIX: (*To* JAX.) Are you trying to offend me?

MISSY: Oh, wait, I skipped the question on gender!

JAX: Let's hear your list for that one.

MISSY: List? Well, it's pretty short. Male or Female.

NIX: But what about other options?

MISSY: There are no other options.

JAX: But, but . . .

NIX: Recognized, you mean, by the US government . . .

MISSY: So, um, Jax . . . what gender do I put for you?

JAX: No gender.

NIX: The fine for not answering is $100?

MISSY: It's even worse if you give a false answer, then it's a $500 fine!

NIX: So . . . you save $400 by refusing to answer?

JAX: Wait, we never finished the race question. You got stuck on Thai.

MISSY: Right, right. Let's see, Native Hawaiian, Samoan, Chamorro—or, uh, last choice: "Some other race."

NIX: Clearly our box!

JAX: Yes! Mark the "X" there!

MISSY: Okay. And now, "print race or origin"?

NIX: S—A—S

JAX: Q—U—A

NIX AND JAX: T—C—H

MISSY: Okay, whew! One down!

NIX: (*To* JAX.) I thought you preferred Bigfoot?

JAX: (*To* NIX.) We "married" people need to stick together!

MISSY: But we do need to go back, there are a few questions we kind of skipped over . . . um, Age, uh, Gender, Same-Sex-Unmarried-Partner . . . ?

NIX: "Same-Sex?" You mean the US government only cares about sexual orientation if you're partnered!?

JAX: Wait a minute! Did you say "Unmarried" Partner?

MISSY: Why, yes, Jax, I have you down as an unmarried partner to, uh, married to . . . This doesn't make sense!

NIX: We need to match.

JAX: Change my answer to "Married!" I don't care if the cactus dies!

MISSY: (*Marking madly.*) And, and Gender?

NIX: Religious exemption.

MISSY: Wait a minute, you can't have a religious exemption to Gender! It just isn't . . . I mean, you can't refuse or willfully neglect to answer, it's—

NIX: But if we stop now, it'll save us $400. Let's call this done! Where do we sign?

MISSY: (*As* JAX *escorts her to the door.*) That Safeway job is looking better by the minute!

JAX: You should stick with the Census, Missy, you'll love our neighbors in 122A.

NIX: Oh, yes. (*As the door closes behind* MISSY.) The unicorns next door.

END OF PLAY

COLOR ME COMPLETE

by Rose-Emma Lambridis

Original Production:
April 19, 2018–April 21, 2018
University of New Haven

Directed by Dalímar Irizarry

Original Cast:
RED: Tim Sheehan
GRAY: Erica Quaedvlieg

Rose-Emma Lambridis is a playwright and actor from Brooklyn, New York. She is a recent graduate of the University of New Haven and is currently challenging society's preconceived notions of existence. Her work *Color Me Complete* has been previously recognized as a semi-finalist in the Kennedy Center American College Theater Festival National Playwriting Program and was featured in the 2019 *riverSedge: A Journal of Art and Literature* at the University of Texas Rio Grande Valley. For business inquiries, contact rlambridis123@gmail.com.

CHARACTERS

RED, an idealist.
GRAY, a realist.

SETTING

A canvas.

TIME

Daybreak.

NOTE

Actors stay in their poses unless otherwise specified, but may move their head to acknowledge one another. The costumes each actor wears should be in their respective color.

• • •

An empty white canvas. The color RED *enters in an extravagant fashion, either through dance, lighting, music, or all of the above.* RED *strikes a fabulous pose. Obviously ecstatic. The color* GRAY *enters a few seconds later with no extra accompaniment, and strikes an unremarkable pose. Obviously unamused.*

RED: Don't you just love the smell of a fresh canvas in the morning? What do you think we'll be?

GRAY: Here we go.

RED: Could we be a landscape? Or maybe a field of flowers? Oh look! She's grabbing another tool . . . it's a flat brush! Oooh, do you think we'll be abstract? That's so interesting!

GRAY: Sure.

RED: Aren't you excited to become part of the "bigger picture"?

GRAY: No.

RED: Oh. (*Realizing.*) Oh! I'm sorry, are you . . . sad? Because you're, you know, Gray? I mean I've never *met* a Gray before. I've only *heard* of the sort.

GRAY: Common misconception, Red: Not all Grays reflect sadness. We actually prefer the term "neutral." For instance, I don't have any particular feelings towards the "bigger picture." We exist as paint to be whatever painting the painter wants us to be. Nothing more, nothing less.

RED: I mean . . . I *guess* that's one way to look at it. But exploring the possibilities is so much more fun! C'mon, try it. Think of one thing you could be.

GRAY: I don't know.

RED: Literally anything! The coolest thing you can imagine!

GRAY: A wall.

RED: I bet you could do better than that. Hey, where did the painter's tools go?

GRAY: In the box.

RED: Oh wow! Maybe she's going to finger paint a rainbow, you know, to show the innocence of childhood or something.

GRAY: I believe she's finished.

RED: Haha, no. That's impossible. We're not finished yet. See? She's grabbing a ruler to outline some cool sketches.

GRAY: She's taking measurements for the frame.

RED: (*Breaking their pose.*) WHAT? Absolutely not. We're not finished yet. Excuse me, but where do you think you're going—NO! HEY! MISS PAINTER! YOU CAN'T LEAVE! WE ARE *NOT* FINISHED YET! COME BACK! (*Beat.*) She really left. She made two lousy streaks and left. We're supposed to be something extraordinary like a radiant sunset or—or—or a field of flowers. This is ludicrous! Is this what art is nowadays? Have we stooped that low? We're not even a bowl of exotic fruit? I'm just one harsh, ugly, Red mark! (*Beat.*) I can't do this. I can't be nothing. I'm leaving.

GRAY: What?

RED: I'm leaving. I'm going to be part of the "bigger picture."

GRAY: That's just silly. You can't leave.

RED: Oh, but I can.

GRAY: (*Matter-of-factly.*) But you can't.

RED: But I can.

GRAY: But you can't.

RED: But I can. Watch me.

GRAY: (*Breaking out of pose.*) Wait!

RED: What?

GRAY: I mean . . . don't you see the "bigger picture" here?

RED: No, because obviously there isn't one.

GRAY: Sure there is. Think about it. There are only two colors here, you and me. So, it's a dichotomy. To show contrast?

RED: *Dichotomy?* I don't want to be part of an idea. I want to be in a *painting*.

GRAY: What you become isn't your decision! You're only the medium through which . . .

RED: Really, it's been a great time, but I'm going to leave before I dry.

GRAY: Please. Don't.

RED: Why?

GRAY: I don't necessarily care. (*Gray does care.*) But the painter . . .

RED: Forget the painter.

GRAY: I'm here to make you look good. My only purpose on this canvas is to show how beautiful and lovely you are. You're bright, I'm dull. Without you, there won't be a vision anymore. Without you I'm just . . . Gray.

RED: But . . . I can't stay. I need to find something to be a part of. Like a mural! Something . . . whole. The "bigger picture."

GRAY: (*Returning to pose.*) Great, we're back to that.

RED: You can't tell me that you have no desires! What's your "bigger picture"?

GRAY: I don't have one.

RED: Use your imagination! If you had the brush, what would you paint?

GRAY: But we're . . .

RED: C'mon . . .

GRAY: I don't . . .

RED: *C'mon . . .*

GRAY: FINE OKAY I'LL IMAGINE.

(RED *and* GRAY *close their eyes.*)

RED: So?

GRAY: Hush. I see wind.

RED: How can you see . . .

GRAY: Wind. Wrapping around itself, in a tunnel. Like a vortex, or a vacuum, or a . . .

(*They open their eyes.* GRAY *breaks their pose to convey the story.*)

. . . Tornado. A tornado just descended from a stormy sky. Its massive magnetic force pulling everything towards it center. There are houses and animals and a wicked witch on a broom and behind the tornado it's clear that the Western landscape has been ripped from its roots. The remnants of its destruction lie in ruin. But the natural disaster has been put to a halt, been stopped in its tracks by the natural beauty that lies in front of it. A small, delicate, red ROSE.

RED: Wow.

GRAY: Wow.

RED: That was . . . !

GRAY: Weird. Never trying that again.

RED: Why not? You obviously have some imagination to spare. Do something with it. Come with me. We could create our own destiny! Make the world our canvas! We could paint the town . . .

GRAY: A dull pink?

RED: Oh c'mon . . .

GRAY: I am paint. Not the painter. I'm going to do what I was mixed to do.

RED: Why are you so afraid?

GRAY: I'm in touch with reality. You have no idea what's out there. What if you become that mural and wash away? Or dry before you become anything at all?

RED: At least I'll know I tried!

GRAY: At least I know I'll only ever be paint!

RED: But you could be so much more!

GRAY: You're *nothing* but paint and when you leave, you'll *still* be paint!

RED: At least I won't be sad! (*Realizing how hurtful this remark was.*) I'm sorry. I didn't mean . . .

GRAY: (*Returning to their pose.*) Not sad, remember? Neutral.

RED: Of course.

GRAY: Don't stay too long now. Like you said, you're going to dry.

RED: Yes. Right. Wouldn't want that.

GRAY: Can't wait to see what you become.

RED: The possibilities are endless.

GRAY: Sure. I hope you find what you're looking for.

RED: Yeah. You too.
    (RED *goes to exit, then turns back to* GRAY.)
It may not be all about the "bigger picture," but sometimes it's enough to want to feel complete.
    (RED *braces for the unknown, then exits. The canvas is blanker than when we began.*)

GRAY: (*Tearing up.*)
Calm down, Gray. Remember, you're indifferent. Not sad. (*Crying.*) Not sad. Neutral. Neutral. Neutral.
    (GRAY *takes one last inhale, and with no release, freezes in place. GRAY has dried.*)

    (*Blackout.*)

END OF PLAY

COUNT DRACULA'S CAFÉ

by Scot Walker

Original Production:
Shafer Street Playhouse, Virginia Commonwealth University, Richmond, Virginia, September 7–9 and 14–16, 2018, produced and directed by Kenn Pridgen, featuring Boris Alexander as COUNT DRACULA, Jase Parker as THE SERVER, and Stephen Lopez as the GAY VAMP.

Scot Walker is a published poet, essayist, novelist, playwright, and short story writer. His plays have been produced both in the United States and in Europe.

CHARACTERS

COUNT DRACULA, 559 years old and yes, he's the original Romanian vampire. For his first half a millennium he drank a mixture of heterosexual and homosexual blood and passed for a man of twenty. Now, however, due to US government policy, which cut off his gay blood supply, he looks old and withered and no longer enjoys the opera or the ballet or the musical theatre. In short, he's withering away.
THE SERVER, 528 years old, although The Server appears to be a teenager. He's/she's an obsequious waiter and second-class vampire who lives for nothing more than serving Count Dracula.
GAY VAMP, 31, a gay man dressed in drag. He is not a vampire.

SETTING

Halloween. A small dimly lit coffee shop in Greenwich Village catering to vampires and homosexuals. A table and two chairs sit center stage.

• • •

The stage is pitch-dark. We hear COUNT DRACULA *singing offstage loudly.*

COUNT DRACULA: Blood, glorious blood, hot plasma and glucose . . .

THE SERVER: Blood? Did you sing about blood, Count Dracula?

> (*Sound of feet shuffling as* COUNT DRACULA *and* THE SERVER *enter the café. Lights come up full.* COUNT DRACULA *fills his lungs deeply as he enters, savoring the taste and smell.*)

COUNT DRACULA: Keep alert. I smell fresh gay blood sauntering nearby.

THE SERVER: Sauntering?

COUNT DRACULA: Yes . . . sauntering . . . or stewing . . . or simmering, it's out there and getting closer . . . and for God's sakes, retract your fangs!

THE SERVER: I'm trying to, but they keep hanging out in antici . . . pation. Besides, I just don't have the energy I used to.

COUNT DRACULA: Then straighten up.

THE SERVER: You mean "gay-en up" don't you?

COUNT DRACULA: Boy, you're messing with the wrong vampire! If you continue your back talk, I'll never turn you into a first-class blood-sucking vampire and you'll have to survive on watered down tomato puree and tangerine juice! Well, what are you waiting for? Set the tables. We don't have all day—the girls will be sashaying in any minute now.

> (THE SERVER *mimes setting tables, putting out coffee pots, etc. without missing a beat.*)

THE SERVER: Sashaying, just like the Sugar Plum Fairies straight out of that glorious Disney Hippopotamus family flick: The Nutcracker Suite. (*He dances.*)

COUNT DRACULA: You make my veins bubble, thinking about those sweet delectable sugar plum fairies!

THE SERVER: Give me an hour with a real nutcracker and that prince will never be the same!

COUNT DRACULA: Are you sure they're coming?

THE SERVER: Of course, the fairies are coming. How could they resist? Besides, you're the one who decided to buy this coffee shop. You figured out how only fresh brewed coffee and mango filled donuts could lure them here. First, we'll fill them with donuts to fatten up their corpuscles. That'll make them sweet and succulent. And then . . . we'll suck them dry! So you tell me, will we suck gay blood tonight or not? I'm so withered, I'm not even turned on by Liza Minnelli. Lady Gaga doesn't even excite me! What am I going to do . . . and don't give me that look . . . (*Humbly, knowing his place.*) I know (*Groveling.*) We're short of coffee cups and that's all I'm good for . . . fetching and serving and serving and sucking and fetching and (*Licking lips.*), sucking, but I need faggot blood!

COUNT DRACULA: Be careful, or you'll be my mid-morning snack!

THE SERVER: (*Exiting.*) Yes master, I know, master. That's all I'm able to do . . . just fetch and serve, fetch and serve . . . fetch and . . .

COUNT DRACULA: The fags will be here, you can count on that!
(THE SERVER *is totally out of vocal range now and* COUNT DRACULA *sits, admiring his new digs.*)
It's coffee shop magnetism, that's what it is—nothing can keep a happy fairy from a hot cup of Drac's cocoa mocha latte . . . nothing! (*Beat.*) I wonder if it's the aroma! (*Beat, laughing.*) Those delicious homos savor smells as much as our nostrils savor their corn-syrup free blood. God, I love their healthy life style! Workouts! Sweat! Vegan diets! Gluten free meals! Only the purest of the pure for these pure-blooded boys! (*Beat.*) Hey, brew a double batch of our vampire delicious cocoa mocha latte and sprinkle some of Tinker Bell's fairy dust on it—that'll get their juices flowing. They'll be prancing their asses in here like good little girls any minute now!

(THE SERVER *enters. He's holding a cross in his left hand and a stake in his right. A huge garlic necklace hangs loosely around his neck.*)

THE SERVER: In the name of Jesus, I condemn you.
(*He takes a few steps toward the Count, brandishing the cross, then pauses a moment and laughs uproariously, joined in by* COUNT DRACULA.)

COUNT DRACULA: What the hell is this? Vampire Comedy Central?

(THE SERVER *hoists the stake above his head and jabs it down into an unseen vampire's heart, making as many gruesome sounds as he can, prolonging the death of the unseen victim and mimes feasting on the blood.*)

COUNT DRACULA: Stop it with that stake! Bram Stoker created that legend centuries ago. It didn't work then and it doesn't work now. Nothing can kill a vampire . . . nothing!

THE SERVER: We both know that . . . but they don't know that. Besides, wouldn't it be fun to keep a pile of stakes next to the coffee urns? It'll give the girls a false sense of security and make their blood flow richer and faster. Think about those extra gallons flowing like . . . Old Faithful!
   (*He lays the cross and stake down, as he brandishes his garlic necklace, rubbing it up and down the Count's face. COUNT DRACULA laughs.*)

COUNT DRACULA: You know neither of us is allergic to garlic anymore—I think it's the Sudafed; it's changed our immune systems.

THE SERVER: That and Dunkin'.

COUNT DRACULA: I forgot about the donuts, they've made my blood too sweet. Look at me. I can't even vamp any more.
   (*He tries to flutter his cape and assume the vampire pose, but fails abysmally in his attempt to "fly" around the room, ultimately collapsing in his chair.*)
If we keep drinking all this sweet heterosexual blood, we'll turn into giant Ho Hos.

THE SERVER: You spell that with an H, right?

   (COUNT DRACULA *laughs again.*)

COUNT DRACULA: Yep. H, O, H, O, just like Santa's laughter.

THE SERVER: I'm not into Ho Ho's, I'm more of a Twinkie lover, myself! Give me all those hot young twenty-year olds and I'll devour them faster than you can say they're as finger-licking good as chicken McFaggots.

COUNT DRACULA: See, that's why you're going to remain a second-class vampire for another five hundred years. You've got to get some macho homo protein. Otherwise, you'll remain a skinny assed vampire for the rest of eternity.

   (THE SERVER *pulls a Little Debbie from his pocket.*)

COUNT DRACULA: And flush that before you turn into a diabetic. It's bad enough that New York homos are sweeter than lollipops, don't add Little

Debbies to the mix. For God's sake, save your appetite for sweet succulent sizzling gay blood!

(THE SERVER *shrugs*.)

COUNT DRACULA: It's bad enough you spend half your life hanging out at Baskin-Robbins and Cinnabon!

THE SERVER: Actually, I hate them both, but it's the only way I can dilute that Godawful heterosexual blood.

COUNT DRACULA: Well, if you keep this up, you'll end up a flabby-assed vampire!

THE SERVER: (*Mumbling*.) Like you . . .

COUNT DRACULA: Can you picture what all those Hollywood actors would look like if they were real vampires? Especially with this gay blood shortage going on?

THE SERVER: Give me a firm, hot, tight-assed homo any day!

COUNT DRACULA: That's for sure, and you'll look five hundred years younger with a homo hottie by your side—God knows you need something to improve your looks. (*Beat*.) I'm just messing with you, boy, I know you don't want to end up in the geriatrics ward with a flabby ass, rotting fangs and wings that won't unfurl, do you?

THE SERVER: That might be better than becoming insulin-dependent. A vampire can only eat so many donuts!

COUNT DRACULA: I guess we should look on the good side, if either of us becomes diabetic, we'll always have Vampire-Care to fall back on.

THE SERVER: Does it come with Medi-Vamp coverage or is that limited to humans?

COUNT DRACULA: Of course it covers us. We've been paying taxes for over five hundred years. We're equal partners under the law!

THE SERVER: (*Under his breath*.) Right, just like we're entitled to suck gay blood!

COUNT DRACULA: (*Oblivious to* THE SERVER'*s previous remark*.) For God sakes, we deserve some bang for our buck! Consider our situation as "no deposit, no return." If the government won't allow us to deposit gay blood into our veins, we'll end up returning to the hospital every night. So, picture, if you can, a hundred thousand anemic vampires filling America's hospitals, sucking up the entire blood supply.

THE SERVER: No deposit, no return! I get it.

COUNT DRACULA: But . . . will they?

THE SERVER: And once the government agrees to our demands, we'll be high-stepping on Broadway.

COUNT DRACULA: With those glorious red-corpuscled girls!

THE SERVER: High-kicking up and down the runway!
    (*He demonstrates his high kick, but quickly fails in his attempt and sits, exhausted.*)

COUNT DRACULA: I guess we could just set up our own version of Leisure Vampire World.

THE SERVER: And fill it with Jacuzzis oozing with blood.

    (*Sound of someone approaching.*)

COUNT DRACULA: Shhhh. Stick with the plan and for God's sake hide that stake! We don't want to freak out the girls.

THE SERVER: Will do, but . . .

COUNT DRACULA: Now what?

THE SERVER: It's makes me feel safe with it in my hand. With all the raids on the blood mobiles and the Food and Drug Administration refusing to accept gay blood, we're becoming more and more defenseless. You saw me just now. I'm too listless to complete a series of high kicks. It's almost like I've become too damned straight for my own good.

COUNT DRACULA: I know, it's all a government plot, but maybe you're right. As long as the FDA forces us to suck nothing but heterosexual blood, we'll lose our sensitivity, our joy de vie, our love of life—we'll end up diabetic farts sitting on our front porches, smoking Marlboros and wishing we could remember the words to those marvelous Liza Minnelli show tunes.

THE SERVER: You're not suggesting that the FDA starts taking faggot blood again, are you? You know it's been over twenty-five years, right?

COUNT DRACULA: Twenty-five straight blood sucking years! And yes, that's exactly my point! As Michael Jackson sang, it's as easy as that stupid alphabet song.

THE SERVER: ABC?

COUNT DRACULA: That's the one. A, our government is destroying creativity by banning homosexual blood. B, America hates vampires almost as much as it hates homos. C, the government is literally sucking all our virility out of us. My God, that's why they're doing it: they're keeping us from breeding!

THE SERVER: I thought something was missing!

COUNT DRACULA: I dream of the good old days when we had gallons of sexy hot American faggot blood. I can picture it now: a sweet young thing floats into the room with his cape unfurling . . .

> (*As* COUNT DRACULA *speaks, the* GAY VAMP *enters. He's dressed in drag with a long cape unfurling behind him. He wears stiletto high heels and seems to float into the room until he stands behind* COUNT DRACULA *and runs his fingers through the Count's hair*

COUNT DRACULA: His stiletto heels scrape across the floor and then he lingers over my shoulder, running his long red fingernails through my thick vampire hair.

GAY VAMP: (*Purring.*) Hi there, big boy. (*Running his fingers along* COUNT DRACULA'*s face.*) Oh my God, you're hotter than hell.

THE SERVER: If you only knew.

COUNT DRACULA: (*To* THE SERVER.) Bring me some Type A—and make it positive, like this sweet young thing.

> (THE SERVER *exits.*)

GAY VAMP: So, you want to be alone . . . with me?

COUNT DRACULA: I'd like nothing better. (*He sniffs the* GAY VAMP, *then, rises suddenly, wheels around and takes the* GAY VAMP *by the arm, pulling him close to his fangs.*) Do you like the ballet . . . the opera? Oh, for God's sakes man, let's dance . . . let's rumba!

> (*Rumba music erupts as* COUNT DRACULA *embraces the* GAY VAMP *and dances with him; they dance madly across the stage, until* COUNT DRACULA *reveals his fangs and closes in on the* GAY VAMP'*s neck.*)

GAY VAMP: (*Pulling away.*): Stop that, you're tickling me!

COUNT DRACULA: (*Sniffing up and down the* GAY VAMP'*s neck.*) Stop what?

> (*The* COUNT *continues sniffing.*) You're just my type, big girl! (*The* COUNT *inhales the Vamp's scent deeply and rubs his hand up and down the Vamp.*) Type A . . . (*Sniffing long and hard*) Positive! That makes you a ten in my book.

GAY VAMP: (*Looking down at the* COUNT'*s crotch.*) And you look more like a size nine yourself!

COUNT DRACULA: (*Looking at his shoes.*) Actually, I'm a size (*Gives real shoe size.*)

GAY VAMP: (*Purring as he eyes* COUNT DRACULA'*s crotch much more intensely*)

I'll say. You're a size (*Repeating* COUNT DRACULA'*s shoe size*) in more ways than one, big boy.

> (*The* GAY VAMP *walks around* COUNT DRACULA, *rubbing his hands briskly up and down the* COUNT'*s ass, then to the* COUNT'*s front, rubbing him romantically before putting his lips on the* COUNT'*s chest and kissing up to the* COUNT'*s face.*)

COUNT DRACULA: Come on, come to papa, give your daddy a big sloppy kiss.

> (*They kiss. Then* COUNT DRACULA *pushes the* GAY VAMP *away gently, eyeing him from head to toe.*)

COUNT DRACULA: On the other hand . . . (*Touches the* GAY VAMP'*s muscles.*) . . . you seem rather strong. (*Inhaling deeply.*) You even smell strong . . . like an aged Pepsi!

> (*He moistens his lips, growing stronger by the moment because he's with a real gay man for the first time in years.* DRACULA *takes another long hard scent.*) I bet you played football in high school, didn't you, big girl?

GAY VAMP: You're half right. I was Wheaton High School's head cheerleader . . . if you get my drift.

(*He kneels in front of the* COUNT, *then jumps up and takes center stage as he leads his high school cheer, complete with arm movements as if he's holding pompoms!*)

GAY VAMP: Boom chicka boom, boom chicka boom. Boom chicka ricka chicka, ricka chicka boom. Hannibal, Cannibal, sis, boom, bah. Wheaton! Wheaton! Rah, rah, rah

COUNT DRACULA: Sweet Mother of Wolfman, you're a full-blooded sissy boy if ever I saw one.

(*He grabs the* GAY VAMP *and pulls him within biting range as he nibbles the* GAY VAMP'*s neck.*)

GAY VAMP: (*Swooning.*) Stop that, big guy; you're going to tickle me to death.

COUNT DRACULA: There's a thousand ways to die, my sweet sexy boy.

(*He continues nibbling the* GAY VAMP'*s neck more and more intensely.*) . . . a hundred thousand ways, actually . . . or I could let you live forever.

(*He starts to bite the* GAY VAMP'*s neck, toying with him, until the* GAY VAMP *suddenly pulls back.*)

GAY VAMP: I'm sure there are more pleasant ways for you to die as I suck your . . .

COUNT DRACULA: Hey! I do the sucking here!

GAY VAMP: So, now you're versatile?

(THE SERVER *enters, carries a massive container.* COUNT DRACULA *flashes his eyes back and forth from the container to the* GAY VAMP, *measuring the* GAY VAMP'*s blood capacity with his eyes.*

COUNT DRACULA: (*To* THE SERVER.) I might not need that, after all.

(*To the* GAY VAMP, *continuing to measure him with his eyes:*) What do you weigh? (*He says a weight commensurate to the actor playing the* GAY VAMP. *Then he nibbles the* GAY VAMP'*s neck.*)

GAY VAMP: (*Mellowing out, becoming more and more blissful.*) Hmmm, sweet thing, I weigh . . . (*Gives his real weight.*) . . . solid as Hard Rock candy, in case you want a better look. (*He starts to move, romantically, seductively gyrating his hips until he finally sinks down to his knees.*)

COUNT DRACULA: You're one hell of a hot-blooded homosexual boy!

GAY VAMP: (*Looking at the huge container.*) And I can devour you by the gallon!

COUNT DRACULA: I'd rather slurp you one pint at a time. (*He licks his lips, his fangs working in and out of his mouth.*) I haven't been with a real man like you in ages. (*He pulls the* GAY VAMP *within neck-biting range and opens wide as the unsuspecting* GAY VAMP *closes his eyes and puckers up his lips.*)

GAY VAMP: (*Pulling away and gently slapping* COUNT DRACULA *as if he's a puppy.*) That tickles, stop it! I'm very sensitive—especially along my neck.

COUNT DRACULA: But I need you . . . And I want you to be a part of me.

THE SERVER: (*Aside.*) He wants you to be a part of him alright, as long as you become the liquid part, gushing red and lustily, oozing down his gullet and dribbling down his lips! I just hope the old Count leaves enough for me to lap up like his puppy dog!

> (*The* GAY VAMP *continues to toy with* COUNT DRACULA *and, in his bantering back and forth, it's hard to determine who's really in charge. Is it this young gay man or is it the aged* COUNT? *The men face each other for the final time as the* GAY VAMP *continues vamping, seductively playing with the* COUNT *and the* COUNT *drools and fawns over his prey. Finally this game ends as the* GAY VAMP *takes control, flaunting all his feminine charms.*)

COUNT DRACULA: I want you to be a part of me.

GAY VAMP: Really? (*He backs up a step or two, sizing up the* COUNT *for one last time.*) I bet you say that to all the girls. (*Swinging his head back, flipping his hair.*) What part of me do you really want? (*Moving his hips sensuously.*) What part do you like the most? (*Wriggling his ass.*)

COUNT DRACULA: Your ass, your lips, your neck! I love it all but mostly I love your spontan-gaiety!
> (*The* GAY VAMP *mellows as his eyes open wider in anticipation of eternal romance with this hot sexy vampire.*)

COUNT DRACULA: I love your build, your walk, your smooth delicious neck . . . but mostly I love your fresh gay smell. It was the same smell we savored in the old days when gay blood ran rampant in the blood banks, when we could walk into any clinic in town . . .

THE SERVER: Without a reservation . . .

COUNT DRACULA: . . . and get an instant transfusion; But that was a long time ago.

THE SERVER: Back in '83 . . .

COUNT DRACULA: Before the gay blood ban, and now . . .

THE SERVER: Without your blood . . .

COUNT DRACULA: . . . without the blood of your gay brothers . . .

THE SERVER: All your gay brothers . . .

COUNT DRACULA: I'm withering away.

THE SERVER: You're withering away? Look at me! Why do you get first dibs on everyone!

COUNT DRACULA: And to be perfectly honest with you, my blood is so heterosexually pure right now that . . . I'm unable to breed . . . I can't even . . .

THE SERVER: Get it up, you old fool, tell it like it is.

GAY VAMP: You can suck all the blood you want, but first I need to tell you a secret.
   (*He reaches inside his pocket.*)

COUNT DRACULA: Anything, tell me anything. I'm yours. Just give me a pint. Half a pint. A tablespoon, anything, anything!

GAY VAMP: I'm going to give you some choices. You can either take me now, convert me into a blood sucker, and make me a fool like him . . .

THE SERVER: I'm no fool!

GAY VAMP: Or . . . fall madly in love and make me your blood brother, or . . .

THE SERVER: There's always another damned "or" isn't there?

GAY VAMP: I can reveal my true identity and tell you why I'm here and what I can do for you.

THE SERVER: Not another twist ending. It's just like a fag. They always have twist endings.

GAY VAMP: (*Ignoring* THE SERVER.) I'm the new Secretary of Health and Human Services, eighth in line to be President, and I just announced our first policy change in decades. As of six o'clock this morning, we only accept homosexual blood. It's taken America too long to realize what our vampire brothers have suffered, and yes, I believe in total equality—even the right of vampires to marry and breed.

THE SERVER: I told you we can't get it up anymore!

GAY VAMP: Well, we're going to end that and end inequality. Vampires are no less human or normal than the rest of us so from now on all minorities will have the same rights as the rest of them. And my vampire friends, that means you can have all the blood you can drink!

THE SERVER: Yes!

GAY VAMP: So, last night we dumped all the heterosexual blood in the sewer.

THE SERVER: Sewer? Which sewer? Where?

GAY VAMP: From now on America will thrive, all of us, vampire and human alike. We'll all be gay and free with the power . . .

COUNT DRACULA: And aroma . . .

THE SERVER: And taste . . .

GAY VAMP: Of fresh, hot, wholesome homosexual blood!

COUNT DRACULA: Let me get this (*Clearing throat.*) straight, I can have a quick transfusion now . . . or I can let you live and you'll provide the vampire community with fresh gay blood for all eternity?

GAY VAMP: In a heartbeat, my sexy vampire friend, we'll provide enough blood for all of us—vampire and human alike—and you can make daily . . .

THE SERVER: Or hourly?

GAY VAMP: . . . withdrawals. Together, as blood brothers, we'll make America the gayest most creative nation on this earth!

THE SERVER: (*Licking lips.*) You mean there are other earths? Other warm-blooded bodies? Glory, glory, hallelujah!

COUNT DRACULA: Wait a minute, what exactly do I have to do to earn this honor?

GAY VAMP: Nothing. I'm a governmental employee. I can't accept gifts or kickbacks . . . but, on the other hand, you could always do something for the cause.

COUNT DRACULA: Anything. Just ask me. What? What is it? What? What?

(*The* GAY VAMP *hands* COUNT DRACULA *a list of names.*)

GAY VAMP: There are seven necks I need you to bite. Once you suck all the blood from their veins I'll guarantee the rights of all Americans: Gay, Lesbian, transgendered, bisexual, Latino, Black, Catholic, Moslem, Hindu, and . . . vampire!

COUNT DRACULA: Because?

GAY VAMP: Boom chicka boom, boom chicka boom. Boom chicka ricka chicka, ricka chicka boom. Hannibal, Cannibal, sis, boom, bah. President! President. Me! Me! Me!

COUNT DRACULA: So all I have to do is bite a few necks. . . and you'll be president!

THE SERVER: When can we start?

(COUNT DRACULA *ponders this, as his fangs go in and out and he sniffs.*)

COUNT DRACULA: Now!

GAY VAMP: Agreed!

(*As the lights fade.*)

COUNT DRACULA: How about a little snack to hold me over?

(*Blackout.*)

END OF PLAY

EXTENDED PLAY

by B. V. MARSHALL

First Performance: Dragonfly Productions, Catherine LaMoreaux Artistic Producer at The DuCret School of the Arts, Plainfield, New Jersey, November 22–24, 2019, with the following cast:

FREDDIE: Arthur Gregory Pugh
ROBYN: Sarah-Elisabeth Stein
GENE: Patrick Serpico
DANCERS: Meghan Coates, Matt Holbert

Directed by Shauni Ramai

B. V. Marshall's plays have earned recognition from HBO New Writers Workshop, New York's Theatre for a New City, Chicago's public radio station WBEZ, and in play festivals from Alaska to Australia. Recently, Plainfield audiences have seen his plays *Five Husbands* and *Incident at Willow Creek*. He has worked as a journalist and published poetry in several small presses. Marshall has received the following awards: five playwriting fellowships from New Jersey State Council on the Arts, fellowships from the Geraldine R. Dodge Foundation, VCCA, NEH, and the Robert Chesley/Victor Bumbalo Foundation. Recently, he received the Bauer-Boucher Award and the Stanley Drama Award for *Incident at Willow Creek*. After studying playwriting at Hunter University, he earned an MFA in creative writing from the University of Massachusetts, Amherst. He is a member of the Dramatists Guild and the New Play Exchange.

CHARACTERS

FREDDIE, 40s, male, been around. Black.
ROBYN, late 20s, female, tries to be cool. White.
GENE, older than 50, doesn't look it, male. White.
RECORDED VOICE, a recorded voice, naturally, on one of the laptops.
If time and budget allow, other dancers.

TIME

Present.

PLACE

The stage and auditorium of a fellowship hall (auxiliary building) of a local church. The stage has been set up as a DJ workstation with a couple of turntables, a few laptops, and a few large speakers facing the audience. The floor of this auditorium serves as the dance floor and the theater audience is on the dance floor.

NOTE

The choice of music I leave to the director and sound designer. I do not have the rights to any of the music. Nowadays, tracks and beats can be found on many laptops. Likewise, at the end of the play, the recorded phrases should not be the unadorned recordings heard earlier in the play. They should be embellished, restructured, and/or mixed to go with the dance music at the end of the play.

• • •

On the stage of an old church, ROBYN *and* FREDDIE *are setting up equipment for the evening's dance.*

ROBYN: I don't like this open stage. I feel exposed. I need the right vibe to do my thing. I guess you heard how good I was at my last gig. I really shone there. I know you usually work with Jimmy G. Did Jimmy G get arrested again? Is that why he's not doing this gig?

FREDDIE: (*Under his breath, pissed off.*) Thirty seconds. Freddie keeps doing what he's doing.

ROBYN: I'm kind of surprised you took this gig. No offense. I mean it's a charity dance. At a fellowship hall. At a church on Saturday night. I would have thought this kind of gig was a little beneath you. Don't get me wrong. Even with their limited equipment. I really appreciate you helping me out like this. I really mean it. But just to let you know, I'm only taking this job because I need to keep my skills on point.

FREDDIE: (*Interrupting.*) Robyn, Jimmy G's' not here. Big Boy and the others were all busy. The people at this gig want two deejays because they want a continuous flow of music. You were the last on my list. I heard you stunk on your last gig and you haven't been working since.

ROBYN: They just didn't like women deejays.

FREDDIE: Sure.

ROBYN: What happened to Jimmy G?

FREDDIE: Let's just spin the tunes. If you're so good, you start them up. I'll bring them home.

> (ROBYN *starts the music. Music comes up and the lights change. They watch the dance floor. In another area,* GENE, *an older man, dances.*)

ROBYN: Not too many people on the floor. Except that one old guy.

FREDDIE: Look at him on the floor all by himself. Takes guts to be the first one on the dance floor.

ROBYN: Fast shuffle. Two-minute spin and then blam! Whiplash. Strategize to mesmerize!

FREDDIE: Wow, girl. That rap is so lame, it needs a crutch and a walker.

ROBYN: It's me doing my magic. You think you can do better?

FREDDIE: I don't have to prove myself to no rookie. You didn't faze him. No matter how you change the rhythm, he keeps the beat.

ROBYN: Oh, I got moves. Let me tear this place up. He can't keep up with me.
> (*She changes the music.*)

FREDDIE: But he does. You need to focus, Robyn. Stop the quick jumps and just play the tunes. People want to get their groove on. They can't do that if

you change the tempo every six seconds. You got to work with the crowd.
With the crowd.

(ROBYN *turns the music up again. Then a speaker abruptly blows.*
GENE *exits.*)

ROBYN: I would, but this sound system's not the best.

FREDDIE: We probably blew a speaker.

ROBYN: I might have a couple of USB cables.

FREDDIE: This is an old speaker, Robyn. It has an electrical plug not USB
cables. There might be some electrical tape and another plug in my tool box.

ROBYN: That's some caveman shit. Real Paleolithic.

FREDDIE: Caveman shit or not, somebody's got to fix it. And I know you can't.

ROBYN: Yeah, but listen to this. I got this effect we can layer this stuff in.
(*She records and it plays back.*)

RECORDED VOICE: USB. USB. USB.
(*It repeats.*)

ROBYN: Pretty cool, hunh? Seriously. This could change your whole style.
'Cause your style was getting pretty stale.

FREDDIE: My Style? Mine? I didn't come up with that "Strategize and
Mesmerize" shit.

(GENE *enters the DJ area. They both jump.*)

GENE: Excuse me. Sorry. Didn't mean to startle you.

ROBYN: You shouldn't be up here.

GENE: (*Ignoring her.*) Give that speaker a good whack. It's not broken. Just
finicky and into a little S and M.

FREDDIE: These days, who isn't?

(*He whacks the speaker and the music comes on.*)

GENE: See? It should work for the rest of the night. In previous years,
someone used to come in earlier and turn on the speakers before the dance
to warm them up.

FREDDIE: That's true. You never know what magic the music sparks.

ROBYN: Okay. Thanks. We got this.

GENE: (*To* ROBYN.) Look. I'm probably older than your father.

ROBYN: So?

GENE: So that gives me the right to make a suggestion or two. Play longer selections. Longer pieces. The music's changing too fast. Me? I'm a music slut. I'll dance to anything. It's rather an important dance tonight. You see—I'll just get out of your hair.
 (*He exits.* ROBYN *adjusts the music.* FREDDIE *works on the speaker.*)

ROBYN: I hate interruptions like that. The last party I worked at. The Beltrand Mansion.

FREDDIE: Last Halloween. That's the gig I heard you messed up.

ROBYN: I didn't mess up! I didn't! See. This old woman in clown makeup comes up to me and asks to play some Michael Jackson. Who the fuck wants to dance to Michael Jackson anymore? That old lady with her wild, white makeup looked like she needed a walker and an oxygen tank.

FREDDIE: Sounds like Baby Jane.

ROBYN: Who?

FREDDIE: The movie. *Whatever Happened to Baby Jane?* Forget it.

ROBYN: Nobody wants to dance to that creepy, child molester music.

FREDDIE: Robyn, the only time other people got up to dance is when we played the extended play. Did you notice that? When people want to dance, they'll dance to whoever's friggin' music they want. That's what we're here for. And that's all we're here for.

ROBYN: I still don't have to play music for their rapist fantasies.

 (*They watch the dance floor as the music plays.*)

FREDDIE: Look at that dude down there. Look at him go again.

ROBYN: That's the same old dude that came up here. He said he was a music slut.

FREDDIE: Now he's dancing with that fine, young thing in the silver dress.

ROBYN: (*Teasing.*) Oh, you think she's fine.

FREDDIE: Up close she's probably got a three-day beard. Look at him go. Bring on those lights.

> (*They turn on some flashing lights.*)

ROBYN: Freddie, let me add some extra layers.

> (*She presses a switch and a recording starts.*)

RECORDED VOICE: USB. USB. USB. Etc.
> (*The recording continues.*)

FREDDIE: That's not music. It's techno noise. Stop that.

ROBYN: Just let me put it in on top of this beat.
> (*She adds the recording to the music.*)

RECORDED VOICE: USB. USB. USB. Etc.

> (*ROBYN adds something else and the result is cacophonous. The dance beat gets lost.*)

FREDDIE: (*Reacting to the dance floor.*) We're down to two dancers. Turn that shit off. TURN IT OFF! Now, put on the one I marked. It's got the same tempo.

> (*ROBYN turns off one song and puts on another. They look at the dance floor again.*)

ROBYN: Man, this shit is so old, it baby-sat Jesus.

FREDDIE: And Jesus can save your ass, white girl. Come on. Get the extended play. More people are dancing. That "Old Dude's" left the silver girl and he's with some guy in a kilt. And the guy in the kilt's got castanets. Now that's what you call some extra layering.

ROBYN: Freddie? What really happened to Jimmy G?

FREDDIE: (*Avoiding the question.*) Look at that guy go. Now he's got somebody's scarf.

ROBYN: It's not a scarf, it's a feather boa.

FREDDIE: Whatever it is, he's working it. He pushes the extreme.

ROBYN: You call that extreme? How you can't put a foot in front of the other. I'll put on the smoke machine. It's not my dance unless I blow the smoke.

FREDDIE: Let him stay in the moment. Robyn. Can't you let other people get back on their feet?

(ROBYN *turns on the smoke/fog machine.*)

ROBYN: If he can handle it, let him handle it.

FREDDIE: Look at him. He's using the smoke. I swear the others are like backup dancers.

ROBYN: Like I said, I make the moments real, Freddie.

FREDDIE: No girl, it's his world, you're just the backup. Sometimes, we're only the backup.

ROBYN: So, did Jimmy G get arrested again? Cause if he needs bail, we can start a Go Fund Me . . .

FREDDIE: He doesn't need bail 'cause he wasn't arrested. Okay? He's got a gig down in Atlantic City. At the Nugget. The Battle Royale of the Dee Jays. That's why he's not working here tonight. Or ever again. That job is for the next few months.

ROBYN: I was up for that gig.

FREDDIE: Like hell you were. Word is out about that Halloween fiasco. I was up for that gig, too.

ROBYN: You should have gotten it. Everybody knows how good you are.

FREDDIE: And do you think anybody cares? I drove Jimmy G down to the interviews. I was all set for my turn. I was down on the list to audition. But they took one look at me and the grey hair and the crow's feet, and they just crossed me out. I saw them do it. Drew a line right across my name. But Jimmy G, he had the rap down. He had the threads down. He had the groove down. He glowed with everything I got him to do.

ROBYN: But. But. You're the best. That's why I was so glad you asked me to help.

FREDDIE: You don't know what it's like, Robyn. I watched him, guided him, and moved him to where he could thrive. He wasn't the first one I took

under my wing. There were others. They move on to the flashier gigs, and I get stuck with birthday parties and charity dances. I can't get ahead. I thought I was doing you a favor. And here you are messing up this gig with your lame-ass rhymes and your fuckin' attitude about how good you are. You can't do shit, except mess up a good, solid gig. And what do I have? Some electrical tape and old plugs. That's it. I can't do this no more.
(*He storms out.*)

ROBYN: Wait a minute. Freddie? Freddie?

(GENE *enters, sweating and a little out of breath and with the feather boa.*)

GENE: Excuse me. Hey—(I know this probably disturbs your set. Where's the other deejay?

ROBYN: Uh, bathroom.

GENE: I just wanted to tell you how good that last set was.

ROBYN: You really went to town.

GENE: Thanks, it's just the box step. Anybody who's done any community theater knows the box step. I just rock the box and send it on different planes. Like this.
(*He demonstrates.* ROBYN *records some things.*)

GENE: Then you change direction. You find a fixed point then you change your orbit. It wasn't just the music. It's the lights and the fog. You guys knew exactly when to bring in the fog. At the last big party like this, at the Beltrand Mansion? The DJ was a real problem.

ROBYN: Yeah, well, if it was the Halloween party, I heard that DJ was pretty good.

GENE: The music was pretty good. But every song was too short. Too hard to get into the groove. You can't dance to those short rifts. Granted, it was Halloween, and I was in costume. I went as Baby Jane. Bette Davis played her. You know, the movie "Whatever Happened to Baby Jane?" I had on white makeup and everything.

ROBYN: Right.

GENE: Every time a song would get going, the DJ would change it. I asked for Michael Jackson and they played the short version of Billie Jean. I mean, it was a Halloween party. What better excuse for "Thriller?" Right? But no. The tunes kept changing.

(*Quietly,* FREDDIE *returns.*)

GENE: You have no idea of what I'm talking about, do you? Do you see this stage? That floor? This is all going to be gone soon. This church is being sold.

FREDDIE: This place has been here since I was a kid. Before that. Must be over a hundred years old.

GENE: Over a hundred and fifty.

ROBYN: Churches don't close, man. They get turned into condos.

GENE: The congregation has moved away or died off. There's not enough to cover basic expenses. They used to rent out this hall for all kinds of functions. Thirty years ago, they even had a gay wedding. Actually, two women renewed their commitment after twenty-five years. That was way back when before we could get married. Eight months later, they had the first memorial service for someone who died of AIDS. Oh, that brought out the warring factions, let me tell you. But look at the dance floor now.

(*The three look.*)

FREDDIE: Everybody's dancing.

GENE: The song's been on for five or six minutes. It's the extended play. People want the extended play, kiddo. They want the song to keep going. That's why I came up. Please keep serving the extended play versions. Please. I'm giving my all because this is the last time they'll ever have a dance here. This is the last time that this tribe will come here to dance. And I'm dancing for all the ones who used to be here but didn't live long enough to see this. I've taken too much of your time. Maybe you're right. Things should change. If you cling to the past too much, you turn into that grotesque Baby Jane. And I just don't look good in ruffles and lace. (*To* ROBYN.) You were at the Beltrand Mansion, weren't you? The Halloween party. Peter Pan. Right? I thought so.

(*At first,* ROBYN *shakes her head no then nods her head as if to say yes.* GENE *exits.*)

FREDDIE: (*Maintaining professionalism.*) It's got nothing to do with you. I signed up to do a job. That's what I'm here to do.

ROBYN: Can I share something with you? I was doing something.

(FREDDIE *gestures "go ahead."*)

RECORDED VOICE: Dance. Dance, dance, dance. Dancing for the ones who used to be here. Dancing for the ones that use to be here. Here! Here! Here! You never know what magic the music sparks. You never know what magic the music sparks. What magic the music sparks.

FREDDIE: Try those lines on top of these beats.

ROBYN: Let's try it on the extended play.

(FREDDIE *hands her a record. She looks at it, nods and puts it on. Music swells. Lights flash. They make magic with the recorded overlays and the old recording.*)

END OF PLAY

FOR A MOMENT, REHATCHED

by Susan Goodell

For a Moment, Rehatched premiered as part of The Orange Players' Acting Up!, An Evening of One Acts, in Orange, Connecticut, October 19–20, 2018, directed by Sara Messore, with the following cast:

ED: Ryan Devaney
PHIL: Tom Ndiaye

Susan Goodell is author of the full-length plays *Hope Throws Her Heart Away* (premiere at Chicago's Genesis Theatrical Productions) and *Heels Over Head* (Tri-State Actors Theatre, Rover Dramawerks). These scripts were developed at theaters including Virginia Stage Company, The Barrow Group, and the Women's Theater Company. Her short plays have been presented on stages worldwide including The Abingdon, the Boston Theatre Marathon, Mildred's Umbrella, and The Changing Scene Northwest. Other recognition: Steppenwolf Theatre Company commission, Djerassi Resident Artist, Denver Drama Critic's Circle nomination, and the Denver Post's ten-best list. A former small-town newspaper editor and Madison Avenue public relations executive, she lives in New England.

CHARACTERS

ED, 20s and up, hapless, unassuming.
PHIL, 20s and up, a seagull with attitude.

NOTE

This play also can cast with teens/students.

SETTING

The sky.

TIME

The present.

COSTUMES

ED's dress is casual, like a pajama bottom and tee shirt or a warm-up suit. PHIL's bird dress is partial and cheesy, like a bird headdress, a color or a tail, so he's more human than bird.

• • •

At rise, ED's eyes are closed. His breathing is soft and comfortable, like he's asleep. He slowly opens his eyes and upon waking realizes the panic of finding himself midair, unable to fly.

ED: Omigawd, Omigawd. I'm not supposed to be . . . oh . . . oh . . . how did I get here?
    (*Frantically begins flapping his arms up and down like a bird working hard to stay in the air, while making hysterical heaving noises.*)
Wow. Long way down.

    (PHIL, *a seagull [or a man with a silly seagull hat, or wings or some bird characteristic], enters. He flies easily as* ED *struggles, circling* ED. ED *finally reaches out for help.*)

You just plan to circle my disaster?

PHIL: That's the instinct.

ED: You're enjoying this. You find it funny to watch some fool who is about to die . . . die . . . die.

PHIL: You are one strange bird.

ED: That's 'cause I'm not a bird. I'm a human person.

PHIL: Thought I didn't recognize your species up here.

ED: (*Struggling with flight, almost slipping.*) Whoa, easy there. Whoa.

PHIL: Where you going, anyway?

ED: Trying to keep from killing myself. I can't fly.

PHIL: You didn't think of that before you took to the air?

ED: Hey, I just woke up doing this.

PHIL: So, you're a dreamer.

ED: Yes! No! Doesn't feel like it.

PHIL: I have some bad news. I'm a real bird.

ED: I thought so. And that worries me.

PHIL: You have no business up here.

ED: Exactly. Humans only fly planes or helicopters after hours of training and licensing.

(PHIL *laughs*.)

ED: What's so funny?

PHIL: I'm imagining birds flying around with little licenses.

ED: Of course, who would even check for them?

PHIL: Exactly. Hey. You told a bird joke.

ED: Pleased I amuse you.

PHIL: You really jumped into the deep end, taking off over the ocean.

ED: Don't say deep end.

PHIL: So sensitive. Somehow you got yourself into this.

ED: Careful what you wish for.

(PHIL *laughs and squawks*.)

What's so hysterical?

PHIL: It's an old seagull expression—careful what you fish for. Isn't that . . .

ED: Hysterical. In return for my straight lines, you might consider lending me a hand. Or should I say, wing.

PHIL: How do I do that?

ED: You're having no trouble up here.

PHIL: True. Like give you . . .

ED: Yeah.

PHIL: Flying instruction?

ED: Yes, yes! Emergency lessons.
   (*Struggles with his flying.*)

PHIL: We're hatched knowing most of this stuff already. What were you hatched knowing?

ED: We're warm blooded. So, we're born rather than hatched.

PHIL: Clearly your first problem.

ED: But you didn't just take off and fly, day one.

PHIL: It took some trial runs, getting in shape. Then it's adios mommy.

ED: Flew the nest.

PHIL: You say that? So do we!

ED: Now that we found our common humanity, sorry, another human expression . . . help! Can't hang on much longer like this.

PHIL: I wouldn't last if I went on like that.

ED: You're enjoying this, aren't you?

PHIL: Squawk!

ED: What do I do? Teach me!

PHIL: Just pass on my sacred, ancient, bird secrets?

ED: Promise to respect them. Oh gawd!

   (PHIL *circles* ED, *looking at him carefully.*)

What are you doing?

PHIL: Analyzing your form.

ED: (*Discouraged.*) Oh, great.

PHIL: How else am I going to help you? That's what your tennis coaches do, don't they?

ED: How do you know about them?

PHIL: I used to hang at a country club on Long Island Sound. Members thought I was cute and fed me bread.

ED: So, what's wrong, what's wrong with my form?

PHIL: The biggest problem . . .

ED: Yeah?

PHIL: You're just not a bird.

ED: Can't do anything about that now. What can (*Struggling.*) I do? (*Starts to fall but recovers.*)

PHIL: Whoops. Almost lost you. (*Analyzing.*) OK, can you take in more oxygen?

ED: Taking in, oxygen.

PHIL: More slowly. Like an eight-count exhale.

ED: Eight count . . . what are you giving me, yoga?

PHIL: Probably. I perched in on a beachside class once.

ED: Great.

PHIL: Do it! Or do you want to look for another teacher?

(ED *does his best to flap, trying* PHIL's *instructions.*)

Geesh. Relax!

ED: Relaxing. Never *worked* so hard relaxing.

PHIL: You are where you are.

ED: Yoga class?

PHIL: Seagull expression. OK, important. Slightly rotate, forward and down, with your resistance on the downstroke, letting air through on the upstroke. Feel the thermal lift.

ED: (*Improving his technique.*) Hm. Like flapping, rowing.

PHIL: Exactly. Make the wing an airfoil, creating low pressure above, high pressure below.

ED: What does that mean?

PHIL: No idea. I daydreamed through the theory explanation.

ED: Then skip the theory.

PHIL: Fine. You look a little better. You're getting it.

ED: Feels . . . less like dying. Yeah. Sort of fun. Work . . . but fun.

PHIL: Build your technique, 'cause you'll need a fishing maneuver sooner or later.

ED: You do this and fish at the same time?

PHIL: Duh.

ED: I'm in awe.

PHIL: We watch your species too. Not much impresses us.

ED: You at least could return the compliment.

PHIL: Seagulls have no social graces.

ED: Somehow, I knew that. All right if I try something more advanced?

PHIL: Go for it.

(ED *swoops.* PHIL *swoops. They have fun in swooping maneuvers.*)

ED: Really, really cool. Realize what fun your species has?

PHIL: Remember we work most of the day. Someone does *your* fishing for you.

ED: No one appreciates what he is. Or what he has.

PHIL: So true.

ED: So, I still don't know if I'm a flying human or . . .

PHIL: This might be a dream?

ED: Hope it isn't. Would love to soar with the eagles. Gulls. No offense.

PHIL: That's an expression? Soar with the eagles? What do you say about gulls?

ED: Bad public relations mostly.

PHIL: No one likes a scavenger. If your food wasn't delivered, you'd be right out there with us.

ED: So, what do gulls dream about?

PHIL: The worst is when we dream, we're a fish, and a bird is going to eat us. And we have dreams like yours.

ED: Really!

PHIL: Over and over. We have to fly, and we're just not ready to leave the nest.

ED: Like we have a final exam, and we never enrolled for that class?

PHIL: Exactly! Dream that for years after we're fledglings.

ED: So do we! Long after we're out of school. You don't dream you're in public in your underwear?

PHIL: Er . . . no.

ED: Guess not, if you don't have . . .

PHIL: Right. No underwear dreams.

ED: If this is a dream, I'll wake up and forget all this, you know.

PHIL: Depressing after the time I put into your instruction. You're taking shape as a passable bird.

ED: I'd take passable as a high compliment from a bird with no social graces.

PHIL: It is.

ED: Worse yet, if I have another flying dream, I start over with no memories of this dream.

PHIL: I hope you remember something. Soaring is a useful skill, even if you find yourself back on two feet.

ED: I'll write this down so I'll remember everything you taught me. At least the fundamentals.

PHIL: OK. And remember. Final lesson. Stay tough. Keep moving, spread your wings, aim for the clouds.

ED: That's . . . inspiring. So, birds spout philosophy?

PHIL: (*Lightly.*) Shut up.

> (ED *and* PHIL *soar contently in silence.* PHIL *backs out of scene and flies off in the direction he entered.* ED *flies center where he slowly flaps until he can't go any slower, and lights begin fade.* ED *puts his arms down and closes his eyes, putting him in starting position from top of show. Light continues to fade. Alarm clock rings.*)
>
> (*Blackout.*)

END OF PLAY

GO TO THE LIGHT

by Laurie Allen

Produced originally January 31–March 1, 2020, at the Snowdance Ten-Minute Comedy Festival by the Over Our Head Players at the Sixth Street Theatre in Racine, Wisconsin. Managing artistic director Rich Smith.

The cast was as follows:
DADDY: Ron Schulz
SOPHIE: Melissa Zeien
ROXIE: Kristin Althoff
WILL: Jimi Turek

Director: Michael Retzlaff

Laurie Allen is a West Texas playwright with nine books of plays and scenes published for young adults. Book titles include: *Power Plays*, *Acting Duets for Young Women*, and *Comedy Scenes for Student Actors*. Her ninth book, *22 Comedy Ten-Minute Plays*, was released in August 2019 by Pioneer Drama Service. Also, her one-act play, *Web of Deception,* was released in January 2020 by Pioneer Drama Service. Laurie has plays published by Meriwether Publishers, Contemporary Drama, Brooklyn Publishers, Eldridge Publishers, Off the Wall Plays, and Original Works Publishing. Her plays have been produced at Lakeshore Players Theatre, Nylon Fusion Theatre Company, West Coast Players, Towne Street Theatre, The Actors Studio of Newburyport, Phoenix Stage Company, Image Theatre, Two Muses Theatre, Paw Paw Village Players, Sunshine Brooks Theatre, Borough of Manhattan Community College, and elsewhere. Laurie's works include a wide spectrum of interests from comedy to intense drama with noted popularity for teens and young adults. For more information, visit www.laurie-allen.com.

CHARACTERS

DADDY, 70s–80s. On death's door.
SOPHIE, 30s–40s. Daddy's daughter.
ROXIE, 30s–40s. Daddy's daughter.
WILL, 30s–40s. Daddy's son.

SETTING

A hospital room.

• • •

A hospital room. SOPHIE *sits at* DADDY's *bedside as he lies motionless in a hospital bed. She stares at her phone.* ROXIE *rushes in.*

ROXIE: Oh, my God! Is he dead?

SOPHIE: (*Stands.*) Oh, Roxie!

(*They embrace.*)

No. He's still hanging in there. The doctors say it could be any minute now.

ROXIE: (*Rushing to his side.*) Oh, Daddy! I'm here! It's Roxie, your little Snuggle bear! (*To* SOPHIE:) Do you think he can hear me?

SOPHIE: I don't know.

(DADDY *mumbles.*)

ROXIE: He said something! (*Leans in.*) What is it, Daddy? What is it?

SOPHIE: (*Rushing to the bed.*) We're here, Daddy! It's okay! Just relax! And if you need to go to the light . . .

ROXIE: Sophie! Don't tell him that!

SOPHIE: Why not? I'm giving him permission to let go.

ROXIE: Daddy doesn't need our permission. Why would he need our permission?

SOPHIE: (*Waves her phone.*) I read that it helps.

ROXIE: Well, that's dumb. He can just hold on. (*Leans over.*) Hold on, Daddy! Hold on!

(DADDY *mumbles.*)

ROXIE: (*Leans in.*) What did you say, Daddy?

DADDY: (*Mumbling.*) Take my picture.

ROXIE: What? You want me to take your picture?

SOPHIE: Why would he want you to do that?

ROXIE: I don't know. But if it's his last dying wish . . .

SOPHIE: Maybe it's his way of saying goodbye.

ROXIE: Maybe. Okay, Daddy. I'll take your picture.

(DADDY *gives a thumbs up.* ROXIE *holds up phone.*)

Okay, Daddy. One the count of three. One . . . two . . . Three . . .

(WILL *bursts into the room.*)

WILL: Oh my God! Is he dead?

ROXIE: Smile! (*Takes picture.*)

WILL: Roxie! Why are you taking Daddy's picture at a time like this?

SOPHIE: Oh, Will! (*Gives him a quick hug.*) You made it!

WILL: What's going on?

ROXIE: Daddy wanted his picture taken. We don't know why, but it's his last dying wish.

DADDY: (*In a weak voice.*) Post it.

ROXIE: (*To DADDY.*) Post it? (*Looks at WILL and SOPHIE.*) He wants me to post it on Facebook. (*Shrugs.*) I guess it's his way of saying goodbye to all his friends. (*To DADDY.*) Okay, Daddy. I'll post it. I'll say, "Goodbye, my friends!" (*Taps on phone.*) There. Posted. (*She puts the phone back in his hand and kisses him.*) I love you, Daddy. Now rest.

SOPHIE: Yes, rest. And if you need to go . . . well, you've said your goodbyes now.

ROXIE: Stop it, Roxie! Stop pushing him. Let it happen naturally.

WILL: Oh, my gosh! Can he not stay off Facebook long enough to . . .

ROXIE: Don't say it, Will!

WILL: I'm sorry! But really?

ROXIE: I think it's sweet that he wanted to send out a last goodbye. He loves his friends and he loves Facebook. You know, it's kept him from being lonely since Mom died.

SOPHIE: That's true. He loved sharing those posts. And rambling. About everything. Dinner. The weather. Memories. Then of course there were those annoying shared posts. Hundreds of them every day. "Let's see if we can keep this moving. If you don't agree, just delete. If you do, pass it on! Share if you support our President. Share and you'll become wealthy. Share if you love JESUS." (*Shakes head.*) It was too much! So much that I unfriended my own dad. Oh! Did I just say that out loud?

ROXIE: You, too?

WILL: You both unfriended Daddy? Well, don't feel bad, because I did too. And look at him now! It's ridiculous. The man can't stay off Facebook even during his last few breaths. So, how long does he have?

SOPHIE: The doctors say it could be any minute now.

WILL: (*Goes to* DADDY.) I love you, Daddy. And I want you to know that I thought you were the best dad ever. And with that said, you now have my blessing to put on your wings and fly away.

ROXIE: Will! Don't pressure him! Let it happen naturally.

SOPHIE: I think it's fine, Will. Wish him on his way. Bye, Daddy! (*Waves.*) We love you! We'll miss you! See you on the other side! Later! Yeah . . . much later.

ROXIE: Would you both stop! He'll go when he's ready!

    (DADDY *mumbles.*)

SOPHIE: What did he say?

ROXIE: What did you say, Daddy? (*Leans in, listens, then stands, shaking her head.*) He wants to know how many likes he got on Facebook.

WILL: What? Are you serious?

SOPHIE: Well, tell him, Roxie! Maybe that'll make him happy and he'll feel free to make his exit.

ROXIE: All right, all right. (*Looks at DADDY's phone, then gives it back to him.*) Daddy, you got 182 likes.

WILL: 182 likes already?

SOPHIE: He has a lot of friends.

(DADDY *raises his hand a gives a thumbs-up.*)

ROXIE: Daddy, you need to rest.

SOPHIE: And if you need to drift off to that bright light, we understand.

ROXIE: Why are you both pushing Daddy off the ledge?

WILL: No one's pushing him, Roxie. We love him. But what kind of life is this?

SOPHIE: Exactly. His body is worn out, and so is mine. I'm tired. I'm so tired. I've been up here for days. And every day the doctors say it could be any minute now. Day after day. Hour after hour. Minute after minute. And he's a little demanding, you know? I'm cold! I'm hot! I need water! I want Jell-O! Where's my ice cream? Turn the TV up! Turn the TV down! Then finally, I get him all settled in and he goes to sleep. Then I start drifting off, but always with one ear open. Then all of a sudden, the snoring stops! Silence. Not a single sound. I jolt up, panic and scream for the nurse to come in here! "Oh, my gosh! Oh, my gosh! He's gone! He's gone!" I'm pacing the floor. The nurse runs in. And then I hear this! (*Stops, facing audience, imitates him snoring loudly.*) False alarm!

ROXIE: Oh, Sophie, I'm so sorry. I know you're tired. You've been here for days. You're such a trooper.

SOPHIE: Yes, but I need a break! So, Roxie, I think it's your turn to stay up here for a few nights so I can get some rest. Then it'll be your turn, Will.

ROXIE: Me? But I'm busy! The twins have cheerleading practice, piano lessons, ballet, voice lessons . . . Sophie, I'm busy trying to be mother of the year!

WILL: And I can't be here! I live out of town. And my job! Meetings! Appointments! Deadlines! Oh, no! I can't! I'm sorry, but I can't!

SOPHIE: That's too bad. We all have to share the load. I know we didn't anticipate this, but if Daddy is going to hang in there, then we need to take turns and be here for him.

ROXIE: You're right, but . . .
(*Leans over* DADDY. *Firmly.*)
Daddy, it's time! It's time to go to the light!

WILL: Yes. Don't fight it anymore!

(*A long pause. They stare at* DADDY. *Deafening silence. They exchange looks.* SOPHIE *and* ROXIE *begin to cry.* WILL *drops his head.*)

SOPHIE: (*Trying to catch her breath.*) I think . . . I think . . . Oh, my God . . . I think he's gone! Oh, Daddy!

ROXIE: I can't believe it! Our daddy is gone!

(SOPHIE *and* ROXIE *cling to each other as they look at* DADDY. WILL *wipes his eyes. Pause.* DADDY *mumbles.*)

SOPHIE: (*Matter-of-actly.*) He's not dead.

WILL: Nope. What did he say, Roxie?

ROXIE: (*Irritated.*) What, Daddy?

(DADDY *mumbles.* ROXIE *leans in, listens, then stands and looks at them.*)

SOPHIE: What? What did he say?

ROXIE: He wants to post a status update.

WILL: You've got to be kidding?!

SOPHIE: What does he want to say?

(ROXIE *leans in, listens, then takes the phone.*)

ROXIE: Okay, Daddy. I'll do it. (*Looking at phone, she updates Facebook.*) "Not dead yet."
(*She places the phone back in his hand.*)

WILL: Oh my gosh, Roxie! I can't believe you posted that!

ROXIE: Why not? I couldn't say no! It's his last, *last* dying wish. Besides, he can't have much longer. Look at him. He's barely breathing.

SOPHIE: He's fighting it. That's for sure.

(*They nod, watching him for a moment.* ROXIE *picks up her phone.*)

ROXIE: I need to make a status update myself. (*Taps on phone.*) "This is the hardest thing I've ever had to do . . ." (WILL *takes out his phone.*)

WILL: Me too. "How can you say goodbye to a parent? I've done this before, and I can't believe this is happening again . . ."

SOPHIE: (*Making a status update.*) "My dad was my hero . . ."

ROXIE: "When my dad is gone, it'll be as if I'm an orphan . . ."

WILL: "I don't know how to deal with this!"

SOPHIE: "My heart will break into pieces."

(DADDY *mumbles. They all stop posting and look at him.*)

ROXIE: Yes, Daddy? What? I can't hear you! (*Leans in, then raises her voice.*) I don't know, Daddy! Let me look!

WILL: What now?

ROXIE: He wants to know how many likes he got on his status update! (*Looks at his phone. In a sharp tone:*) 227, Daddy! 227!

SOPHIE: Look. He's grinning.

ROXIE: I'd like to wipe that grin . . .

SOPHIE: Roxie!

ROXIE: I'm sorry. I didn't mean that. Well, I kinda did.

WILL: He's obsessed with Facebook.

ROXIE: Yeah. Addicted.

SOPHIE: Ridiculous.

(*They go back to their phones.*)

WILL: Wow . . . I already got seventy-five likes. And a lot of sad faces with tear drops.

SOPHIE: I have eighty-nine.

ROXIE: Oh, I've got lots, too. Ninety-nine. Just one more and . . . Okay, I'll like my own status to get to one hundred. Done. One-hundred likes! Go me!
    (*Smiles.*)

WILL: Wow. Amy sent her condolences. She said we should get together after the funeral. Wow. I'd like to get together with that little hottie.

SOPHIE: Aunt Jane said her Sunday School class can bring food over. Those ladies are great cooks, too. That'll be good.

ROXIE: Aw . . . Jay and Dina are planning to come to the funeral. And they live so far away.

SOPHIE: That's sweet. It'll be nice to see our cousins. A little family reunion.

WILL: Maybe I'll invite Amy to the funeral. Do you think that'd be appropriate? I can reach out and take her hand . . . for comfort, of course. And afterwards, well . . . I might need more comforting.

ROXIE: I'm not sure that's appropriate, Will.

    (*As they continue to stare at their phones,* DADDY *sits up in bed and begins taking dramatic selfies with a huge smile on his face. After a while, they finally look over and notice him.*)

SOPHIE: DADDY! WHAT ARE YOU DOING?

ROXIE: DADDY!

WILL: OH MY GOD?! REALLY?

    (DADDY *takes another selfie, smiling.*)

SOPHIE: DADDY STOP IT!!

ROXIE: LAY DOWN! YOU'RE GOING TO PASS OUT AND . . .

SOPHIE: (*Matter of factly.*) And what? (*Looks at them and shrugs.*) Die?

(*They shake their heads and go back to their phones as* DADDY *continues taking pictures and posting on Facebook.* WILL *looks at phone.*)

WILL: "Tough guy is still hanging on."

SOPHIE: (*Updating Facebook.*) "Fighting for each last breath."

ROXIE: (*Updating Facebook.*) "Labored breathing. Motionless.

(*Pause.*)

SOPHIE: (*To* ROXIE *and* WILL.) I think services should be at ten o'clock. What do you think?

ROXIE: Sounds good.

WILL: Yeah. Sounds good.

SOPHIE: And I say open casket. Daddy would like that. (*Looks at* DADDY.) Wouldn't you, Daddy?

(DADDY *smiles and gives a thumbs-up.*)

DADDY: (*Looking at his phone.*) Oh, this is a good picture of me! I'm going to post it! Oh, look! Barbara said she's going to miss me! And Sandra. And Syble. And Doris . . . (*Smiles.*)
I'm a popular old geezer! (*Suddenly, he grabs his chest, moans, then falls back on the bed.*)

(SOPHIE *rushes over*)

SOPHIE: Daddy?! Daddy?!

(ROXIE *rushes over.*)

ROXIE: Daddy?

WILL: I think he's a goner.

(SOPHIE *steps back.*)

SOPHIE: (*In a calm tone:*) Oh, good. (*Goes back to her phone.*)

(ROXIE *steps back.*)

ROXIE: Finally. (*Goes back to her phone.*)

WILL: I need to send Amy a message.

(*They all stare at their phones.*)

ROXIE: "Daddy has passed away peacefully."

SOPHIE: (*Calmly.*) "We are all so heartbroken. I can hardly stop crying."

WILL: "Amy, I could really use a friend right now."

ROXIE: "Please remember our family in your prayers."

SOPHIE: "If I could just stop the tears."

WILL: "Amy, I really appreciate your support. And if you find your way close to my apartment tonight. I'll leave the door unlocked, so please feel free to come in . . ."

(DADDY's *hand goes up as he looks at his phone. He bolts up.*)

DADDY: 589 likes! Wow-wee!

(*They all turn and look at* DADDY.)

SOPHIE, ROXIE and WILL: DADDY! (*They point heavenward.*) GO TO THE LIGHT!

(DADDY *falls back on the bed. The lights begin to fade.*)

DADDY: I bet I get a million likes!

(*Blackout.*)

END OF PLAY

GREATER THAN NINA

by Bruce Bonafede

Greater Than Nina was produced originally in October 2019 as part of the New Short Play Festival at the John DeSotelle Theatre, 754 9th Avenue, New York, New York. The director was Pierre Guy. The cast was Elena Clark and Eric Michael Gillett.

Bruce Bonafede is a playwright based in Palm Springs, California, and has been a member of the Dramatists Guild since 1981. His longer plays include *Advice to the Players* (Heideman Award, Actors Theatre of Louisville, 1985), *Crusade* (Baltimore Playwrights Festival, 2019), *The Desert of Love, Ellie, North,* and *Quarantine.* His ten-minute plays have been produced in New York, San Diego, Atlanta, Minneapolis, Kansas City, and Los Angeles.

CHARACTERS

ROKOSSOVSKY, 40s, a Russian man.
ALISA (Zinovyevna Rosenbaum), 20, a Russian-Jewish woman.

SETTING

Lubyanka Prison, Moscow, headquarters of the Soviet secret police and intelligence services.

TIME

1925.

• • •

ROKOSSOVSKY's *office in the Lubyanka Prison. A desk and chair with a second chair facing it. The flag of the Soviet Union on the wall behind the desk or standing next to it.* ROKOSSOVSKY *sits at his desk. He wears a brown military-style tunic with large red stars on its epaulets.* ALISA *sits facing him. She is a thin (undernourished) young woman with short, dark, straight hair. She wears a shabby dress and shoes, and holds a tattered purse.*

ROKOSSOVSKY: (*Offering a cigarette box.*) Cigarette?

ALISA: No thank you, comrade.

ROKOSSOVSKY: (*Taking one himself.*) You have been in the Lubyanka before?

ALISA: Never, comrade.

ROKOSSOVSKY: Colonel.

ALISA: Excuse me?

ROKOSSOVSKY: Colonel. In our glorious Soviet workers paradise, all men and women are equal, but . . . some of us are colonels.

ALISA: Yes Comrade . . . Colonel.

ROKOSSOVSKY: Do not be afraid. You are not here because you have done anything wrong.
   (*He strikes a match and lights his cigarette.*)
I am told you wish to become an actress.

ALISA: I do.

ROKOSSOVSKY: But you have not much experience.

ALISA: No, sadly. So far only . . . amateur theatricals. Comrade Colonel.

ROKOSSOVSKY: That is fine. It serves our purpose. We require someone who has not yet made a name for herself. A young woman who is unknown, yet shows promise.

ALISA: You think I show promise?

ROKOSSOVSKY: I am told. One of my men saw you perform. A Gorky play.

ALISA: Ah yes, a great play. I prefer Chekhov.

ROKOSSOVSKY: Chekhov? You have played Nina?

ALISA: No, only Masha. I would love to play Nina. It is my life's dream. You know the work of the great Chekhov?

ROKOSSOVSKY: Before the revolution my wife used to drag me to the theater. I hate Chekhov.

ALISA: My goodness, but why?

ROKOSSOVSKY: Because bourgeois theatre serves no purpose. Because plays about the landed gentry do nothing to advance the revolution. And because . . . I never understood what was going on.

ALISA: Comrade Colonel, I am sure you would love Chekhov if you understood him.

ROKOSSOVSKY: Well, I will not get that chance. And you will not get the chance to play Nina. Art must now serve the revolution. And you—yes, you, Alisa Zinovyevna—you are going to get the chance to do just that.

ALISA: I? How?

ROKOSSOVSKY: You are going to play the role of a lifetime, a great character we will create.

ALISA: I do not understand, Comrade Colonel.

ROKOSSOVSKY: You are going to America.

ALISA: America?

ROKOSSOVSKY: And there you will become a great actress.

ALISA: I will?

ROKOSSOVSKY: In a manner of speaking. You will play a part, but no one will know you are doing so. No one will know you are actually working for the Soviet people.

ALISA: Am I . . . to be a spy?

ROKOSSOVSKY: A spy? No, no. We already have enough spies in America.

ALISA: I do not think I would make a good spy.

ROKOSSOVSKY: You will be much greater than a spy.

ALISA: Comrade Colonel, I am very confused.

ROKOSSOVSKY: That is why my plan is so brilliant. No one will ever figure it out.

ALISA: May I have that cigarette now?

ROKOSSOVSKY: Certainly.

> (*He holds out the box.* ALISA *takes one and he lights it for her.*)

ALISA: Comrade Colonel, I do not think I can go to America. I do not even speak English.

ROKOSSOVSKY: You will be taught rudimentary English. You leave in a month.

ALISA: A month? Comrade Colonel, I am in school. My studies . . .

ROKOSSOVSKY: Your studies are over, Alisa Zinovyevna.

ALISA: I am enrolled in the Technicum for Screen Arts.

ROKOSSOVSKY: Another factor that recommends you. However, your term has ended. It has been arranged. You have withdrawn from school.

ALISA: I have? But Comrade Colonel, Moscow is my home. My family is here. I cannot just up and leave the country.

ROKOSSOVSKY: Of course, you can. People do it every day . . . people who do not wish to live in our workers' paradise. Counter-revolutionaries. Enemies of the people. You are not an enemy of the people, are you?

ALISA: No, Comrade Colonel. I am a loyal Soviet girl.

ROKOSSOVSKY: I am glad to hear it.

ALISA: But what am I to do in America?

ROKOSSOVSKY: You will become the foremost proponent of capitalism.

ALISA: Capitalism? But capitalism is the enemy of our socialist revolution.

ROKOSSOVSKY: Exactly right. That is the whole point. First we will send you to Hollywood. You will become a film star. Americans love their film stars. They listen to whatever they have to say. No one knows why.

ALISA: A film star? Really?

ROKOSSOVSKY: Who knows? They may even put you in a Chekhov film. Perhaps you will get to play Nina.

ALISA: Nina? That would be wonderful. But what if they do not? What if I do not become a film star?

ROKOSSOVSKY: It does not matter. You will still achieve fame and become a great influence.

ALISA: How?

ROKOSSOVSKY: We will execute Plan B. You will write books.

ALISA: Books?

ROKOSSOVSKY: Novels.

ALISA: Comrade Colonel, I do not think I can write novels.

ROKOSSOVSKY: No matter. We will write them for you. They will be all about how wonderful capitalism is. They will not be very well written, but that does not matter either. They will be hugely popular.

ALISA: They will? Why?

ROKOSSOVSKY: Because they will tell Americans what they want to hear. That greed is good. That selfishness is a virtue. That all that matters is the individual, and to care about others more than yourself is sheer folly.

ALISA: But none of that is true.

ROKOSSOVSKY: Of course it is not true.

ALISA: Is that what Americans believe?

ROKOSSOVSKY: Some of them. And you will become a great icon to these. They will turn your books into bestsellers. But most Americans? Most of them are not sure, and your mission will be to show *those* Americans how wrong such thinking is.

ALISA: How am I to do that?

ROKOSSOVSKY: By promoting your philosophy in the most obnoxious way possible. By carrying it to such an extreme that any sane person with an ounce of goodness in them will be disgusted by you and your ideas.

ALISA: I am to be hated?

ROKOSSOVSKY: Loved by some—worshipped even. But hated by most, yes. Or at least greatly, greatly disapproved of.

ALISA: That sounds terrible.

ROKOSSOVSKY: You will revel in it. You will call all who disagree with you stupid. You will mock them. You will constantly refer to your own intellectual superiority.

ALISA: Pardon my language, Comrade Colonel, but it sounds as though I will be a great ass.

ROKOSSOVSKY: Oh yes. But remember, the more you succeed, the more people you offend, the greater your success.

LISA: That seems . . . backward.

ROKOSSOVSKY: Not at all. By pretending to champion capitalism, you will expose its ugly face. You will take the philosophy we oppose, and you will promote it in such an extreme, offensive way that you will actually make people more likely to agree with us.

ALISA: I see. At least, I think I see.

ROKOSSOVSKY: It will be a great test of your acting ability. It will be a role far greater than Nina.

ALISA: Greater than Nina?

ROKOSSOVSKY: You will have to play this character day and night. You will have to *become* this hideous woman, and you will never be able to be yourself, except for those moments when you are alone with your handler.

ALISA: My "handler?"

ROKOSSOVSKY: One of my officers will be near you at all times. To pass you instructions, to help you when you are in need. And . . . to make sure you do as you are told.

ALISA: I see.

ROKOSSOVSKY: Do not be alarmed. It is standard procedure. Just be sure you follow his orders.

ALISA: I am sorry, Comrade Colonel, I do not think I can do this.

ROKOSSOVSKY: Excuse me?

LISA: You take over my life. You withdraw me from school. You say I must leave Russia and perform some mission for you. This is wrong.

ROKOSSOVSKY: Wrong?

ALISA: You have no right to make such decisions for me! These should be my decisions! I should be free to decide what I want to do for myself!

(*Pause.*)

ROKOSSOVSKY: Excellent.

ALISA: I am sorry?

ROKOSSOVSKY: You already sound like the character. Such passion. Such blind selfishness. Bravo!

ALISA: Comrade Colonel, I am not acting!

ROKOSSOVSKY: No?

ALISA: No. I do not want to go!

ROKOSSOVSKY: I see. You would rather go to Siberia?

ALISA: Siberia?

ROKOSSOVSKY: That is your choice, Alisa Zinovyevna. That is how the revolution works—either you serve or you suffer. Either you go to America, or you and your family go to Siberia. That is the only decision you get to make.

ALISA: Well, if you put it that way . . . I suppose I will go to America.

ROKOSSOVSKY: I am glad. I did not want to have to send you to Siberia. I do that to people all day long. It gets old.

ALISA: But Comrade Colonel . . . please tell me. When can I come home?

ROKOSSOVSKY: Home?

ALISA: To Moscow.

ROKOSSOVSKY: You will not be coming home, Alisa Zinovyevna. You will become an American. You will stay there the rest of your life, in your new home, with your new name.

ALISA: I am to have a new name? What is it?

ROKOSSOVSKY: I have selected one much easier for Americans to say. And easier to put on a poster or book cover. Ayn Rand.

ALISA: "Ayn Rand?" I do not like it. It is not a pretty name.

ROKOSSOVSKY: No, it is not. I am quite proud of it. It fits the character perfectly.

(*Pause.*)

ALISA: May I have another cigarette?

ROKOSSOVSKY: Of course . . . Miss Rand.

(*He holds out the box.* ALISA *takes one. He lights it for her, smiling.*)

(*Blackout.*)

END OF PLAY

THE HOME FOR RETIRED CANADIAN GIRLFRIENDS

by John Bavoso

The Home for Retired Canadian Girlfriends was first performed May 24–June 16, 2019, as part of Fells Point Corner Theatre's 10x10x10 Play Festival, directed by Steve Goldklang.

Cast:
RUPERT: Tom Piccin
TIFFANY: Grace O'Keefe

John Bavoso is a Washington, DC-based playwright, book and theater reviewer, marketer, and aspiring wrangler of unicorns. He mostly writes plays about women and queer people who are awkwardly attempting (and generally failing) to engage with serious subject matter using only dry wit and impeccably timed combative taunts. John is a member of the Dramatists Guild of America, a Pinky Swear Productions company member, a 2019 Lambda Literary Fellow, and the recipient of District of Columbia FY18 and FY19 Arts and Humanities Fellowships. For more info, please visit www.john-bavoso.com.

CHARACTERS

RUPERT, a man of any age and any race. Skilled typist, clipboard enthusiast, generally high on life.
TIFFANY, a woman in her early 20s, any race. Half-formed and searching.

SETTING

The reception area of a retirement home.

TIME

October 11, National Coming Out Day.

• • •

> *Sometimes we think people are like lottery tickets,*
> *that they're there to make our most absurd dreams*
> *come true.*
> Carlos Ruiz Zafón, *The Shadow of the Wind*

Lights up on the reception area of a retirement home. RUPERT *stands behind a desk, holding a clipboard. There are a few empty chairs lining the wall. Perhaps some diva pop classic plays quietly in the background. After a moment,* TIFFANY *enters, clearly bewildered and befuddled.* RUPERT *lights up when he sees her and rushes to greet her.*

RUPERT: Hello! Welcome! Name?

TIFFANY: What?

RUPERT: I need your name, dear.

TIFFANY: Um, I don't . . .

RUPERT: Most only have the one, but if you've got a surname, I'll take that, too.

TIFFANY: I . . . I'm not . . .

RUPERT: Rachel? You look like a Rachel. Or perhaps a Jennifer? We used to get a lot of those back in the day.

TIFFANY: I'm sorry . . . who are you?

RUPERT: Oh, gosh, look at me getting ahead of myself! (*Pointing to his name tag.*) My name is Rupert. I'll be your Intake Specialist and Orientation Coordinator. Today is going to be a very busy day, so if I could just get your name . . .

TIFFANY: It's Tiffany. Just Tiffany . . . I think.

RUPERT: Oh, like the singer! (*Elbowing her gently.*) Don't worry, you won't be alone now.

TIFFANY: I don't know what that means.

RUPERT: Really?! What are they teaching you kids in school . . . ohhhhhh. Never mind.

TIFFANY: I'm sorry, I don't mean to be rude, but . . . what is this place?

RUPERT: This is a retirement home, sweetie. The best in the Great White North. You live here now. So, if I could just get a bit more info from you, I'll get you all squared away.

TIFFANY: Retirement home? But I'm only like . . .

RUPERT: Twenty-one? Twenty-two, maybe? Yeah, most of our residents get put out to pasture in their late college years, especially now that social media's so ubiquitous. Some hold on a lot longer, but, really, it just gets sadder the older they get.

TIFFANY: I don't . . . I don't remember . . .

RUPERT: Oh, don't worry about that—it's not that you've *forgotten* your life; it's that you never had one in the first place!

TIFFANY: Is that supposed to be comforting?

RUPERT: Most of our ladies just show up on our doorstep with a name and location. Speaking of which—where you from, girl? Toronto? Winnipeg? Vancouver?

TIFFANY: Saskatoon.

RUPERT: Ohhhhh, rustic! But they do grow a great beard there. Please, come with me.

> (*He leads her back to the desk, takes his place behind it, and begins furiously typing at his laptop. Way too much typing. What could he be typing?* TIFFANY *follows reluctantly, taking in every inch of the place.*)

And can I get the name of your former employer, please?

TIFFANY: My what?

RUPERT: Oh, duh, sorry. The name of your (*Air quotes.*) "boyfriend."

TIFFANY: (*Perking up.*) Patrick?! Is Patrick here?!

RUPERT: Oh no, dear. I'm afraid you'll never see Patrick again.

(TIFFANY *becomes visibly agitated.*)

TIFFANY: Look, I don't know who you are or how I got here, but I want to see my Patrick. Right now. Right now!

(*She begins to pace.* RUPERT *looks alarmed and comes back around from behind the desk to comfort her.*)

RUPERT: Tiffany! Tiffany. Please. You must calm down. I'll explain everything if you just take a few deep breaths.

(*She eyes him suspiciously, but reluctantly inhales and exhales deeply.*)

There. That's better, right? Come here, sit with me.

(*They move to the chairs and take a seat.*)

Now, what's the last thing you remember?

TIFFANY: Well, I was at home, waiting for my boyfriend, Patrick, to call, and then, suddenly . . . *poof*, I'm here!

RUPERT: Yeah, that sounds about right. I've heard some version of this story about a million times. Especially today—today is basically our Black Friday.

TIFFANY: What's so special about today?

RUPERT: It's October 11. (*Beat.*) National Coming Out Day in the States.

TIFFANY: Okay, but I don't know what that has to do with . . .

RUPERT: Can you tell me a little more about Patrick? How did you two meet?

TIFFANY: Oh, it was very romantic. (*Beat.*) Wait, hold on. That's strange . . .

RUPERT: What is?

TIFFANY: Everything's a little . . . fuzzy. I can't remember the exact day we met . . .

RUPERT: But it feels like you've known him your whole life?

TIFFANY: Yes, exactly! Do you think I hit my head or something?

RUPERT: No, this isn't amnesia. The reason you feel like you've known Patrick your whole life is because, well . . . you have. Because you weren't born, per se, so much as *willed into existence.*

TIFFANY: That doesn't make any sense.

RUPERT: You see, this isn't just any assisted living facility. This is the Home for Retired Canadian Girlfriends. You don't remember your life before Patrick because you're a product of his imagination. A prop. A ruse.

TIFFANY: You're insane. Am I being punked?

RUPERT: I wish! That Ashton Kutcher is a dreamboat. (*Beat.*) I know this is a lot to take in, but I'm telling you the truth.

TIFFANY: Prove it, then.

RUPERT: Okay. What was your childhood like? Tell me about primary school.

TIFFANY: Well, it was . . . you know. It was fine.

RUPERT: Was it? Because I don't think you remember anything before your eighteenth birthday.

TIFFANY: Even if what you're saying is true—*if!*—then why? Why would an American materialize a Canadian woman out of thin air?

RUPERT: Typically, it's because a young man goes away to university, finally acts on his attraction to men, then comes home and isn't ready to tell his friends and family the truth, and so he invents a girlfriend—one they will never meet because she lives abroad.

TIFFANY: But why Canada?

RUPERT: Because it's just remote enough to explain your absence, but not so exotic that it invites further questions he'd have to improvise the answers to.

TIFFANY: And I'm here, in this place, because . . .

RUPERT: Patrick is finally living his truth! It's so inspiring! My Patrick was named Gabe, by the way. I still miss him sometimes.

TIFFANY: *You* were a Canadian girlfriend?

RUPERT: Oh, no! That wouldn't be very effective. I was a (*Air quotes.*) "Roommate Who Watched Gay Porn on Gabe's Computer While He Was Out of Town, Now Please Stop Looking at His Search History . . ."

TIFFANY: So, that's why you're such a good typist . . .

RUPERT: Guilty! I'm retired, too; this is more of a volunteer position.

TIFFANY: So, that's it? I'm never going to get to meet Patrick in person? I'll never get to visit Utah? (*Beat.*) He's just thrown me out like last week's trash?!

RUPERT: He hasn't discarded you, Tiffany—he's freed you! This may be a retirement home, but it's where your life really begins. You can do anything you'd like here.

TIFFANY: And there are other women here? Like me?

RUPERT: Tons! Some even look *exactly* like you—for a long while, they used the same stock photo in all the picture frames at Walmart . . .

TIFFANY: And what do people around here *do* all day?

RUPERT: Oh, um, whatever they want, really. Knitting. Low-impact water aerobics. Mahjong is all the rage these days . . .

TIFFANY: Are you serious?!

RUPERT: Is there a problem?

TIFFANY: Yeah, there's a huge fucking problem, eh?

RUPERT: Shhhh! This is Canada . . . I don't think we can swear here.

TIFFANY: Some man—some *American*—wishes me into being to cover his cowardly ass, and now I'm stuck spending the rest of my non-life trapped in some facility doing needlepoint and Jazzercise? How is that fair to me?!

RUPERT: Well, some find the relaxation very soothing . . .

TIFFANY: Relaxation?! I haven't even *done* anything yet! What am I relaxing from?!

> (*There's a moment of silence, during which RUPERT seems to be weighing options in his head. Then he looks around, checking to make sure no one's within earshot.*)

RUPERT: Well, there is a special . . . let's call it a club . . . for ladies who want to be a bit more active.

TIFFANY: Zumba?

RUPERT: No, a little more exciting than that. But it's rather . . . clandestine.

TIFFANY: Oh, great, more secrets!

RUPERT: Yes, but this group is in service of *tearing down* closets, not building them.

> (TIFFANY *shoots him an intrigued look. She retakes her seat warily beside* RUPERT.)

TIFFANY: Okay . . . I'll bite.

RUPERT: So, you know how the permits for the heterosexual pride parades keep getting rejected? Or how conservative politicians keep getting outed? Oh, remember the time the power went out at the Super Bowl?

TIFFANY: You're telling me Canadian girlfriends are responsible for all that?

RUPERT: Of course.

TIFFANY: That's insane.

RUPERT: Is it? Ladies like you make the perfect covert team members—you have no families or attachments, no paper trail or record, no fingerprints . . .

> (TIFFANY *looks at her fingertips with horror.*)

But that's all from your life before. You'll have meaning now, a purpose.

TIFFANY: But I don't know how to fight . . . I have no real skills at all, that I know of.

RUPERT: Not to worry! We'll train you on everything. You gals are like clay just waiting to be molded. Besides, at this point, we really have to take what we can get.

TIFFANY: What's that supposed to mean?

RUPERT: You, my dear, are an endangered species. As the world becomes more open and accepting, fewer of you girls show up on our doorstep. A decade ago, this place would have been busier than a Tim Hortons on Christmas morning!

TIFFANY: But doesn't that mean fewer men are coming out of the closet? How is that a good thing?

RUPERT: No, it means fewer are going into the closet in the first place— they don't need Canadian girlfriends anymore, because they don't have anything to hide. They're not waiting decades to live their lives fully and exactly how they want to.

(TIFFANY *stands up and starts to pace.*)

TIFFANY: If I join this—I don't even know what to call it, a *rainbow* ops squad—what happens when I retire from that? Where do I go? Back here?

RUPERT: Huh. I . . . don't know, actually. I don't think we've ever had a girl leave the service.

TIFFANY: So, that's it then?

(RUPERT *stands, and walks to the front desk.*)

RUPERT: That's it! How simple is that?! It's not often that you get your mission in life handed to you on a silver platter—and this is your second time! How lucky!
(*He assumes his position behind the computer, and waits for* TIFFANY *to join him at the front desk. She does not.*) Now, I'm going to need to schedule you for a physical.

TIFFANY: No.

RUPERT: It's very standard, I promise, no big deal.

TIFFANY: I said no! No physical, no castoff-beard hit squad, no wasting away in this sad little box!

RUPERT: What are you saying?

TIFFANY: I'm saying no! I understand that Patrick was scared, but I deserve to have a life of my own! I did my duty, and now I'm going to live for myself.

RUPERT: But you're not even a real person.

TIFFANY: Nobody in their twenties is a "real person!" But I'm going to turn myself into one, not some indentured servant. Haven't you ever wanted that for yourself?

RUPERT: Why would I? It's a mean, scary world out there.

TIFFANY: It's *Canada* . . .

RUPERT: Why else would we need a hit squad? In here, I know my place. Everything is ordered and makes sense. (*Beat.*) I've already been abandoned once . . . why would I want to open myself up to that again?

(TIFFANY *goes to him.*)

TIFFANY: Because the other option is to stay here and play cruise director for the rest of your life?

RUPERT: And what do you intend to do with this brand-new life of yours?

TIFFANY: I'm going to travel—I'm going to see Niagara Falls and Banff and Whistler . . . Jesus, is there anything man-made in this country? (*Beat.*) And I'm going to meet some men—and maybe some women—and *use them* for a change. Or, fall in love; real, mutual, honest love! I'm not wasting one more minute of my life—I'm outta here!
    (*She runs to the door, but stops short when she hears* RUPERT *speak.*)

RUPERT: But you can't go!

TIFFANY: I'm sorry, Rupert, but you can't stop me. No one can. Not anymore.

    (*She exits, joyously.* RUPERT *runs after her, but is too late.*)

RUPERT: Tiffany, wait!
    (*He gets to the door, but she's long gone. He waits a minute, contemplating. He walks slowly back into the middle of the room, and after a moment, throws his clipboard on the floor, startled by the clatter it makes. After another moment, he pulls out his cell phone and dials 4-1-1.*)
Hello, yes, I'd like to place a call to the United States. (*Beat.*) Gabe Manzo, yes, with an M. Panama City Beach, Florida. (*Beat.*) Yes, I'll hold . . . but not for long.

    (*Lights out.*)

END OF PLAY

IF WE ONLY KNEW

by Aren Haun

If We Only Knew was first produced by the FUSION Theatre Company (FUSIONnm.org) as an award-winning entry in their annual original short works festival, THE SEVEN, June 6–9, 2019, at The Cell Theatre and KiMo Theatre in Albuquerque, New Mexico. Festival producer: Dennis Gromelski. Festival curator: Jen Grigg. Directed by Michael Counts. Lighting and scenic design by Richard K. Hogle. Sound design by Edward Carrion. Properties design by Robyn Phillips. Production stage manager: Robyn Phillips. The cast was as follows:

HE: Gerome Olona
SHE: Rhiannon Frazier

Aren Haun is a playwright, director, and teacher. He is the playwright of *Kill the Editor*, which premiered at Exit Theatre and was published by Exit Press. Other workshop productions include *The Mating Instinct* at 5th Wall Productions in Charleston, South Carolina and *Expecting* at the Players Loft in New York City. He received an MFA in playwriting from Columbia University and teaches playwriting at the Ruth Asawa School of the Arts.

CHARACTERS

HE, a college student, 27 years old.
SHE, a college student, 22 years old.

SCENE

A university cafeteria.

TIME

1968.

• • •

1968. University cafeteria. A student is seated, with a tray of food in front of her. SHE *is reading* Nine Stories *by J.D. Salinger. An older student enters, with his own tray of food.* HE *sits across from her. A few moments pass.*

HE: "She was a girl who for a ringing phone dropped exactly nothing." Isn't that a great line?

> (SHE *looks up, confused.*)

"A Perfect Day for Bananafish." "She looked as if her phone had been ringing continually ever since she had reached puberty." It's one of my favorites.

> (SHE *smiles, nods. Brief pause.*)

SHE: I used to carry *The Catcher in the Rye* around with me all through high school.

HE: You know they're starting to make that book required reading?

SHE: Oh no. They shouldn't teach that book in school. We need Holden Caulfield as an antidote *from* school.

> (HE *smiles. Slight pause.*)

HE: You're not at the protest. Aren't you against the war?

SHE: Of course I'm against the war. We should be looking at what's wrong at home before fighting some stupid war thousands of miles away. I would be . . . I just don't like big crowds.

HE: Neither do I.

SHE: Oh well. We'll all be dead soon from the atomic bomb, anyway. I think humanity deserves to wipe itself out.

HE: Every generation thinks the world is coming to an end.

SHE: No. It's really going to happen this time.

HE: Listen . . . what are you doing Saturday night?

SHE: Saturday? Oh, um, uh . . . nothing. Nothing.

HE: Want to hear some music? I heard of this place that's supposed to be pretty good. Do you like Joan Baez?

SHE: I love Joan Baez.

HE: They've got a singer who sounds just like her.

SHE: Um, yes, I . . . I'd like that.

HE: Shit. I'm sorry . . . I didn't realize . . .

SHE: Why would you . . . what makes you think I'd like a place like that?

HE: I didn't know what it was . . .

SHE: All those naked girl's bodies. Do you like that kind of thing?

HE: I'll take you someplace nicer next time, I promise.

SHE: Thank you. So. Do you have any brothers or sisters?

HE: No. I'm an only child. Do you?

SHE: I have a brother. He's very smart. They gave him a full scholarship to go to college at sixteen.

HE: Look, I know it's a little soon, but . . . do you . . . do you want to get married?

SHE: Married? Gee, I . . . I don't know. I mean, we haven't known each other that long.

HE: I feel ready. Don't you?

SHE: I'm only twenty-two. I wasn't planning . . .

HE: This is what I'm thinking. We both finish our degrees here at Davis and then we'll move to Berkeley where I can finish my PhD and you can support us with a teaching job.

SHE: Is that what you really want? A PhD?

HE: You have to have a PhD if you want to teach philosophy.

SHE: Are you sure you want to teach? Or are you only trying to avoid the draft?

HE: You're right, mostly it's to avoid the draft. Let the politicians go and fight their own fucking war.

SHE: I'm scared. How are we going to raise a baby when we're still in school?

HE: I've been talking to some people . . . it's simple. They just fly you down to Mexico in a little plane . . .

SHE: A little plane! I can't go in a little . . . I'm afraid to fly!

HE: It'll be over before you know it.

SHE: But I want to keep it. I've always known I wanted to be a mother.

HE: The timing isn't right. Once we both get teaching jobs, we can think about starting a family.

SHE: I don't know . . . I don't know what I was thinking. The principal is a very kind man. But the kids don't listen to me. I can't control them. And Back-to-School night was a fucking nightmare.

HE: Are you going to eat these fries?

SHE: Help yourself.

HE: Thanks. Let's face it, I was never cut out for philosophy, anyway.

SHE: You don't give yourself enough credit.

HE: This new job will be good for us. Computers are a growing industry.

SHE: We do need money for the baby.

HE: Having a baby is all you think about. Is it really that important to you?

SHE: Of course it is! I thought we were going to start a family!

HE: Fine, I'll just kill myself in a job I can't stand so you can have everything you want in life.

SHE: I've been thinking . . . maybe we should get counseling. I think you need to see somebody and find out what's wrong with you.

HE: I'm doing the best I can. Okay? That's all I can do. The best that I can. I can't do any better than that.

SHE: It doesn't make sense. The therapist told me you were the most well-adjusted man she'd ever met.

HE: Well, that's good, isn't it?

SHE: But it isn't true, you *aren't* well-adjusted. You have serious issues with your father who abused you even though you won't talk about it and your mother is a cold woman, I know she can't stand me . . . and you aren't kind to me anymore. I feel like you resent us. When the baby was born you just shrugged like you couldn't care less. Who reacts that way to their own son being born?

HE: The thing is . . . I don't know if I love you anymore.

SHE: What are you . . . ? I don't . . . Are you . . . ?

HE: I need some time. Some time to . . . Christ, everything's happening so fast.

SHE: And meanwhile, I'm just supposed to sit around while you decide whether or not you want to stay with us? Fuck you. It's another woman, isn't it?

HE: It's not . . .

SHE: Of course it is. That woman in your office. Go ahead. Have your little fling.

HE: I admit it, okay? I made a mistake. A terrible mistake!

SHE: And you just expect me to go back to the way things were? I'm not going back to that hell!

HE: Listen to me. Things are going to change.

SHE: How? Why should they? I shouldn't even be having this conversation with you. I should be out protesting with everyone else!

HE: Will you just listen to me for one goddamn second? I got a promotion. They've got me working on the new mainframes. You should see these things, they take up entire rooms!

SHE: I'm not forcing you to do anything, you know. This is your life. You can do anything you want with it. If you hate working in computers so much then quit!

HE: I want to come home. I miss you. I love you.

SHE: Can I have a sip of your soda?

HE: Go ahead. So, guess what? I've got a surprise.

SHE: Oh no. What is it?

HE: I put a down payment on a house in the suburbs.

SHE: Why would you . . . ? You're going to hate it there!

HE: Wait till you see it. It's beautiful. And the schools are very safe.

SHE: But I can't stand it. None of the other parents like me. These people are living in a fucking time warp. You'd think the sixties never happened.

HE: You have to make an effort.

SHE: Everyone at the PTA meeting was rude to me.

HE: All you do is lie around in bed all day. It isn't healthy.

SHE: I get migraines. Why aren't you ever home anymore?

HE: What do you expect? I have a two-hour commute each way.

SHE: You're smoking too much dope. It used to be recreational. But now you're using it practically every day.

HE: A little in moderation never hurt anyone.

SHE: Moderation! You've got Advanced Emphysema. How do you think it feels getting a call in the middle of the night that your husband passed out on the Bay Bridge from mixing drugs and alcohol?

HE: When you stop popping pills and maxing out the credit cards, I'll cut back on the pot.

SHE: I'm trying to cut back on spending but I can't help myself! I'm so unhappy!

HE: Getting high is the only thing I've got left in my life. It reminds me of the sixties.

SHE: What's so fucking great about the sixties? It's an overrated decade.

HE: It's about taking back the system. It's about saying fuck you to the establishment.

SHE: The establishment? We *are* the establishment! Face it: you don't care about the sixties. You just like the bands and the free love and getting stoned and those experimental foreign films. The truth is you're afraid to truly experience the sixties. That's why you're not out at the protest, you're afraid you'll get hurt or arrested. You're afraid of everything!

HE: Our accountant thinks the best thing to do is sell the house, pay off our debts, and file for bankruptcy.

SHE: Bankruptcy?

HE: It isn't as bad as it sounds.

SHE: What are we going to do? What's going to happen to us?

HE: Let's just not talk about it.

SHE: That's your answer for everything.

HE: I said I don't want to talk about it! (*Pause.*) Oh Jesus.

SHE: What's the matter?

HE: I'm not feeling . . . I think my . . . I might be having a heart attack . . .

SHE: Okay, stay calm, keep breathing, just keep breathing. I told you not to eat so many french fries . . .

HE: You were right. They're packed with cholesterol.

SHE: How are you feeling?

HE: Like a truck hit me.

SHE: They said the operation was a complete success. You had four bypasses. They took veins from your legs and created new arteries for your heart.

HE: Everything is going to change now. You'll see.

SHE: I hope so. We almost lost you.

HE: I'm going to eat right, start exercising . . . How are the kids?

SHE: They're outside. They're worried about you.

HE: Here. Get these fucking french fries away from me.

SHE: After the way you've treated me I don't know if I can go through the next months of taking care of you, feeding you . . .

HE: Haven't I always given you everything you wanted?

SHE: You gave me everything . . . everything except *you*. You've never really been here with me. You just liked the idea of having a family. I knew you wanted to get married but I could never tell if you really wanted to marry *me*. You've missed it. You missed it all.

HE: I've failed you, haven't I?

SHE: Don't worry about it. Over a lifetime everybody fails everybody.

HE: You've been the love of my life.

SHE: You don't have to say that.

HE: It's the truth. The only thing I ever did in my whole life was sitting down at this table in this cafeteria to talk about J.D. Salinger.

SHE: I don't regret anything. That's not true. I regret almost everything. But it happened. It happened.

HE: If only you knew what you were getting yourself into, huh?

SHE: Maybe I did. Maybe we both did. Maybe we all know everything all the time.

(HE *takes her hand.*)

HE: You're such a beautiful girl.

(*Lights fade.*)

END OF PLAY

JUDAS ISCARIOT'S DAY OFF

by David MacGregor

Premiered at Short + Sweet Hollywood, September 27–29, 2019, Marilyn Monroe Theatre at the Lee Strasberg Institute.

Directed by Taji Coleman

JUDAS ISCARIOT: Peter Trencher
DEBRA HORTON: Bridget Oberlin
OMAR BAQRI: Mario Barra
ARCHANGEL GABRIEL: Christopher Guyto

David MacGregor is a playwright and screenwriter. He is a resident artist at the Purple Rose Theatre in Michigan, where seven of his plays have been produced. His plays have been performed from New York to Tasmania, and his work has been published by Dramatic Publishing, Playscripts, Smith & Kraus, Applause, and Heuer Publishing. He adapted his dark comedy, *Vino Veritas*, for the silver screen, starring Carrie Preston (Emmy-winner for *The Good Wife*). Several of his short plays have also been adapted into films, and his screenplay *In the Land of Fire and Ice* was a 2016 Athena List Winner (best screenplays featuring female protagonists). He teaches writing at Wayne State University in Detroit and is inordinately fond of cheese and terriers.

CHARACTERS

JUDAS ISCARIOT, disciple and betrayer of Jesus Christ, 30s–50s.
DEBRA HORTON, attorney, 30s–50s.
OMAR BAQRI, attorney, 20s–30s.
ARCHANGEL GABRIEL, winged seraph, indeterminate age.

SETTING

A law office.

TIME

Now and then.

• • •

Lights up on a law office. Sitting in a chair is JUDAS ISCARIOT, *wearing clothing from around 30 A.D. He looks around the office curiously as* DEBRA HORTON *enters in a rush.* JUDAS *stands up.*

DEBRA: I'm incredibly sorry to keep you waiting! I had to file a last-minute brief at the courthouse and the traffic is just terrible at this time of day.

JUDAS: It's fine . . . although I am a little pressed for time.

> (*While his attire gives her pause, she snaps on a smile and extends her hand.*)

DEBRA: I'm Debra Horton.

JUDAS: Judas Iscariot.

DEBRA: Oh, I see! And you're certainly dressed for the part! Now please, sit.

> (JUDAS *sits back down and* DEBRA *moves around the desk and sits down. She picks up a pen and a legal pad.*)

So, I'm happy to refer to you by any name you're comfortable with, but for legal purposes I will need your real name.

JUDAS: That is my real name.

DEBRA: Judas Iscariot? (*Off his nod.*) Oh, I see! You legally changed it for . . . professional purposes?

JUDAS: No, that's the name my parents gave me. I was named after my Uncle Judas.

DEBRA: Your parents gave you the same name as the man who betrayed Jesus Christ?

JUDAS: Oh, I understand your confusion! No, I am the man who betrayed Jesus Christ.

DEBRA: You betrayed Jesus.

JUDAS: That's correct.

DEBRA: Well, I hate to be a stickler for details, but that would make you over two thousand years old.

JUDAS: Give or take.

DEBRA: You are aware that I charge three hundred dollars an hour.

JUDAS: Absolutely! And I'm happy to pay.
(*He pulls out a canvas bag and pours thirty pieces of silver on the desk.*)

DEBRA: Nice. Thirty pieces of silver.

JUDAS: It's kind of my thing.

DEBRA: Is this . . . ? (*Looks around, then closely at* JUDAS, *who is mystified.*) I'm looking for the hidden cameras . . . for whatever prank show this is for, or practical joke my staff is playing on me.

JUDAS: I'm not sure I understand what you're talking about. Could we get to my case? Like I said, I don't have a lot of time and . . .

DEBRA: Of course! Can you just hold on a second? (*Hits a button on her desk phone.*) Omar, could you come in here, please? (*She smiles at* JUDAS. *A moment later,* OMAR *enters.* JUDAS *stands up.*) Omar, this is Judas Iscariot.

(JUDAS *extends his hand and they shake.*)

JUDAS: Very nice to meet you.

OMAR: Likewise.

DEBRA: (*To* OMAR.) Do you know anything about this?

(OMAR *shakes his head.*)

JUDAS: Excuse me, my case?

DEBRA: Yes, of course! I'm very sorry. Please, sit down. Would you mind if Omar sat in on your case? He's one of our junior partners and I always like to share interesting clients with him.

JUDAS: Fine by me.

(*They all sit.*)

DEBRA: Now then, what can I do for you, Mr. Iscariot?

JUDAS: Well, here's the situation. As you may know . . . wait, are both of you Christians?

DEBRA: Used to be.

OMAR: Muslim.

JUDAS: Then maybe I should just catch you up real quickly. I'm the disciple of Jesus Christ who betrayed him for thirty pieces of silver, after which he was crucified by the Romans. Because of that, I am condemned by God to spend eternity in the ninth circle of Hell, which is pretty much as far down as it goes. However, thanks to an act of kindness that I once performed, I am allowed to leave Hell for one day every thousand years.

DEBRA: And today is that day?

JUDAS: Today is the day!

OMAR: (*Taking out his phone and tapping at it.*) And you decided to spend it in a lawyer's office?

JUDAS: Well, I do have some other plans; but yes, this is my first stop.

DEBRA: So, this would only be the second time you've been released from Hell since . . . ?

JUDAS: The incident.

DEBRA: The incident, right.

JUDAS: Yes. The first time was during the Dark Ages, and that did not go well. My big mistake was still only speaking Aramaic. I should have learned Latin if I wanted to get anything accomplished.

OMAR: I was going to say that your English is excellent for a Middle Eastern man who died two thousand years ago.

JUDAS: Thank you! I've been practicing, and I have a lot of time on my hands. Mark Twain has been a tremendous help to me.

OMAR: Mark Twain is in Hell? The Tom Sawyer, Huckleberry Finn guy?

DEBRA: Well, he would be. He was an atheist back when there weren't too many atheists.

JUDAS: Wonderful man! Such a sense of humor! He really lightens things up down there. And he's been advising me as to what I should do today . . . him and Mahatma Gandhi, Oscar Wilde, Hypatia of Alexandria, George Carlin, and so on, and they all agreed that I should see a lawyer to try and . . .

(*There is a knock at the door. It opens a crack and the head of the* ARCHANGEL GABRIEL *appears.*)

DEBRA: Excuse me, we're having a private meeting. Could you please wait in the lobby?

(GABRIEL *comes into the office, clad all in white, with a pair of wings.*)

GABRIEL: Do not be afraid.

DEBRA: Oh boy. Must be a full moon. (*To* JUDAS.) I take it this is your partner in . . . whatever this is?

JUDAS: My partner? Can't you see his wings? He's an angel!

GABRIEL: Archangel, actually. Hello everyone. I'm Gabriel.

JUDAS: What are you doing here?

GABRIEL: Nothing. Just . . . in the area.

JUDAS: God sent you.

GABRIEL: Maybe yes, maybe no. His ways are inscrutable.

JUDAS: That means He's worried about me visiting a lawyer.

GABRIEL: Nooooo . . . God doesn't worry. He's just interested in . . . things.

DEBRA: Would you excuse Omar and me for a moment?

JUDAS: Of course.

(DEBRA *and* OMAR *get up and huddle together. Behind them,* GABRIEL *points to his own eyes, then to* JUDAS. JUDAS *stands up and he and* GABRIEL *circle one another like two playground antagonists.*)

DEBRA: Okay, what do you make of this?

OMAR: What do I—oh, I see! This is a test, isn't it? You want to know how I would handle a bizarre and unusual case as an attorney. To see if I would be a good fit as a full partner.

DEBRA: Omar, no.

OMAR: Well, here is my analysis. Either this is a test of some kind or a practical joke created by someone in the firm. Or, let's not forget that Greenvale Performing Arts College is only a few blocks away. This could be two actors trying out parts, or even a fraternity prank of some kind.

DEBRA: What were you looking up on your phone while Judas was talking?

OMAR: Just checking the details of his story. He's completely correct. Judas Iscariot is allowed to leave Hell for one day every thousand years. Oh, and you'll find this interesting. Do you know the first thing an angel says when he encounters human beings?

DEBRA: Do not be afraid. (*Off* OMAR's *nod.*) So, they've clearly done their research, or . . . you know what? Let's see what else they have to say. (*Turning back to* JUDAS *and* GABRIEL.) I'm very sorry! Do go on with your story.

JUDAS: Well, I'm happy that Gabriel is here, because he can back me up on this. So, point number one. Is God all-knowing?

GABRIEL: Of course!

JUDAS: And God, Jesus, and the Holy Spirit; that is, the Trinity, are all one?

GABRIEL: Yes!

JUDAS: Which would mean that Jesus is all-knowing too, right?

GABRIEL: Where are you going with this?

JUDAS: It's quite simple. My sin was that I betrayed Jesus Christ, correct?

GABRIEL: Which you did!

JUDAS: Ah, now that is where you have fallen into my trap! How can you betray someone who is all-knowing? You see? God and Jesus are all-knowing. That means they knew that I was going to betray him. Clearly, since they allowed it to happen, that was part of their plan all along. I was merely the scapegoat in their scheme.

DEBRA: Hang on. So, you're saying . . . what you're saying is that you were caught up in a sting operation.

JUDAS: I don't know what that is.

OMAR: It's when the authorities, the police, or God purposely allow a crime to be committed. In this case, Jesus played the role of the victim, knowing full well that you would betray him. It's a form of entrapment, which is basically illegal.

DEBRA: And you know, I remember enough from Sunday school that during the Last Supper, Jesus did predict that one of his disciples would betray him, just like he predicted that the Apostle Peter would later deny knowing him. That definitely suggests that Jesus knew the future.

JUDAS: Exactly! So I ask you, based on your expertise and experience in law, am I guilty? Should I have to spend eternity in the ninth circle of Hell?

OMAR: Absolutely not.

DEBRA: I agree. Any decent defense attorney would be able to get your charges reduced, if not dismissed completely.

GABRIEL: What? No! He betrayed our Lord and Savior for money! Jesus died on the cross because of you!

JUDAS: Which was their plan from the very beginning! Without me, without my so-called "betrayal," there would have been no crucifixion, which means there would have been no resurrection, which means that Jesus would never have brought salvation to humanity through his death.

DEBRA: So, what you're saying is, if I'm understanding you correctly, is that in terms of the whole story, you're actually kind of the hero . . .

OMAR: . . . that JESUS: the son of a carpenter wouldn't be Jesus the savior of mankind without you and your actions.

GABRIEL: Hold on! Just hold on one minute here! Are you on his side?

DEBRA: We're on the side of justice.

GABRIEL: But he's the bad guy! Judas has always been the bad guy!

OMAR: Only because he didn't have a decent lawyer.

GABRIEL: That's your attitude? Seriously? You know God is watching all this, right?

DEBRA: Is that a threat?

JUDAS: Yes, that's exactly what it is! That's how they operate! Threats! Intimidation! Do what we say or you're going to Hell!

GABRIEL: Listen, you . . .

JUDAS: What? What are you going to do to me? I'm already in the ninth circle of Hell and that's as far down as it goes!

GABRIEL: You know what? I give up. There are some people you just can't save. (*He shakes his head in disgust and storms out, slamming the door behind him.*)

DEBRA: Well, Mr. Iscariot, while we're both clearly sympathetic to your case, I'm still not sure if I understand how we can help you.

JUDAS: Just a formal legal letter would be nice . . . pointing out that you can't betray someone who is all-knowing and how I never had any decent representation.

DEBRA: I'd be happy to write that up. Do you think it will help?

JUDAS: Not really. God's pretty fixated on the whole being infallible thing. I'm just making a point, I suppose. But who knows, maybe I can move up to the fifth or sixth circle of Hell. A change of scenery would be nice.

DEBRA: I'll have that letter for you by this afternoon.

JUDAS: Wonderful! (*Shaking hands with* DEBRA *and* OMAR.) And thank you so much for seeing my side of things. It really means a lot. (*He heads for the door.*)

OMAR: So . . . any other big plans for today?

JUDAS: (*Turning.*) Oh, absolutely! I want to find a decent meal and a prostitute.

DEBRA: Well, we'd be happy to recommend a restaurant or two, but just so you know, prostitution is illegal these days.

JUDAS: Seriously? So, what do men do when they want to have sex with a woman who isn't their wife?

DEBRA: Omar, maybe you'd like to escort Mr. Iscariot to the elevator and tell him a little bit about the internet.

OMAR: The . . . oh! I'd be happy to.

(*He escorts Judas out the door, then turns back to* DEBRA.)

OMAR: I know this might sound ridiculous, but you don't suppose that / / / ?

(*They share a look for a beat, then . . .*)

OMAR and DEBRA: Noooo . . .

(OMAR *exits, closing the door behind him.* DEBRA *picks up one of the pieces of silver on her desk and looks at it pensively, her gaze shifting to the door as lights fade.*)

END OF PLAY

LAST DANCE WITH MJ

Lindsay Partain

Originally produced at Iowa State University in January 2020; directed by Jobe Free, featuring Jess Fenton (MILLY), and Rachel Ward (JOHANNA).

Voted "The Next J. K. Rowling" at Banks High School, **Lindsay Partain** is an Oregon playwright, a graduate of Pacific University, and a member of the Dramatists Guild. She is the vice president and editor for the online literary magazine, *Cascadia Rising Review,* which features works by Pacific Northwest artists. Recently, her work has been produced by the Whisper Skin Theatre (*Until the Earth Breaks Open*), Otherworld Theatre Company (*Monsters Beyond the Midnight Zone,* and at the Daisy Dukes Festival in Portland, Oregon (*Penny for Your Traumas*). Most recently, Lindsay's full-length play *Sabrina and the Thunderbird* was a top four semi-finalist for the 2019 Portland Civic Theater New Play Award and her play *The Message of Pain* was presented at the 2020 Mid-America Theatre Conference in Chicago, Illinois. Lindsay's ten-minute play *Shimmers* was recently chosen as first place winner for *Smith & Kraus' Best Ten-Minute Plays of 2019,* as were her monologues *Curves* and *Backfired,* which are included in their *Best Female Monologues of 2019.* You can contact her at lgpartain@gmail.com or via her New Play Exchange page.

CHARACTERS

MILLY, late teens-early 20s. Jo's sorority "little sister."
JOHANNA, late teens-early 20s. Milly's sorority "big sister."

SETTING

Milly's dorm room.

TIME

Morning. Present day.

• • •

MILLY *and* JOHANNA *are in* MILLY'*s dorm room.* JOHANNA *is sitting on the bed listening to her friend rant.* MILLY *is fuming to the point of full-blown meltdown. She's been going for a while.*

MILLY: Why do they do this? Why are boys so *fucking stupid*?! Why do they think they can treat people like this an-an-an an just *treat* you, make you believe that- they think you're beautiful or smart or whatever the fuck and then just- stop? Why do they do it, Jo? Why do they always—I'm just—I don't—I'm so—(*Screams.*)

JOHANNA: (*Taken aback by her friend's outburst, she needs a minute to process the rage.*) I . . .

MILLY: I think it's just that they're *obsessed* with themselves and with "the chase" whatever that fucking means. I mean, I'm not a deer. I'm not a wild animal, I'm a person! This happens every time and I don't understand. I just don't . . . I don't understand. I don't get it I . . .

JOHANNA: Okay, Milly.

MILLY: What . . .

JOHANNA: Do me favor and take a big breath.

  (MILLY *does; she doesn't let go*).

O- okay, Mill . . . Milly, you gotta exhale—you're turning bright red, honey.

  (MILLY *exhales but only because she is rage-sobbing.*)

Men are just . . . they're assholes.

MILLY: No!

JOHANNA: No?

MILLY: *Men* are not the problem. It's the boys that look grown up and say nice things—like when you say you're chilly and they say (*In a "douche boy" voice.*) "hey sit next to me" because they always run warm, and you think it's the warmth that burns from the kindness of their bleeding romantic hearts when really it's the dumpster fire inside of them, the blazing trash heap they really are—warm hands: it's a warning.

JOHANNA: Okay—what happened?

MILLY: Fucking Tinder happened! Bumble-Feeld-Hinge-Grindr!

JOHANNA: Why are you on Grindr?

MILLY: I'm lonely!

JOHANNA: Woah, okay, sorry I didn't . . . fuck boys.

MILLY: No, don't fuck boys! To hell with boys. Grind them up into dog food. They aren't worthy of my time or my breasts, they aren't worth any of this . . .

JOHANNA: Hey, Milly. Can you just, what are we?

MILLY: Friggin furious?

JOHANNA: No. We are Alpha Phi . . . what are Alpha Phi?

MILLY: (*Depressed.*) Alpha Phierce.

JOHANNA: Right. So. Why don't you just sit down and tell me what happened. Calmly.

(MILLY *doesn't sit down.*)

MILLY: I was talking to this boy—Andrew

JOHANNA: 'Kay . . .

MILLY: God he's so sexy, he's got these abs that are just . . . he's like the real-life Peter Parker, it's fucking obscene. We're talking and we're clicking (*Snapping her fingers.*) and things are so easy and fun (*Turns into air punches.*) and after a week or so we trade some sexy pictures and he's all about it—still writes me back the next week—nothing changes!

JOHANNA: You haven't met this person though? You haven't actually gone on a date with this Parker guy?

MILLY: He *looks* like Peter Parker, his name is Andrew, and that's the thing. We did go out. We went out to dinner and he sat down in his chair like Riker does in Next Gen and we spent an hour just talking about, all of the incredible foreshadowing in Battlestar Galactica and—it was *perfect*. We drove around for a while and saw how fast his car could go (*A little turned on.*) and then he came back to my place and next thing I know he's pushing me up against the door and we're kissing and having a good time and literally he unzips my dress to kiss my shoulder blades. This fucking asshole . . .

JOHANNA: Skip ahead, please.

MILLY: We didn't sleep together. I told him I wasn't quite there yet but that you know, soon. I really wanted to but I had to be up early for Logic and my room was a disaster and I only had bread and soup for dinner so all I really wanted was to dive headfirst into my bag of bacon Cheez-Its.

JOHANNA: Awww. This is why we're friends. 'Kay, so you didn't sleep with him.

MILLY: No! I didn't sleep with him! And the day after I didn't hear from him at all—I even wrote him and asked him like how his day was or something and barely got a response. And then same thing the next couple of days. Just barely responses. He never starts a conversation anymore. Just . . . I even went out of my way to be like "I really liked what we did the other night, we should do that again sometime soon" and all he had to say was something like "aww that's so nice" or some stupid shit like that. I mean. What the fuck did I do, Jo? I know he's sleeping with other people. That he's not "dating exclusively" right now. I know this wasn't going to turn into a, a, a thing. I've *known* this! So why am I still so fucking upset about being told "you're so sexy" "so beautiful" "God, I can't wait to wrap up with you all weekend" and then being completely discarded? Am I allowed to be this upset? Am I . . . I just . . . *uuughhHHHH-HUH-HUHH.*
   (*Defeated, she flops down and tries not to cry.*)

JOHANNA: Have you thought about just deleting the apps? Getting rid of the temptation all together? I mean, it sounds like maybe you need a break from relationships for a while. Maybe it's just not the right time to be putting yourself out there.

MILLY: But it wasn't a relationship, it was just straight up sexual rejection! And besides . . . I don't want to delete them.

JOHANNA: Why? It's just a stupid app. Give it here, I'll do it for you . . . What are you doing?

MILLY: Nuh-nothing.

JOHANNA: Did you just . . . Are you protecting your phone from me?

MILLY: No.

JOHANNA: Yes you did! You just held your phone from me like Tarzan's gorilla mother did from that jaguar that tried to eat him!

MILLY: No I wasn't!

JOHANNA: Really? Then give it to me.

MILLY: But . . .

JOHANNA: Let me see it, Milly!
  (*She climbs on top of* MILLY *and fights for the phone.*)
Oh my God you have a serious attachment issue!

MILLY: You think I don't know that!

JOHANNA: Give me one good reason why I shouldn't sit on your chest, pry that thing away from you, and delete that stupid app.

MILLY: Don't . . .

JOHANNA: Twenty seconds.

MILLY: What if he messages me!

JOHANNA: Milly! What the fuck?!

MILLY: I'm weak!

  (JOHANNA *pinches* MILLY. *Hard.* MILLY *yelps.*)

OUCH! Jo! What the fuck?! That fucking hurt! Owww!!!!

JOHANNA: (*Shaking a finger at* MILLY.) Bad! Bad Milly!

MILLY: What are you . . .

JOHANNA: No!
  (*She pinches* MILLY *again.*)

MILLY: YOW-OW-OW-OW!! Stop pinching me! What's the matter with you?!
(*Tries to slap* JOHANNA *away.*)

JOHANNA: What's the matter with you?!

MILLY: Stop pinching!

JOHANNA: I pinched you because you are being a dumbass.

MILLY: Because I want him to call me? I mean, message—it's weird when people call, right?

JOHANNA: Why are you so obsessed with some douche bag who's totally left you hung out to dry?

(MILLY *gets on her phone to open the app.*)

No, I don't need to see . . .

(MILLY *holds up her finger and continues in silence until she finds the photos. She holds the phone up to Johanna, who is speechless.*)

JOHANNA: Woah. (*She swipes through.*) *Woah* . . . are these . . . are those real? *Daaaaaaamn*! You got to meet this guy? In real life? You touched this?

MILLY: And he's even prettier in person. How unfair is that?

JOHANNA: That's just . . . oh god.

MILLY: The one with the puppy, right?

JOHANNA: No, he's like, laying down in bed or something. The ab shot with just a little bit of the top of the goods—god, I want to lick hummus off his stomach. I wanna . . . no, no take it away. Get that thing away from me before it sucks me into the same sad hole it got you into.
(*She has an idea. She hops up and paces around the room.*)

MILLY: You see! I told you!

JOHANNA: All you said is that Spiderman felt you up a little.

MILLY: Was I wrong?

JOHANNA: He does bear a striking resemblance . . .

MILLY: He's so beautiful it makes my pussy ache.

JOHANNA: Ewwuuuughck—god, gross—don't use that word.

MILLY: She *aches*, Jo! I am not a crazy person.

JOHANNA: (*Pause. She's thinking.*) You aren't a crazy person.

MILLY: Huh?

JOHANNA: Let me see your phone again.

(MILLY *hesitates*.)

I'm not gonna delete anything, good lord.

(MILLY *gives* JOHANNA *her phone*.)

MILLY: He makes me feel crazy though and I hate it. Not being able to speak like a human. I have an extensive vocabulary and I can only access 20 percent of it right now because the blood that used to power that part of my brain is currently swelling around my thighs! What are you doing?

JOHANNA: Take a picture with me.

MILLY: I look like a trash fire . . .

JOHANNA: Neck down. No faces. Get close to me, get . . . come over here.

MILLY: What? Why?

JOHANNA: Ready?

MILLY: I mean, I . . .

(JOHANNA *takes a picture of the two of them*.)

JOHANNA: Perfect . . .

MILLY: What are you doing?

JOHANNA: Getting revenge.

MILLY: By sending him pictures of our tits?

JOHANNA: Shh. What do you think?

MILLY: "Hey you. What are you up to tonight?" He isn't going to resp . . . wait, did you just send that picture?

JOHANNA: Yea. He only gets to see it for ten seconds, big deal. It's going to take him three just to realize what it is.

MILLY: He's going to think we're inviting him to a threesome . . . Oh my god he's going think we're inviting him to a threesome!

JOHANNA: Good job, my Little. That's the plan.

MILLY: I don't know about this, I mean, we're besties, I don't know if I could do that with you though, I mean, that could just be awkward and . . .

JOHANNA: Stop speaking. Tonight, let's invite him out for dinner. We'll get dressed and made up—that dress you wore to the Britney concert in Vegas, wear that. We are going to go out on a date, the three of us . . . just listen. We'll have to really sell it at dinner. Touch his arm and tell him how funny he is, rub his leg under the table—make it so painfully obvious that he could have both of us. I want him begging for the check. We should sit really close together, hold hands. I'll probably kiss your shoulder a little to sell it.

MILLY: Sell it?

JOHANNA: We'll leave the restaurant, get a ride back here—oh, he wrote back.

MILLY: He what? What did he say?

JOHANNA: "Not much. What are you up to?"

MILLY: I can't believe he actually . . .

JOHANNA: "Damn, you look good."

MILLY: Did he . . . ?

JOHANNA: He wrote it, I'm just saying it.

MILLY: BAM! I know I look good! I look so good! You could have *had* so good.

JOHANNA: Are you going to be able to do this tonight? You aren't going to have second thoughts or anything?

MILLY: Yeah! What's the game plan? We go to restaurant, get all sexy, make all sexy, get a ride, get home . . .

JOHANNA: We get home, we all three of us get out of the car, we walk up to the door, I am going to whisper in your ear the code word, and then you will say: "That was a lot of fun, I had a great time tonight." And then I will *yawn*, I will lean my head on your shoulder, smile at him my biggest *fuck-you-*

smile, and say "Let's go inside, Milly, I'm so tired." And then we will go inside, turn on Queer Eye, and the night will be over.

MILLY: That. But. But that's it? That's your master plan? I still don't get to sleep with him?

(JOHANNA *raises her hand to pinch and* MILLY *flinches.*)

Please, please don't pinch me again.

JOHANNA: We are going to blue-ball this pathetic fuck-stick so hard. I want him to cum in his pants on your porch steps just thinking that he might have had you. He can ride home in soggy disappointment when he realizes that he hasn't earned the right to sleep with you. He. Is not. Worthy. (*She picks up the cellphone.*) "Thanks, winky-face, we're having a good time. Want to join us?"

MILLY: You did not just . . .

JOHANNA: Oh, I did just. Milly, repeat after me.

MILLY: After me.

JOHANNA: I am a strong independent woman who don't need no man.

MILLY: I am a strong independent woman who don't need no man.

JOHANNA: Comic book characters are not allowed inside of me.

MILLY: Come on . . .

JOHANNA: Say it.

MILLY: I won't let comic book characters inside me—tonight. I frequent Cons, it's gonna happen.

JOHANNA: What do you think?

MILLY: Where should we tell him to meet us?

JOHANNA: Waitwaitwait—he responded. You ready?

MILLY: What does it say???

JOHANNA: "Join the two of you? Sounds great. Where at?"

MILLY: Italian food is sexy.

JOHANNA: I never understood that. What other food is sexy? None.

MILLY: Weird.

JOHANNA: What about Nona's?

MILLY: It's kind of spendy.

JOHANNA: If we do this right we won't be paying for dinner.

MILLY: Nona's. Let's go to Nona's. (*Types in the location and sends the message.*)

JOHANNA: THUNDERCATS ARE GO!

MILLY: I gotta get ready.

JOHANNA: It's eleven o'clock, we have some time.

MILLY: Dinner, ride back, get home, cock-block—wait. Code word. What's the code word? Do we have a set code word, Jo? Have you been using a code word all this time and I just didn't know it was a code word?

JOHANNA: God, please stop. (*She thinks a moment.*) When we get back to the house, I am going to push your hair back off of your shoulder, and I am going to whisper into your ear, "Go get em, Tiger." Then, initiate operation cock-block. Do you get it? The code word?

MILLY: Yea it's really, it's so, no, not really.

JOHANNA: It's from the movie.

MILLY: What movie?

JOHANNA: Spiderman! With Toby McGuire? You just spent all morning raving about how much he looks like Spiderman, I just assumed you'd seen the movie.

MILLY: I just like the costumes.

JOHANNA: "Go get em, Tiger" is MJ's line. It's what she always tells Peter before he leaves. It's her sexy catch phrase.

MILLY: Oooooooohh! I get it . . .

JOHANNA: Wait—what's he say?

MILLY: "See you girls tonight." God, we're evil. The worst.

JOHANNA: Never trust an app that makes you swipe for sex. People will use it for money, attention. It's too easy to abuse that kind of power.

MILLY: With great power comes great responsibility.

JOHANNA: And I am responsible for you, little sister. Alright, one more picture to seal the deal—come closer, get your face right there, right by my boob—peeerfect. Filterrr . . . Aaand . . . Sent.

(*Lights out.*)

END OF PLAY

THE LOBSTER QUADRILLE

by Don Nigro

Among the most frequently published and widely produced playwrights in the world, **Don Nigro** has continued to build a deeply inter-related, diverse body of dramatic literature, including the long cycle of Pendragon County plays, which traces the history of America from the eighteenth century to the present, and has written a long cycle of plays about Russian writers. Nigro's plays have been produced in every state, including at the McCarter Theatre, Actors Theatre of Louisville, the Oregon Shakespeare Festival, Circle Rep Lab, Capital Repertory Company, the People's Light and Theatre Company, the WPA Theatre, Manhattan Class Company, the Hudson Guild Theatre, the Berkeley Stage Company, Milwaukee Rep, Nylon Fusion Theatre Company, and many others. Internationally, his plays have been produced in London, Athens, Moscow, St. Petersburg, Warsaw, Krakow, Prague, Vienna, and Munich, and in Spain, France, the Netherlands, Canada, Belgium, Iran, Mexico, Argentina, Ukraine, the Czech Republic, Belarus, Finland, Estonia, Kazakhstan, Kyrgystan, Slovenia, Moldova, Hungary, Australia, New Zealand, South Africa, Singapore, Hong Kong, and Beijing, and toured in Delhi and Calcutta, India. His work has been translated into French, Italian, Spanish, German, Polish, Greek, Russian, Slovenian, Dutch, Persian, Lithuanian, and Chinese. John Clancy's production of Nigro's *Cincinnati*, featuring Nancy Walsh, won Fringe First and Spirit of the Fringe awards at the Edinburgh Fringe Festival, Best of Fringe at the Adelaide Fringe Festival, and later toured in England, Ireland, and Wales. *Seascape With Sharks And Dancer*, translated into Spanish by Tato Alexander, and featuring her and Bruno Bichir, was produced in Mexico City and toured in Mexico. In recent years Victor Weber's Russian translations of many of

Nigro's plays have been produced all over Russia and in other Eastern Euro-pean countries, including *Mandelstam* at the Roman Victyuk Theatre in Moscow, which toured to Israel and France; *Don Giovanni* in Moscow, *Gor-gons* in St. Petersburg and Moscow, *Iphigenia* in Kiev, *Maddalena* in Chis-nau, Moldova, and *Animal Tales* at Theatre Fontanka in St. Petersburg.

CHARACTERS

BEN, middle aged.
ROSE, 30.

SETTING

A bed, late at night.

• • •

—change lobsters, and retire in same order—
Lewis Carroll, *Alice's Adventures in Wonderland*

Late at night. Sound of crickets and a clock ticking in the darkness. Then lights up—ROSE has turned the light on. BEN and ROSE are in bed.

ROSE: Before we do this, I need to ask you a couple of questions.

BEN: Okay.

ROSE: Would you love me if my name was Assvogel?

BEN: Assvogel? Who is named Assvogel?

ROSE: I don't know. Somebody must be. That's not the point. The point is, would you love me if I had an ugly or stupid name? Instead of Rose, which is a very beautiful name.

BEN: I think so, yes.

ROSE: But you're not sure.

BEN: I'm pretty sure.

ROSE: What if I wanted to move to the Congo? Would you follow me to the Congo?

BEN: What would you do in the Congo?

ROSE: I don't know. Sell speed boats. I need to know a man would follow me to the Congo to sell speed boats if I'm going to have sex with him. Would you follow me to the Congo to sell speed boats or wouldn't you?

BEN: Is this a trick question?

ROSE: Yes.

BEN: Then no.

ROSE: Good. Honesty is good. Do you scream in your sleep? Or like, throw your arms and legs all over the place and kick box or something?

BEN: I don't think so.

ROSE: Well, I do. Can you live with that? Because sometimes I can get pretty violent. I wouldn't want to poke out your eye or anything.

BEN: I'll wear a catcher's mask.

ROSE: I have an extremely active dream life. Last night I dreamed I was having sex with the Angel of The Bottomless Pit. He liked to do it from behind. He gave me pearls and we ate gastropods. But then he tried to smother me with a dead octopus and I woke up screaming and I must have kicked the cat because she's still hiding behind the toilet. I think I was nervous about tonight. Because I kind of thought we'd probably finally get together tonight. I have some inhibitions. Not many, but they're serious. I have trouble abandoning myself. I'm always commenting on my performance in my head. Life is a ship without enough life boats. Like the Titanic. I always feel abandoned. But not in a good way. Sometimes I want to give myself up to evil. I used to sneak into abandoned buildings with boys and fool around. I liked kissing but I had mixed feelings about fornication. I've dated a lot of bastards. Well, not on purpose. I mean, I don't wake up in the morning and think, where can I find a bastard to date? It just turns out that way. But in a way, it's actually easier to date bastards. That way when I dump them, I won't feel guilty. I'm going to feel really guilty when I dump you.

BEN: So, you plan on dumping me?

ROSE: No. I don't plan these things. They just happen. I dump everybody. It's my trademark. Some people think I'm kind of wild, but in fact I'm actually very shy. But I do like being naked. Except in church. Although once I dreamed I was naked in church, laying on the altar, and this vampire flies in the window and bites my neck. It was actually pretty sexy. I think it stopped raining. I like the rain. I mean, I don't like getting soaked on the way to band practice, but I miss the rain when it stops. If I went back to my husband, would you go berserk?

BEN: Do you want to go back to your husband?

ROSE: No. But I might. I have a history of unexpected behavior. You seem very steady. Reliable. It's one reason to go for an older man. Security. I'm wild but I'm also insecure. But also you scare me because you're kind of weird.

BEN: How am I weird?

ROSE: I don't know what you're thinking. You don't babble when you're nervous. You listen. That makes me nervous. Sometimes I dream dogs are chasing me in the woods. I'm naked and I'm running through the woods and these dogs are going to tear me to pieces because I've been unfaithful to my lover. What kind of underwear do you think the Pope wears?

BEN: I've never thought about it. If you have his number, we could call him up and ask him.

ROSE: Oh, I don't want to bother him. I'm sure he's busy. Engaging in Papal activities. But let's not talk about the Pope.

BEN: Okay.

ROSE: You probably think I'm stalling. The thing is, I don't know you. I mean, we've known each other for a fairly long time, technically, off and on, but I don't really know you. Tell me some things I don't know about you.

BEN: Like what?

ROSE: Do you have a lot of casual sex?

BEN: No.

ROSE: How often do you have casual sex?

BEN: Never.

ROSE: Never?

BEN: I'm not a very casual person. If I'm not really pretty deeply involved, emotionally, it just doesn't feel right.

ROSE: So, you feel pretty deeply emotionally involved with me?

BEN: Yes.

ROSE: I was abducted by aliens.

BEN: Really?

ROSE: That's the reason I turned out this way. The alien abductions.

BEN: There's been more than one?

ROSE: They keep coming back for more. Of course, it's possible those were just dreams. I mean, who really knows if they're dreaming or not? I think there's a kind of telepathy where you have other people's dreams. I think maybe I've been having H. P. Lovecraft's dreams. Are you getting pretty anxious to get to the sex?

BEN: Don't do anything you don't want to do.

ROSE: You're a nice person. That's not a good sign.

BEN: Why is it not a good sign?

ROSE: Because for the most part I'm only attracted to assholes. Tell me something dangerous about yourself.

BEN: I hear voices.

ROSE: What kind of voices? You mean like dogs telling you to push old ladies in wheel chairs down staircases?

BEN: No. It's more like a radio in my head. I hear it especially clearly just before I'm falling asleep.

ROSE: What do the voices say?

BEN: I don't know. Nothing very profound. It's like picking up the phone and hearing somebody on the line in the middle of a conversation.

ROSE: So, it's like telepathy?

BEN: I don't know what it is.

ROSE: It's difficult to know anything. We think we know things, but we're just guessing. We think we want somebody, but maybe we don't.

BEN: What are you worried about, Rose?

ROSE: I don't want to be casual, either. I've done that, and it doesn't make me happy. But on the other hand—on the other hand, the thing is, you're too old. I don't mean that you're not attractive. It's that if I get all tangled up with a person like you, emotionally, then some day you're going to drop over dead, and then what will I do?

BEN: That's a good point.

ROSE: I know. This is why lovers should probably be about the same age. So they can drop over dead together instead of one of them dropping over dead and the other one left stuck with the gas bill and the car payments and the rest of her life. I don't want to lose you. And I'm going to lose you. Because you're so old. I mean, you're not ancient. You're just a lot older than me. Do you ever, I mean, as you get older, do you ever think, this could be the last person I ever love? I mean, that you might die before you find the next person you love? Do you ever think about that?

BEN: Yes.

ROSE: Doesn't it bother you?

BEN: Yes. But what am I supposed to do about it? You can't choose who you love or when you love or when you don't love. It happens for all sorts of reasons that are buried so deep in who you are that you can never really be sure what they are, really. You get older, and you begin to see a pattern, the particular way in which your relationships seem to fail. And even if you try to change the pattern, say, by getting involved with somebody who's different than the other people who've broken your heart, the universe tricks you, and they turn out to be pretty much the same sort of person you've always found yourself in love with. It happens when we're kids, I think, and then it just keeps happening, no matter what we do. But we just keep hoping the next person will somehow be different. That they won't go away like the others. But everybody goes away, eventually.

ROSE: So, what am I supposed to do about that?

BEN: I don't know. Love who you can't help loving, and hope for the best.

ROSE: But what if the best is waking up and realizing you're stuck with some old guy who's going to drop over dead and leave you alone again? What if that's the best you can do?

BEN: It just depends on what you want. What do you want?

ROSE: I think I just want to cuddle. Is that all right?

BEN: Sure.

ROSE: My father never liked to hold me. I think it made him nervous. I've decided seventy-eight percent of pretty much everything is Freudian bullshit. (*Pause.*) You're not mad?

BEN: No.

ROSE: Thank you.
    (*She snuggles under his arm, her face on his chest. They lie there together.*) I'm going to choose to pretend that I believe you because I'm tired and I want to go to sleep and I'm too comfortable to get up and go home. (*Pause.*) It's like the lobster quadrille.

BEN: The what?

ROSE: In *Alice In Wonderland.* The lobster quadrille. You dance for a while with one lobster.
And then eventually, you need to change lobsters. It's just how it works. Otherwise, the dance is over. And you don't want the dance to be over.

BEN: No.

ROSE: So, you just keep changing lobsters.

BEN: Uh huh.

ROSE: Even if you're really fond of one particular lobster.

BEN: Um hmm.

ROSE: That's just how the dance works. The aliens told me. When they abducted me. That was the wisdom they needed to share with me. About changing lobsters.

BEN: Okay.

ROSE: So, don't let me be the last one, okay?

BEN: I'll do my best.
(*Pause.*)

ROSE: It's raining again. Can you hear it? There's nothing better in the world than lying safe and warm in the dark in the arms of somebody who loves you while it's raining outside. (*Pause.*) I think those aliens might have done something to my brain.

BEN: Your brain is fine.

ROSE: I don't know. Sometimes it feels like there's things crawling around in there.

BEN: It's all those lobsters.

(*She snuggles up in his arms.* BEN *turns out the light.*)

END OF PLAY

MEANWHILE AT THE PENTAGON

by Jenny Lyn Bader

Meanwhile at the Pentagon was originally written for and performed by La Jolla Theatre Ensemble on January 26–27, 2020, as part of their presentation of Jenny Lyn Bader's short play cycle *The Age of Trump* in La Jolla, California. It was directed by John Carroll Tessmer, with the following cast:

THERESA: Julia Giolzetti
MARVIN: Geoffrey Graeme

Jenny Lyn Bader's recent productions include *Mrs. Stern Wanders the Prussian State Library* (Luna Stage) and *Equally Divine* (14th St. Y). Other plays include *In Flight* (Turn to Flesh), *Manhattan Casanova* (Hudson Stage), and *None of the Above* (New Georges). One-acts include *Worldness* (Humana Festival), *Miss America* (NY Int'l Fringe/"Best of Fringe" selection), and *Beta Testing* (Symphony Space). She co-founded Theatre 167, where she co-wrote *The Jackson Heights Trilogy.* For This Is Not a Theatre Company, she wrote the audio play *The International Local* (Subway Plays app) and co-authored *Café Play* (Cornelia St. Café). A Harvard graduate, she has received the "Best Documentary One-Woman Show" Award (United Solo); 2019 Athena Fellowship; Lark Fellowship; and the O'Neill Center's Edith Oliver Award for a playwright who has, in the spirit of the late *New Yorker* critic, "a caustic wit that deflates the ego but does not unduly damage the human spirit." Her work has been published by Applause, Dramatists Play Service, Smith & Kraus, Vintage, W.W. Norton, and *The New York Times,* where she served as a frequent contributor to the "Week in Review." She belongs to the Dramatists Guild. For more, see jennylynbader.com.

CHARACTERS

MARVIN MARKS, a General, 60s–70s.
THERESA AYLES, a Lieutenant Commander, younger than the General but
   at least mid-30s.

TIME

January 2020.

PLACE

The Pentagon

• • •

GENERAL MARVIN MARKS *is in his office.* LT. COMMANDER THERESA
AYLES *enters carrying a piece of paper and a laptop or other device.*

THERESA: General Marks.

MARVIN: Mmmf. Lieutenant Commander Ayles.

THERESA: Permission to enter.

MARVIN: Granted.

THERESA: There's a letter, Sir.

MARVIN: What does it say?

THERESA: Hard to do it justice. I think you should look at it.
   (*She shows him the letter.*)

MARVIN: I see.

THERESA: What would you like me to do about it?

MARVIN: Well, obviously don't sign it, don't approve it, and don't send it
to anyone.

THERESA: Right.

MARVIN: Why don't you shred it too. Anything else?

THERESA: Yes. Um. It's already been sent.

MARVIN: Sent?

THERESA: Leaked. It's been leaked.

MARVIN: To the press office?

THERESA: No . . .

MARVIN: Newspapers?

THERESA: Not exactly, but . . .

MARVIN: Fox News? Because they would send it right back to us if we asked, no questions.

THERESA: If only. No.

MARVIN: Who has it?

THERESA: Somehow—it was sent to the Iraqi government.

MARVIN: What?

THERESA: I know.

MARVIN: Is there a way to get it back?

THERESA: They've read it.

MARVIN: The Iraqi government. Read an unsigned, unfinished draft memo. Of an ill-advised, half-baked possible plan. That we are not pursuing.

THERESA: That's correct, sir. And they've shared it with the media.

MARVIN: But look at it! It was never even proofread!

THERESA: I'm painfully well aware of that sir. Though in fairness, the experienced proofreaders were the first to quit or be fired under this— regime.

MARVIN: (*Furious.*) Please. You don't need to be an experienced proofreader to see this letter makes no sense, grammatically or strategically! We obviously can't withdraw all the troops! Or rather the "trops" as it says here. It says "trops" instead of troops!

THERESA: I'm sorry!

MARVIN: I'm assuming you are not the one who sent or leaked it!

THERESA: Correct.

MARVIN: Then do not apologize!

THERESA: Okay!

MARVIN: Instead, do something! Quickly! Tell me something comforting.

THERESA: General! You do not require comforting.

MARVIN: No but that's changing. Every moment. Tell me. Something, anything comforting.

THERESA: That's a lovely photograph of your grandchildren.

MARVIN: Children are not comforting! They are loud, misbehaved, and often inappropriate.

THERESA: They looked so sweet! Um . . . something comforting. The hurricane on the coast of the Carolinas is no longer heading this way.

MARVIN: No, I mean something comforting, about this situation!
     (*Pause.*)

THERESA: Of course, sir. I'm thinking. (*Pause.*) There have been no declarations of war as a result of this letter.

MARVIN: Hmm.

THERESA: No major international mockery of this letter so far.

MARVIN: Okay.

THERESA: Oh, wait, I got it. Here's comforting: The typos will probably not be noticed by the Iraqi brass, most of whom speak a first language other than English. Usually Gelet Mesopotamian Arabic, Qeltu Mesopotamian Arabic, or Northern Kurdish. They'll be coming at it . . . from a remove.

MARVIN: Yes, that actually is a little bit comforting. Many of them won't know just how atrocious this letter is!

THERESA: Just think on that.

MARVIN: Until a translator explains it to them!
     (*This is a setback. But only momentarily.*)

THERESA: *Although* . . . hundreds of their translators have been assassinated since the Iraq War because the administration only granted two Visas to interpreters who worked with us! All the others—have been in a lot of danger since then.

MARVIN: Right. Not completely comforting but a silver lining of sorts. There could be some confusion generated.

THERESA: Yes.

MARVIN: And you know what we at the Pentagon do about confusion.

(*A beat as she is not sure what to guess.*)

THERESA: Try to create more?

MARVIN: Very good.

THERESA: What course of action would you like to take?

MARVIN: Hm. It's funny, I always know what to do.

THERESA: I know, that's why I'm here.

MARVIN: I always tell everybody what to do!

THERESA: Yes! We're counting on that, General!

MARVIN: Oh God, what do you think we should do?

THERESA: Me? Um. I can give you some options: We could say the letter is an unfinished work in progress, as evidenced by the fact that no one signed it . . . We could say it's an old letter from a previous time, maybe a previous administration? And our policy plans have changed since that time . . . Or we could say it's real but there are a number of careless mistakes in the letter that make it wrong . . .

MARVIN: Yes!

THERESA: The last one?

MARVIN: All of them. The letter is wrong. It's old. It's a draft. It's unfinished. It's not signed. It wasn't approved. It was written shoddily with amateur grammar and punctuation. It was sent by accident.

(THERESA *is typing notes.*)

THERESA: . . . "sent by accident." You want to admit to all of those errors? At once?

MARVIN: Yes. If we say everything went wrong, then we don't have to admit that a particular thing went wrong. Confusion. Distraction. The more wrong things you can fit in, the better. The letter was written by mistake, poorly worded by mistake, unedited by mistake, sent mistakenly by people who don't work here anymore.

THERESA: Right. Though it was drafted by the U.S. Military Command in Baghdad and sent by the Defense Department.

MARVIN: How? Who would do this? Was it in an envelope?

THERESA: I believe it was an email.

MARVIN: I knew we shouldn't have started using email!

THERESA: But think of this: now it's good we have it. We can use email now. To get our message out.

MARVIN: Yes, I suppose that's good. Little silver linings are abounding.

THERESA: Here, I've drafted your statement. Do you want me to get it proofread?

MARVIN: No time for that. Let me see. This is fine. Just one thing, let's change "careless mistake" to "honest mistake."

THERESA: (*Typing.*) I like that! That way we sound like we're not careless. And we are honest. "Honest mistake." That's nice.

MARVIN: Very good. Send it to the Iraqis. And the major news outlets.

THERESA: General. I hate to say it, but I should probably also release your statement . . . on Twitter.

MARVIN: We've talked about this!

THERESA: If we don't, it will get put in other words for us. By people—who don't care about words at all.

MARVIN: Fine. But I don't like it.

THERESA: What?

MARVIN: I don't like "Social Media." It revolts me.

THERESA: Yes sir. There, how's that for the tweet?
(*Shows him tweet on screen.*)

MARVIN: Can you add a few words or are you at limit?

THERESA: This is the limit. But I can link to the whole statement.

MARVIN: Ridiculous! How are people who are clarifying what they said supposed to do it in such a tiny number of words? Who would enjoy such an absurd form of communicating?
(*A pause that gets long as they both think of who but don't say it.*)
And you know what I really dislike? The phrase "Twitter Wars." I'd like to show them "Wars!"

THERESA: You could. Shall I press send?

MARVIN: You realize there's one more option.

THERESA: No. What?

MARVIN: Just pulling out of Iraq. Because we said we would in the letter. And saving face.

(*Silence.*)

THERESA: I know. I keep thinking that.

(*Another silence as they both imagine it some more.*)

But we've seen the map!

MARVIN: Press send.

(*A glum moment. Then she checks her phone.*)

THERESA: Twenty responses so far . . . and the President liked our tweet!

MARVIN: He's on there again?

THERESA: Always. Um . . . the President also liked a tweet where someone reposted the original letter we're saying is wrong!

MARVIN: He can't go endorsing alternative policies!

THERESA: Oh, he's shown he can. He can do anything we thought presidents couldn't do. Just by doing it.

MARVIN: See if you can get it taken down. The thumbs up or whatever it is they do in Twitland.

THERESA: Twitter. It's not a thumbs up. It's a heart.

MARVIN: See if you can get his people to un-heart the heart. If you can't, see if you can get the guy who posted the link to take it down, so the president's heart does not appear.

THERESA: I'm trying. But moving his heart—his hearts—that's always tricky. Because . . .

MARVIN: I know, because he listens to no one! That's the problem.

THERESA: It seems he sometimes listens to a late-night anchor or infomercial.

MARVIN: Do you think the Pentagon could produce an infomercial?

THERESA: There are over a hundred responses now. Some people are angry. Some say they like the policy in the letter, we should pull out of Iraq . . .

MARVIN: Yeah, those people haven't looked at a map.

THERESA: And a lot of them are giving us advice.

MARVIN: And the president?

THERESA: Doesn't like any of the advice. He's arguing against the advice. Oh wait, there's one piece of advice he likes!

MARVIN: What does it say?

THERESA: Someone named HelpfulPundit4710 says, "When I want to make sure I don't send a message by accident, I don't type the whole email address till I'm done. The Defense Department should try that." Oh, he's got another one. "In fact, I often copy the address into the body of the email until I'm finished, then put it back when the whole thing's written."

MARVIN: Very sensible. Of course, wouldn't have helped here because we had a leaker.

THERESA: The president is following this person.

MARVIN: What?

THERESA: And he's liked this person's advice before!

MARVIN: Such as?

THERESA: "The Congress and the White House should talk more behind the scenes instead of fighting in public. My family has tried this and it works."

MARVIN: That would have softened the impeachment a bit. What else?

THERESA: Hmm . . . HelpfulPundit talks about how loud a speech should be, how many lines you should yell, best ways to close an umbrella in the wind, why the chief executive should in fact get more ice cream than everyone else. This person's views overlap with the president's but modify and soften them and sometimes even nullify them . . .

MARVIN: How many likes has the President put on this account?

THERESA: Dozens.

MARVIN: Let me see. Reasonable. A calming point of view. With the ear of the President! Is it a man or a woman? It doesn't matter. We need this person in the Pentagon.

THERESA: Let me see . . .

MARVIN: This person could be very important.

THERESA: Not a man or a woman.

MARVIN: Non-binary? Gender-fluid?

THERESA: No, I mean, the adviser seems to be . . .

MARVIN: What?

THERESA: Don't be mad. A child.

MARVIN: A child?

THERESA: According to what I've found so far by cross-checking Twitter and Instagram, 4710 is actually the helpful pundit's date of birth. He or she, hard to tell from the haircut, is nine years old.

MARVIN: Oh.
   (*A bleak pause, then:*)
It's the end of civilization as we know it. The Commander in Chief getting feedback from a child . . . And me asking for advice from a woman. No offense.

THERESA: None taken. And I appreciate your asking me for my input. It meant a lot to me. Even if it made you feel civilization might be ending.

MARVIN: Of course. Glad to hear it.
  (*Beat.*)

THERESA: So, we've seen the map. We can't actually pull out of Iraq. I realize you're not fond of children. I'll just keep checking the feed.
  (*She picks up her phone slowly to return to Twitter.*)

MARVIN: No don't give up! Let's get in touch. This nine-year-old could save the Republic.

THERESA: I'll try to find a way to have the child brought to the Pentagon?

MARVIN: It's worth a shot.

END OF PLAY

MOST WONDERFUL

by Jennifer O'Grady

Original production by OnStage Atlanta
Merry Little Holiday Shorts
December 11–21, 2019
Scottdale, Georgia

Managing Director, Barry West
Director, Melissa Simmons

ADDIE: Ellerie Daube
JAKE: Fontez Brooks

Jennifer O'Grady is an award-winning playwright and poet. Her plays include *Charlotte's Letters* (Henley Rose Award; Newvember Festival Dublin; O'Neill Semifinalist and other honors); *Paranormal Love* (MTWorks Newborn Festival; Newvember Finalist; Pandora's Box runner-up); *Ellery* (selected for The Best Women's Stage Monologues 2017 and a Bechdel Group selection); and *Persephone* (selected for *The Best New Ten-Minute Plays 2019*). Her work has won many playwriting competitions and been selected for festivals across the United States, as well as in the United Kingdom and Dublin, Ireland. Producing theaters include Rover Dramawerks, 6th Street Playhouse, Heartland Theatre Company, The Hive Collaborative, Gi60, OnStage Atlanta, Lowell Arts Theater, Monster Box Theatre, and others. Her work has also been developed at various theaters including Off-Broadway at the Irish Rep. Additional publications include *The Best New Ten-Minute Plays 2021, The Best Ten-Minute Plays 2017, The Best Ten-Minute Plays 2016,*

The Best Women's Stage Monologues 2014, Best Contemporary Monologues for Women 18-35, Stage It 3: Twenty Ten-Minute Plays, and *Feels Blind Literary*. In 2018, Jennifer was selected as Mentee in Playwriting by AWP's Writer2Writer program. Jennifer is also a widely published poet and author of the poetry books *White* (Mid-List First Series Award for Poetry) and *Exclusions & Limitations* (Plume Editions/MadHat Press). Her poems are taught, anthologized, set to music, and featured in numerous places including Harper's, The New Republic, The Kenyon Review, Poetry, The Writer's Almanac, Poetry Daily, BBC Radio 4, and American Poetry: The Next Generation. Born and raised in New York City, Jennifer earned a BA from Vassar, where she won awards for her writing, and an MFA in poetry from Columbia University. She lives near New York City with her husband, son, and daughter, two dogs, two cats, and a rabbit. For more about Jennifer, see www.jenniferogrady.net.

CHARACTERS

ADDIE, 20s/30s. An unemployed female actor and JAKE's roommate.
JAKE, 20s/30s. An unemployed male actor and ADDIE's roommate.

PLACE

A small town outside of a city.

TIME

Christmas Day.

• • •

> *With the kids jingle belling*
> *And everyone telling you "Be of good cheer"*
> *It's the most wonderful time of the year*

Late afternoon, Christmas Day. ADDIE *and* JAKE *in their living room. No decorations. Snow outside.*

JAKE: Chicken dumplings?

ADDIE: Nope.

JAKE: Sesame chicken?

ADDIE: No.

JAKE: Moo goo gai pan?

ADDIE: I don't even know what that is.

JAKE: It's what they always ate on TV.

ADDIE: What TV?

JAKE: Old TV. Like, old people's TV.

ADDIE: That was chop suey.

JAKE: And moo goo gai pan.

ADDIE: I don't want Chinese, Jake.

JAKE: Nothing else is open, Addie.

ADDIE: We can eat snow, then.

JAKE: I can't eat snow. Anyway, it's all full of dog piss.

ADDIE: I think we have a can of beans.

JAKE: Beans are not a festive meal.

ADDIE: Neither is moo goo gei pei or whatever it is. (*Beat.*) Or Chinese. (*Pause.*)

JAKE: I could go see if Julio is . . .

ADDIE: He isn't.

JAKE: How do you . . . ?

ADDIE: I was there yesterday. He said he'd be closed today.

JAKE: Julio is never closed.

ADDIE: Well, he's closed today.

(*Beat.*)

JAKE: How about pizza?

ADDIE: They're closed too.

JAKE: Marcello's is closed?

ADDIE: They're Italian, Jake. They like Jesus.

JAKE: There are Jews in this town. They must eat too.

ADDIE: Presumably, they've all prepared. Unlike us.

JAKE: There's McDonald's . . .

ADDIE: Why not just pour toxic salt down my throat?

JAKE: Anything else would mean a long highway drive and it's snowing. I'll let you have my fortune cookie?

(*She doesn't answer.*)

Well, how about this? I'll get Chinese and you can watch me eat it.

ADDIE: You'd make me go without dinner? On Christmas Day?

JAKE: Then it has to be Chinese.

ADDIE: I don't want Chinese!

JAKE: But Addie . . .

ADDIE: No! Every other Friday we order Chinese, and you know why? Because I don't have a boyfriend and you don't have a boyfriend, neither of us has a family that is in any way sane, and all our friends, every single one of them, is either dating or working some Carnival cruise, or at least community theater for God's sake, and you're sitting here talking about CHINESE! AGAIN!

(*Pause. Then* JAKE *gets up and goes off.* ADDIE *is alone and sort of crumples inside. We hear a kitchen cabinet bang, then newspaper-rustling sounds. Jake returns with a small gift half-wrapped in old newspaper.*

What's that?

JAKE: Open it.

ADDIE: We said no gifts.

JAKE: I know, but you'll like this.

ADDIE: (*Looking at it.*) The theater section, thanks. Oh, look: everyone else is taking more of our jobs away.

JAKE: Open it.

(ADDIE *unwraps it. It's a can of beans. Beat.*)

ADDIE: *Beans?*

JAKE: I thought . . .

ADDIE: You're giving me *beans??*

JAKE: I just . . .

ADDIE: And you used the stupid *theater* section!!

JAKE: I thought it would make you laugh.

(ADDIE *puts it down and moves away. A silence.*)

It's just another day, Addie. (*Pause.*) Why don't we play cards, or . . .

ADDIE: Why do you like me, Jake? (*Beat.*) Why do you live with me?

JAKE: Because . . . you're my friend?

ADDIE: You hesitated.

JAKE: It was a weird question.

ADDIE: But you hesitated. That means you couldn't think of anything to say.

JAKE: That isn't true. I just said you're my friend, and you're a good one.

ADDIE: Right.

JAKE: You are. Remember when I was sick and you made cookies?

ADDIE: You threw them all up.

JAKE: But you were here. You had that party and you stayed home with me.

ADDIE: You like me because I took care of you? Get a nurse!

JAKE: That isn't the only reason. I can tell you things.

ADDIE: You never tell me anything.

JAKE: Well, you aren't nosey. I like that.

ADDIE: Nothing you said has anything to do with me or who I am.

JAKE: Come on . . .

ADDIE: None of it!

JAKE: Okay. You're smart. You're really good at Improv. You make great grilled cheese.

You have excellent taste in clothes. You knew Brandon was a jerk before I knew. You're . . .

ADDIE: We don't have a stupid Christmas tree!
  (*Beat.*)

JAKE: You said you didn't want a tree.

ADDIE: Do you have to do everything I say?

JAKE: I don't, but . . .

ADDIE: Do you have to do every single thing THAT I SAY??

JAKE: I don't do every single thing that you say.

ADDIE: Then why don't we have a tree??

JAKE: You didn't want one.

ADDIE: See what I mean?!

JAKE: This is absurd!

ADDIE: And now you're calling me absurd! Jesus!

JAKE: Yes! It's his birthday! Let's bake him a cake, or throw him a surprise party! Let's slaughter a calf! This is a completely made-up artificial day. Do you know how many people can't stand this day? Everyone pretends that they like it, but they don't. We're not stuck singing for dumb cruise-ship people, or performing the endless hell of another *Christmas Carol*. We're not sitting with awful relatives eating nasty food and unwrapping ugly socks. We're here and with each other, so get over it!
  (*A silence. Then:*)
It isn't too late.

ADDIE: What?

JAKE: For a tree. It isn't too late.

ADDIE: It's almost Christmas night.

JAKE: They're on sale. We could get a big one. (*Pause.*)

ADDIE: What would we put on it?

JAKE: (*Thinks.*) Beans?

ADDIE: I'm not putting beans on a Christmas tree.

JAKE: I have three cans of olives.

ADDIE: Why?

JAKE: They were on sale.

ADDIE: You're hoarding olives?

JAKE: They were on sale, okay? I was hungry.

ADDIE: What could we hang them with?

JAKE: Got any thread?

    (ADDIE *shakes her head no.*)

I have dental floss.

ADDIE: Me too.

JAKE: Go get your coat.

ADDIE: I only have thirty.

JAKE: I have forty. We'll be fine.

ADDIE: What about dinner?

JAKE: (*Slight pause.*) Chinese?

ADDIE: Okay. (*Beat.*) Merry Christmas, Jake.

JAKE: Merry Christmas, Addie.

    (*They exit.*)

END OF PLAY

THE ONES WHO ADAPT

by Greg Lam

Original Production:
Wishing Wind Creations
Midlothian, Virginia

January 15–25, 2020

Directed by Brendon Watts

Cast:
JOGGER: Hunter Wenner
THE ALIEN CREATURE: Stone Casey
FEMALE HUMAN: Jenny Sappington

Greg Lam is a playwright, screenwriter, and board game designer. He is the cocreator of the *Boston Podcast Players* podcast (bostonpodcastplayers .com) Boston's virtual podcast stage for new works by local playwrights. He is the cofounder of the Asian-American Playwright Collective and a member of The Pulp Stage Writer's Room. *Last Ship to Proxima Centauri* premiered digitally at Kitchen Dog Theater in March 2021 and will premiere onstage at Portland Stage Co. in 2022 after winning the Clauder Competition. His full-length play *Repossessed* received its world premiere at Theatre Conspiracy in 2018. In 2019, he was named a fellow in the Dramatic Arts by the Mass Cultural Council and the inaugural Pao Fellow of the Company One PlayLab. Greg was a member of the 2016 Company One PlayLab Unit for the development of Boston area playwrights. His works have been produced by Company

One, Fresh Ink Theatre, Pork Filled Productions, The Depot, The Boston Theatre Marathon, Open Theatre Project, Post Meridian Radio Theatre, Other World Theatre Paragon Festival, theatre@first, Navigators Theater, Fantastic.Z, Project Y, The Hive Collective, Culture Park, Silverthorne Theatre, The Pulp Stage, Ixion Theatre Ensemble, Eagle and Beaver Ensemble, 4th Street Theatre, Midwest Dramatists Conference, Tiny Theatre, Pear Theatre, The Best of All Possible Podcast, Baldwin Wallace University, Aching Dogs Theatre Company, Shadow Boxing Theatre, and others. You can see works of his that have been filmed at https://tinyurl.com/greglam. For more about Greg, see https://greglam.wixsite.com/home.

CHARACTERS

JOGGER, a male human in his 20s or 30s.
ALIEN CREATURE, age unknown. Species unknown.
FEMALE HUMAN, appears to be a female human in her 20s or 30s.

TIME

The early 90s.

SETTING

A public park near the woods.

• • •

At sunrise: A public park. Pause. Nothing happens for a while. Then, an ALIEN CREATURE *creeps across the stage, on all fours. It's like no lifeform seen on earth. It makes unearthly snarling/gurgling noises. A* JOGGER *trots onto the stage listening to an old-school Discman. Perhaps we hear the song that is playing for him, a song from the 1990's. Perhaps Nirvana's cover of "The Man Who Sold the World." He stops, jogging in place next to the* ALIEN CREATURE, *not noticing it. He checks his pulse. Eventually he notices the* ALIEN CREATURE. *The* ALIEN CREATURE *is looking right at him. They stare at each other for a long moment.*

JOGGER: Aaaaah!

> (*He suddenly runs off the stage. The* ALIEN CREATURE *bounds off after him. Pause. A* FEMALE HUMAN *enters. She holds a shopping bag. She walks towards to where the* JOGGER *and* ALIEN CREATURE *ran.*)

FEMALE HUMAN: Hey.

(*The* JOGGER *leaps back onto stage, disheveled and with the posture of the* ALIEN CREATURE. *He snarls.*)

JOGGER: Grrrr!

FEMALE HUMAN: Calm yourself! It's me. I'm one of us. I see you've acquired a local body. Well done.

JOGGER: Rrrruuu . . .

FEMALE HUMAN: Come on now. Access the creature's language center. You'll find it in the front of his little brain. I'll wait.

(*The* JOGGER *pauses, his eyes dart back and forth for a bit. Finally, he smiles.*)

JOGGER: Got it! That was tricky. These "humans" have a lot of useless things inside their brain spaces, don't they?

FEMALE HUMAN: OK, now, try standing up like me on your hind limbs. Humans don't scuttle about like that.

(*The* JOGGER *slowly stands up on two feet. It's awkward. He tries to get the hang of balance.*)

JOGGER: Like this? Wow, is this uncomfortable or what?

FEMALE HUMAN: You get used to it. Look at me. I even figured out how to walk on these pointy-foot sheaths.
(*She indicates her high heel shoes.*)

JOGGER: How long does it take to learn? You seem to have mastered it.

FEMALE: Well, I hatched weeks ago. I'm fairly assimilated.

JOGGER: How did you find me?

FEMALE: Are you serious? You made enough noise to alert the entire hemisphere.

JOGGER: So, you came to make sure I was safe?

FEMALE: Please. You are expendable, but I had to make sure that the nest was not discovered. Luckily human ears can't pick up the higher frequencies, but the canines in the town—best to stay away from those. Here, I brought you coverings.

(*She hands him the shopping bag. The* JOGGER *looks at his running clothes.*)

JOGGER: Am I not sufficiently covered already?

FEMALE HUMAN: You are attired for intensive activity, necessary for physical maintenance. Lower level everyday activity requires different coverings which advertise the wearer's level of inactivity.

JOGGER: Explain further.

FEMALE HUMAN: The less practical the coverings, the more high-status the wearer. If you want privilege, display the coverings of the privileged. People will assume you deserve them.

JOGGER: I'll take your word for it. It is far too cold for my tastes. Hmmm . . .
(*He begins to put on more clothes. It's a trial and error process.*)

FEMALE HUMAN: Hurry. Before any humans approach.

JOGGER: Are we not leaving this world, soon? We are hatched.

FEMALE HUMAN: Negative. According to the latest climate readings, under the current rates of warming the doorways won't appear until the year . . . 2043 by the local calendar. That's another fifty years away.

JOGGER: Fifty years?! That's alarming. Why did we hatch so early?

FEMALE HUMAN: Unknown. There's something off with this world. It's too cold, too many competing lifeforms. Still, it'll be many years before we will be able to find a new mating ground. We'll have to keep ourselves whole until then.

JOGGER: OK. Hibernating underground again. I can do that.

FEMALE HUMAN: No, no. That body you're wearing will start to rot unless you regularly feed it. They're quite fragile and need constant upkeep. I'm afraid we have to join human society for the time being.

JOGGER: Us? Join them? Look, we might be a race of interdimensional coldblooded spineless parasites, but we have standards. From the memories I can access from my host, these humans are clearly steering their society into the path of destruction. They're selfish, short-sighted, and very bad at math. And their mating procedures? Oh, goodness! (*He visibly recoils.*) Utterly repulsive!

FEMALE HUMAN: Actually, I was somewhat curious about that last item. It seems that there could be some . . . side benefits to their mating procedures.

(*The* JOGGER *looks at her, aghast.*)

Look, it's not like we have a lot of options. We were awoken too early, and we have no choice but to survive as best we can until the planet warms and the doorways open. This world is strange, but like they always say,

FEMALE HUMAN AND JOGGER: ". . . the ones who adapt are the ones who survive."

JOGGER: Yes, yes. The primary doctrine endures. Alright, then. FIfty years, on a cold, hostile planet with stupid hosts. How do we survive until we can leave this place?

FEMALE HUMAN: Access your life information. Does your host have a purpose?

JOGGER: A purpose?

FEMALE HUMAN: Yes. Many human adults are given a purpose, a series of menial tasks which they perform on a daily basis. If they successfully achieve these, they are given the means to obtain basic necessities.

JOGGER: Really? How do they assign these purposes?

FEMALE HUMAN: Very inefficiently. Many humans are dissatisfied with their purposes but lack the drive to obtain improved ones.

JOGGER: Do you have a purpose?

FEMALE HUMAN: Yes. My host is a "Real Estate Agent." I "show houses" for "entitled Yuppies" with "big trust funds."

JOGGER: Fascinating.

FEMALE HUMAN: Do you have a purpose you can access?

(*The* JOGGER *searches in his head.*)

JOGGER: I believe . . . I am a "lawyer."

FEMALE HUMAN: Oh dear.

JOGGER: What?

FEMALE HUMAN: Lawyers are quite unpopular. There are many jibes.

JOGGER: I can't help what I am.

FEMALE HUMAN: "What do you call a hundred lawyers buried up to their necks in sand?"

JOGGER: An ideal nesting situation.

FEMALE HUMAN: No—Well, yes. Never mind. Human humor is exhausting.

JOGGER: So. Fifty years living in a world that does not suit us, surrounded by apes with poor social skills.

FEMALE HUMAN: I'm afraid so.

JOGGER: Unless . . .

FEMALE HUMAN: Unless what?

JOGGER: You said that climate would not be warm enough to support the doors opening for fifty years, correct?

FEMALE HUMAN: Correct. Under the current rates of planetary warming. Why?

JOGGER: What if instead of adapting ourselves to suit the world, what if we were to adapt the world to suit us?

FEMALE HUMAN: How?

JOGGER: If we were to promote activities that warms this planet to our liking? Could that trigger the conditions that would open the doorways early?

FEMALE HUMAN: How would we do that?

JOGGER: Well, my host in addition to being a lawyer had plans to "run for office" in his ambition file. It occupies much of his brain space.
   (*He points to his head.*)

FEMALE HUMAN: So? Those are even more disliked than lawyers. You should hear the jests they make at the expense of their leader, "Clinton."

JOGGER: Yes, but they would be able to promote activities that increase the level of ambient warming, correct? As I understand it, "politicians" are able to choose amongst options which affect their future. If we were to gain high office, we could begin to encourage activities that would speed the rate of planetary warming. We could leave this hellhole decades earlier than projected.

FEMALE HUMAN: It would never work. Humans have mechanisms to remove politicians which do not serve their interests.

JOGGER: But look at the humans! Their brain spaces are filled with unreason and superstition and detritus. They're unable to free their brains from caveman instincts. Look at me! I'm repulsive, all fleshy and short-sighted and small brained. If we could get more humans to be as terrible as me, we could rule the world into its destruction!

FEMALE HUMAN: I admit, it's tempting. However, we are just two individuals. How much damage could we possibly do?

JOGGER: I think it's worth rousing more of our nestmates. We can work together. Grow our influence. Invest in political power. If we had a constituency of spineless, cold-blooded, parasites, we could make America safe for Greblaks everywhere!

FEMALE HUMAN: I don't know. I think we'd eventually be found out. I think it's safer to just assimilate and let them destroy themselves, as we know they will. The doorways will open eventually. Patience and camouflage has always been our kind's way.

JOGGER: My aggressive approach would allow us to progress to the spawning grounds decades earlier.

FEMALE HUMAN: If successful!

JOGGER: It will be successful! Look inside your host's brain. Do you see a rational thought in there? Any bit of judgement that would guard against a charlatan saying that someone else is to blame for their unsatisfactory life? Not only will it work, it will be easy! These humans have been waiting for someone like us to arrive.

(FEMALE HUMAN *thinks, then nods.*)

FEMALE HUMAN: Alright. You've convinced me. Let's rule this misbegotten ball of mud. On one condition.

JOGGER: Yes?

FEMALE HUMAN: Your host has no mate, correct?

JOGGER: That is correct.

FEMALE HUMAN: Every politician needs a mate, correct? A visual prop that you hold hands with triumphantly, that displays your virility and "family values." You will mate me.

JOGGER: Oh. Do we actually have to perform the actual mating?

FEMALE HUMAN: Yes. It's much more effective with prop children.

JOGGER: I suppose you're right. It's distasteful, but I'll do it for the good of the species. I'll just lay back and think of Greblak!

FEMALE HUMAN: Then we have an agreement. Shall we perform the human ritual of agreement?

JOGGER: Alright.

(*He holds out his hand to shake.* FEMALE HUMAN *swoops in for an intense kiss.*)

FEMALE HUMAN: Now we are agreed.

JOGGER: That will take getting used to. Alright, I think we will enjoy this. Decades of lies, hatred, skullduggery, and destruction lie ahead of us. Together we will weaken societies, erode trust, and make people act against their own self-preservation. It starts here today, with one blood-sucking parasite meeting his soul mate. It will not end until the Earth has come under our heel. (*As he speaks it turns into a campaign speech.*) Ladies and gentleman I accept your nomination! As a proud . . . American, I will fulfill the promise I made those many years ago to my beautiful wife, mother of my five children, on the day we met. We will bring about a new, warmer morning in America! A temperature change that we believe in! In this year 2020, are you going to be like the dinosaurs, unable to adapt to a changing world? Or are you going to join us, and be the one who adapts?

END OF PLAY

RECONCILE, BITCH

by Desi Moreno-Penson

Reconcile, Bitch was presented as part of an evening of short comedy plays, Dark Planet: Not Your Mother's Valentines Day, which took place at the Theater at the 14th Street Y. Associate artistic director: David Stallings. It was produced by Planet Connections Theater Festivity in New York City; opening for previews on Thursday, February 6, 2020, with its official opening Friday, February 7, 2020. The director was Glory Kadigan, sound design was by James O'Connor, costume design was by Janet Mervin, lighting design was by Joshua Langman, press representative was Jay Michaels, Arts and Entertainment, and the production stage manager was Charles Casano.

The Cast was:
LENNY: Charles Everett
EMMA: Mary Monahan

Playwright's note: *Reconcile, Bitch* was originally commissioned and developed by Tiny Rhino Theater Company, Brooklyn, New York.

Desi Moreno-Penson is a playwright/actor based in New York City. Her plays have been developed/produced at Ensemble Studio Theater (EST), INTAR, Perishable Theater (Providence, Rhode Island), Henry Street Settlement, SPF-Summer Play Festival, The Downtown Urban Theater Festival (DUTF) @the Cherry Lane, Urban Theatre Company (Chicago), among others. She is the winner of the 2017 MultiStages New Works Contest for her play, *Ominous Men*. Another play, *Beige*, was a finalist for the 2018 Bay Area

Playwrights Festival (San Francisco, California), received Honorable Mention on The Kilroys List 2017, was the winner of the 2016 National Latino Playwriting Award sponsored by the Arizona Theater Company, a finalist for the 2016 Eugene O'Neill National Playwrights Conference, a semifinalist for the 2016 Princess Grace Award for emerging artists, a finalist for the 2017 New Works Festival at Kitchen Dog Theater (Dallas, Texas), and a semifinalist for the 2017 Blue Ink Playwriting Award sponsored by the American Blues Theater in Chicago. *Beige* was also nominated for the 2018 Mentor Project at the Cherry Lane Theatre, and was selected for the inaugural list of 50 Playwrights Project Top 8 Best Unproduced Latinx Plays 2017. In summer 2020, she won Outstanding Playwriting in the Short Form (One-Act) for Snipped/Cut/Tied: *Una Noche de Magia*, an evening of three short magical-realist plays; *Genesister, Let Mezaluca Buy Your Car*, and Dead Wives Dance The Mambo, produced by Step1 Theatre Project and featured as part of the Planet Connections Theater Festivity at the Clemente Soto Velez Center. Her play *COMIDA DE PUTA (F%&king Lousy Food)* was the winner of the 2013 MultiStages New Works Contest, a finalist for the 2014 O'Neill National Playwrights Conference, received Honorable Mention on The Kilroys List 2015, and was given its world premiere at the West End Theater in New York City, produced by MultiStages Theater Company, and directed by Lorca Peress. In addition, her play *Devil LanD* was a semifinalist for the 2007 Princess Grace Award and one of only seven finalists for the first annual Ball Grant sponsored by the Playwriting Collective (New York City). Performance monologues include *A Latina Prepares* (excerpt featured in the documentary; "The Theater of Rice and Beans" (Tribeca), selected as Best Performance Short at 2004 Downtown Urban Theatre Festival at Henry Street Settlement, New York), *And Don't Knock It 'Til You Try It* (Puerto Rican Traveling Theatre, New York). Both monologues were presented together in a solo show, *Dos Mujeres*, as part of the tenth annual soloNOVA Arts Festival produced by terraNOVA Collective, New York. Her plays *Devil Land, Ghost Light, Lazarus Disposed, 3 To A Session: A Monster's Tale* are published through Broadway Play Publishing. A short play, *Spirit Sex: A Paranormal Romance* was published by Smith and Kraus as part of the anthology *The Best Ten-Minute Plays Of 2010*, and a scene from *Comida De Puta* has been selected for an upcoming anthology of scenes from plays written by Latinx playwrights, *Scenes for Latinx Actors: Voices For the New American Theatre*, also published by Smith and Kraus. Desi is a proud member of The Dramatists Guild, SAG-AFTRA, and the Going To the River Writers Unit at the Lark New Play Development Center.

CHARACTERS

LENNY, race-neutral, male, early to late 30s. Passionate, controlling, more
than a little thoughtless. Perhaps too much macho swagger for his own
good. But there's a good guy in there. Somewhere.

EMMA, race-neutral, female, early to late 30s. Passionate, determined, more
than a little fearless. Perhaps too much volatility for her own good. But
it's what makes her a badass. Somehow.

TIME

The present.

PLACE

A fire escape. The kind you will find in any urban city.

• • •

> *Oh yes! You are the ruin—the ruin—the ruin—of me!*
> *I have no resources in myself, I have no confidence in*
> *myself . . . I have no government of myself when you*
> *are near me or in my thoughts. And you are always in*
> *my thoughts now. I have never been quit of you since I*
> *first saw you. Oh, that was a wretched day for me!*
> *That was a wretched, miserable day!*
> Charles Dickens, *Our Mutual Friend*

> *"Well," said she, after a pause, "if you despise my love,*
> *I must see what can be done with fear. You smile, but*
> *the day will come when you will come screaming to*
> *me for pardon.*
> Sir Arthur Conan Doyle, *The Parasite*

*An autumn evening. The fire escape of an apartment building. Let's say we're in
New York, but we could easily be in Chicago . . . certainly any urban city. Present time. We see an angry LENNY is being pursued by a determined EMMA,
who's holding two plastic red cups. She seems to have cornered him, and now
he's trapped.*

EMMA: Lenny . . .

LENNY: (*Waving her away*.) Back, go back!

EMMA: But you . . .

LENNY: I said, *go back*!

EMMA: . . . You left your beer.

LENNY: Just turn around, go back inside—and leave me alone. I need some air, alright?

EMMA: Out on the fire escape? It's dangerous.

LENNY: No. *You* are dangerous, Emma, okay? You're *psychotic*. You terrify me.

EMMA: You like being terrified by me.

LENNY: Bullshit.

EMMA: You used to call it, "sex-dreading." What made you forget that?

LENNY: Can't believe you showed up tonight. No, what am I saying—I *can* believe it!

EMMA: I used to live here, too, you know.

LENNY: Yeah, and you moved out THREE MONTHS AGO, remember? Then you show up here again with Hector?

EMMA: Hector is my friend, too. What's the big deal?

LENNY: (*Exasperated*.) *Oh my God!*

EMMA: He told me you were having a party, and asked me if I wanted to come, and I said yes! So what?

LENNY: (*Flustered*.) What . . . why do you think I'm having this tonight, huh? It's a *celebration*, Emma, a festivity heralding the return of my freedom—*freedom*! From YOU. It's supposed to be a joyous event shared amongst all those who love and understand me. You never understood me. You were in love with someone who didn't exist. My gifts . . .

EMMA: Your what?

LENNY: My gifts . . . my gifts, okay? My gifts!

EMMA: No. I'm the one with gifts, Lenny. Unlike you, God in his infinite wisdom has blessed me with a sacred endowment. The ability to love . . .

LENNY: The only endowment God's put in your possession are your tits!

(*Offstage, we hear the familiar sounds of a typical, disgruntled urban dweller.*)

(*Voice-over: Yo, shut the fuck up out there!!*)

LENNY: (*In the direction of the voice.*) Fuck you! (*Lowers his voice; points.*) You see? See what you did? Can't do it. I can't live like this anymore. You can keep your drama for your mama. So, turn around . . . go back to the party and quietly make your exit.

EMMA: I can't. (*Short beat.*) I want you back.

LENNY: (*Shaking his head.*) We broke up. Accept it.

EMMA: I can't.

LENNY: You can.

EMMA: I won't.

(*A beat. Angrily,* LENNY *snaps his fingers at* EMMA *in frustration.*)

LENNY: I'll kill you.

(EMMA *stubbornly snaps her fingers back.*)

EMMA: I love you.

LENNY: (*Snaps again.*) I'll kill you.

EMMA: (*Snaps again.*) I love you.

LENNY: (*Snaps again.*) I'll kill you.

EMMA: (*Snaps again.*) I love you.

LENNY: *I don't love you!*

EMMA: But I'm your puppy. Let me be your little puppy.

LENNY: (*Confused.*) What the hell?

EMMA: When I see you walk into a room, I want to throw my little puppy paws up in glee. I want to nip, nip, *NIP* at your ankles! Please let me rub my cold, wet, little puppy snout up against your arm and feel the hairy, grizzly warmth through your smooth and ruddy skin . . .

LENNY: Get away from me!!

EMMA: (*Moving even closer to him.*) Use me, Lenny . . . please!! I love you so much. I want to tuck in my little puppy ears and feel my tail between my puppy legs as I walk back into my dark, little puppy corner for you. Nip! Nip! Nip!
(*She bites him.*)

LENNY: Ow! Jesus, what the hell . . . ? (*A short, shocked beat.*) Did you just fucking bite me?

EMMA: I want us to reconcile.

LENNY: Yeah?
(*He crudely grabs his crotch.*)
Well, "reconcile" this, bitch.

(EMMA *brandishes a blade.* LENNY *stops moving and stares in shock and amazement at her. A strange, anxious beat.*)

LENNY: (*Very careful.*) Oh . . . Shit! Okay, look . . . let's both take a deep breath here. Let's both breathe deeply, all right?

EMMA: I *am* breathing.

LENNY: No reason to lose our heads here, okay? It's cool. (*Short pause.*) I get now that you want to talk. I'm sorry for making this weird. We'll go back to the party; we'll sit down, have ourselves a couple of espressos and talk this whole thing out, calmly and rationally.

EMMA: I don't like espresso.

LENNY: Not a problem. I can make you a cappuccino.

EMMA: Too sweet.

LENNY: It doesn't matter, *damn it!*
(*Catches himself; attempts a small, nervous chuckle; tries to recoup some masculine swagger.*)
I was wrong. I shouldn't have assumed you wanted either an espresso or a cappuccino. That was *my* mistake, okay?

(EMMA *nods.*)

LENNY: (*Choosing his words carefully.*) Good. Okay. Beautiful. Listen to me. You done good, honey. I'm proud of you. You know that, right?

(EMMA *nods.*)

LENNY: (*More confident.*) Okay, *now*—here's what we're going to do. At the count of three, you're going to slowly put the knife down . . .

(EMMA *shakes her head.*)

LENNY: You're shaking your head at me. Why are you doing that? D-don't shake your head at me. I need you to do this, Emma. Put the knife down,

EMMA: No.

LENNY: (*Furiously.*) So, help me God—DON'T be a fucking crazy trick bitch now, alright?!!

EMMA: I'm a woman that won't stop.

LENNY: (*High dudgeon.*) Well, I am A MAN, okay? That means I'm gonna fight you . . . Oh hell yes! I'd never raise my hand to a woman, but Emma— you have pushed me beyond the limits of human endurance, and if I have to, I SWEAR TO GOD, I will beat your ass and stomp your face right into the fucking ground, alright?

EMMA: If I put the knife down, you'll grab it and then you'll stab me.

LENNY: Put it down!

EMMA: Stop screaming at me. My hands are shaking!

LENNY: (*Shakes his head; unyielding.*) I won't beg. I won't give you the satisfaction. I'm glad I cheated on you.

EMMA: Lenny, don't . . .

LENNY: (*Sardonic chuckle.*) Oh man . . . you were so easy to con, you know that?

EMMA: Stop it.

LENNY: Your girlfriend . . . Roxanne? The one I cheated on you with?

EMMA: Shut up.

LENNY: She was better in bed than you.

EMMA: I don't believe you.

LENNY: We used to laugh at you all the time. And then we'd have sex.

EMMA: You're a scumbag.

LENNY: Lots and lots of sex.

EMMA: You miserable, two-timing, rat bastard!

LENNY: Fuck you.

EMMA: Fuck you!

> (*She stabs him.* LENNY *cries out in horror and fear. Perhaps he's being a little over dramatic.*)

LENNY: *What the hell—?!!* (*He sees it; hysterical.*) What the—Oh my God . . . WHAT THE HELL?!! Oh Jesus, I'm—I'm—I'm bleeding, I'm *bleeding*! D'you see it? You do, right? You see it, right?

EMMA: (*Nods.*) Yes, I see it. It's not so bad.

LENNY: (*Flustered.*) Not so—? Are you out of your mind?! You've drawn blood.

EMMA: (*Flatly.*) I think true love should always draw blood.

> (LENNY *stares at her, stunned. A strange beat. As* LENNY *continues to bleed down the front of his shirt, the two of them stand warily observing the other. Then suddenly,* LENNY *laughs out loud. Another strange beat.* LENNY *continues to chuckle until this seems to coax a slight smile from* EMMA. *For a moment, it seems as if they're seeing each other for the first time.*)

LENNY: You know . . . I didn't notice it before . . . but you . . . you look *good.*

EMMA: (*Surprised.*) I do?

LENNY: Yeah. The way you . . . way you're standing there, like that . . . holding the knife.

EMMA: Am I terrifying?

LENNY: (*Almost proudly.*) No. Beautiful. You're reminding me. Of before. (*Nods.*) Oh yeah. This reminds me . . .

EMMA: Of what?

LENNY: . . . Of when I first saw you. I fell in love with you on sight.

EMMA: (*Pleased by this; preens a little.*) No, you didn't!

LENNY: Sure, I did. Why not? Moment I saw you, you became *my* Emma . . . my never-ending, my *endless* Emma . . .

EMMA: Don't call me that.

LENNY: But

EMMA: (*Sharply.*) You don't get to call me that anymore!

LENNY: Shoulda told you, okay? Shoulda told you that when you first looked at me, I fell in.

Right through your eyes, I fell in. Shoulda told you that. Shoulda told you I enjoyed the sounds you make when we made love. Panting and pleading your way like a small ground being up through the soil. Pushing through. Bursting. It's why I call you my *endless*—your body's an endless field of warm seeds, with skin that glows like brilliant dapples. I still see your skin in my dreams, you know . . . skin like a bright charm hiding in shadow.

(EMMA *is overwhelmed by this "confession," but doing her best to remain tough and intractable.*)

EMMA: Lenny, stop it.

LENNY: Stop what?

EMMA: Don't say things you don't mean. You know me. I never say anything I don't feel first.

LENNY: When you said you loved me? I felt it. Felt it when I heard it. Like the sound of water. I *heard* how warm it was. Warm and heavy enough, I could catch it. The wind blew it into my hands. And it made me feel like . . . like my soul's . . .

EMMA: Yes?

LENNY: Like my soul's caught in my throat . . . and my heart.

EMMA: (*Nodding.*) Is throbbing . . . it's pounding below membrane. I think my chest is going to burst.

LENNY: My mouth has gone dry.

EMMA: My nerve endings . . .

LENNY: Yeah. (*Nods.*) They're sparking off like tiny lightning bolts.

EMMA: Like it's ripping a million tiny shreds into my skin. Lenny?

LENNY: Yes, Emma?

EMMA: Jesus Christ, it's like . . .

LENNY: It's like . . .

EMMA: It's like . . .

LENNY: It's like . . .

EMMA: (*Aroused.*) It feels really good!

LENNY: (*Also aroused.*) Oh, man—I've got a hard-on that could chisel fucking granite right now. (*A beat, lewd.*) You want to see?

EMMA: (*Coy smile, short beat.*) Maybe.

LENNY: Okay . . . bring your left hand down . . . like I'm doing with my right hand . . . like this . . . like this!
      (*Still holding his hand against his bleeding wound, he awkwardly begins to show her.*) . . . and then raise your right arm, like I'm doing with my left arm, all the way up, like this . . .
      (*Also shows her.*)

EMMA: What—what are you . . . ?

LENNY: (*Becoming a little impatient.*) Like this, Emma . . . bring your left hand down . . .

EMMA: (*Confused.*) My—my left . . . ?

LENNY: (*A little impatient.*) Your other left, Emma!

EMMA: (*Standing her ground.*) Don't snap at me.

LENNY: I'm sorry.

EMMA: Don't be sorry. Just don't do it.

LENNY: Okay! I'm sorry.

EMMA: If you're gonna act like an asshole, I'm leaving you here, alright?

LENNY: No! D-don't go. I'm sorry. I'm sorry, okay? Look.
(*Tries showing her again.*)
Just like I'm doing with my right. You see? Okay! Yes, yes . . . that's it—*that's it!* Good, Emma. Oh my God, baby . . . that's-that's great. Now, raise your right arm, like I'm doing with my left—See? All the way up, bring it all the way up—AND point the knife towards the sky . . .
(*Thrilled by what he sees.*)
Yes, Emma, that's it. *Oh my God, yes, that's it!*

EMMA: (*Proudly.*) Okay.

LENNY: Now . . . I want you to come towards me . . .

(EMMA *seems finally to notice the condition he's really in.*)

EMMA: I think you should go to the emergency room.

LENNY: (*Strangely matter-of-fact.*) Oh yeah, yeah. Later. We'll go later. Just-just please come over here.

EMMA: (*Concerned.*) Why don't I put the knife down?

LENNY: (*Firmly.*) No! Don't . . v. don't put it down. I like the knife. The knife is *sexy*. The knife stays. Now, come on . . . please . . . stop arguing . . . come to me.

EMMA: No.

(*A beat. LENNY stares at her, hurt and confused.*)

LENNY: (*Indicating his crotch; a little childish, pleading and whiny.*) But baby . . . it feels like it's going to *explode*, you know? I mean, look . . . *I* wasn't the one who got it in this condition, okay? It wasn't me!

EMMA: Don't act innocent. You're the reason for all this.

LENNY: No, baby—that's not fair. *It wasn't me!* (*Indicating the knife.*) *You're* the one that showed up here with it. (*Smiles.*) Didja know you were gonna shank me like a boss?

EMMA: (*Shrugs.*) I didn't bring it with me. I got it from the kitchen. Made sure to get the extra-long, thin one, with the diamond-coated blade and the ginsu handle.

LENNY: (*Sharp intake of breath.*) Oh shit. That's hot. Come on, *sweetheart*—have some pity; I need to be with you right now!

EMMA: (*Stubborn.*) No. If you want me, Lenny . . . if you really want me . . . you can damn well walk towards me, too.

> (LENNY *is stunned by this. At this point, it's possible he might even be bleeding out/dying.*)

LENNY: (*Barely conscious.*) Baby, I don't think I can. I feel like I'm gonna pass out . . .

EMMA: (*Disappointed; almost a little pouty.*) Oh . . . damnit.

LENNY: But I'll tell you what . . . I can put my arms out towards you.

EMMA: (*Surprised.*) Really?
> (*She takes a step towards him.*)

LENNY: (*Shakily raising his arms towards her slowly.*) Sure. I mean, if that's what it's going to take then—I am a practical man. I can be fair.

EMMA: (*Moving towards him; more in love than ever.*) I thought you'd want me to do all the work.

LENNY: (*Still raising his arms; ardently.*) Baby, I just need your ass over here, right now!

EMMA: (*Moving even closer.*) I'm coming, Lenny!

LENNY: Now, that's what I want to hear!

> (*They finally meet, nose-to-nose. They give each other an exuberant high-five and begin to kiss passionately, with* EMMA *still pointing her knife high up in the air. They've reconciled.*)

> (*Blackout.*)

END OF PLAY

ROOST FIRST, THEN FLY

by Mildred Inez Lewis

Original Production Information:
Producing Organization: Playground, LA

Cast:
LITTLE RED: Carolyn Deskin
PENNY: Carla Vega
DOODLE DOO: Tahmus Rounds

Director: Jim Kleinmann
Theater: Broadwater Main State, Los Angeles, California

Date: March 9, 2020

Mildred Inez Lewis is a produced and published writer for theater, film, and the digital space. A member of the Dramatists Guild, she is part of the playwriting units of the Ensemble Studio Theatre-Los Angeles and Company of Angels. Her awards include UCLA's Samuel Goldwyn Writing Award. She was a British Theatre Challenge finalist and part of Humanitas' PLAY LA in 2018. She teaches in Chapman University's English department.

CHARACTERS

LITTLE RED, an exhausted, but still scrappy, hen.
PENNY, 20s–30s, female. An also exhausted hen who has given in to a
   plump complacency.

DOODLE-DOO, 20s–30s, male. A rooster and bit of a dandy. He talks a good
game, but years of servicing up to thirty hens a day has taken its toll.

SETTING

A chicken coop on a chicken farm in Central California.

TIME

Now. Just before dawn on a spring Sunday morning.

• • •

Chickens dreaming. LITTLE RED *and* PENNY *quietly roost and coo.* DOO-
DLE-DOO *dozes in front of them, while "standing" guard.* LITTLE RED *star-
tles awake and checks her wrist chip for the time. They've overslept.*

LITTLE RED: Nooo . . . Wake up. Shield your . . .

(*She tries to shake* PENNY *awake. Too late. An earsplitting buzzer
sounds.* DOODLE-DOO *jumps up and turns in circles.* PENNY *shakes
and hyperventilates.* LITTLE RED *comforts* PENNY. DOODLE-DOO
still spins, discombobulated.)

LITTLE RED: It's okay. Breathe, breathe.

PENNY: One of these days it's going to give me a heart attack.

LITTLE RED: I know.

DOODLE-DOO: Cock-a-doodle-doo!
(*He runs in circles.*)

LITTLE RED: Hey watch it. You're splashing. They haven't flushed our
doody away yet.

DOODLE-DOO: You get so used to it. I forgot it was there. Sorry.

PENNY: It's all right, Doodle-Doo.

DOODLE-DOO: I thought for a minute . . .

PENNY: I know. I was scared too.

(*A harsh light comes on.*)

LITTLE RED: That light always puts me on edge. What's the point of it?

DOODLE-DOO: Something about your cycles . . . and tender meat.
(*He winks.*)

DOODLE-DOO: If I may be so indelicate.

PENNY: You're such a gentleman.

LITTLE RED: Come on. He's banging thirty of us a day.

PENNY: That's his job.

DOODLE-DOO: It doesn't mean I don't have someone special.
(*He stands close to* PENNY *and gently nuzzles her.*)

LITTLE RED: I bet you say that to all the chicks. Actually, I'm sure you do.

PENNY: Don't ruin my moment.

LITTLE RED: I'm not saying—It's this whole set up that's wrong.

PENNY: We have a lot to be thankful for. No one's going to be processing today. It's Sunday.

DOODLE-DOO: That's right.

(*All three heave a sigh.*)

PENNY: Not that I don't want to take my place.

DOODLE-DOO: You always have such a good attitude.
(*He looks pointedly at* LITTLE RED, *who rolls her eyes.*)

PENNY: I see myself being served 'a la king' for a nice family. Three kids, mom and dad. First marriage. Dinner around a big ole wooden table.

DOODLE-DOO: Nice. Old fashioned.

PENNY: It's kinda corny.

DOODLE-DOO: Nothing wrong with that. Mmm hmm. Nothing at all.

LITTLE RED: Oh my god.

PENNY: Have you given yours any thought?

LITTLE RED: I'm not helping them plan my own demise. If it happens, it happens without my help.

DOODLE-DOO: I want to go out at a Sunday afternoon picnic. Fried between the 'tater salad and coleslaw. I see a big group of family and friends, laughing and talking. Gals huddled in their little circles. The men sneaking drinks while little kids play tag.

LITTLE RED: You're too tough to be anything but stewed. Thirteen hours minimum.

DOODLE-DOO: You've got a cruel streak.

LITTLE RED: Humans are the cruel ones.

PENNY: Not this again.

LITTLE RED: We could live to ten or maybe twelve if we were protected.

DOODLE-DOO: There were never any good old days for us. Before there were people, there were foxes.

PENNY: And dogs.

LITTLE RED: They only picked off who they needed to survive. A hatchling, an old man—

DOODLE-DOO: Hey!

LITTLE RED: Even Old Farmer MacDonald never caged us. You know what else? When Ivan came back from the vet that time, the van stopped at KFC.

PENNY: That was just plain mean.

LITTLE RED: He said people piled up their plates with our brothers and sisters. They'd take a few bites, then toss the rest aside.

(PENNY *gasps*.)

DOODLE-DOO: Well I don't believe it.

PENNY: Who would waste food like that? I eat every last pellet.

LITTLE RED: Ivan saw it with his own two beady eyes.

DOODLE-DOO: It doesn't matter. After the humans are gone, there'll be something else. Things can always get worse.

LITTLE RED: How? It's pretty bad now.

PENNY: Everyone says heat's coming. Grandma Ginger says she can feel it in her feet. She's sure it's got something to do with them.

DOODLE-DOO: You hens. Always gabbing. Think. Does it make sense that they would burn themselves down to the ground?

LITTLE RED: Lots of things don't make sense. Does it make sense us living like this?

DOODLE-DOO: No, but you've got to accept our role in the world.

LITTLE RED shakes her head 'no.'

(*A visual standoff.*)

PENNY: Everybody's got a place in the chain of life. Ours just happens to be close to the bottom.

LITTLE RED: The food chain's rigged.

DOODLE-DOO: I get where you're coming from. I'd love to spread my wings like an eagle, spot a salmon, swoop down . . . sushi! Mm. Then I'd be ready for the end.

LITTLE RED: Don't be so quick to accept the status quo. They're grooming us: when to sleep, what to eat. And always more, more, more eggs. Things don't have to be this way.

PENNY: We're not innocent. Don't you think worms mind when we rip them from the ground? Have you ever given them a second thought?

LITTLE RED: We've never been outside.

PENNY: Now you're being defensive.

LITTLE RED: Am not!!

PENNY: When they played Oprah over the PA, you promised you'd try to be more positive.

LITTLE RED: Can you imagine how big flock reunions would be if they'd give up eating us twice a week? Once even.

PENNY: You don't expect them to do that, do you?

LITTLE RED: Why not?

DOODLE-DOO: They don't want to. Simple as that.

(*The blinding light dims.* PENNY *rubs her eyes.* DOODLE-DOO *pats* PENNY's *shoulder. Offstage, the processing machine starts almost imperceptibly.*)

PENNY: What's that?

LITTLE RED: You know what it is, it's the death

DOODLE-DOO: processing

LITTLE RED: machine

PENNY: But it's Sunday.

(*The sound shuts off.*)

ALL: WHEW!

DOODLE-DOO: See? It was probably maintenance. You know us men. We love to tinker.

(*The sound kicks up again. It's still low, but ominous.*)

LITTLE RED: Nope. It's happening.

DOODLE-DOO: We're not scheduled. It's Sector 118's turn.

(*Lights flash slowly three times. It's their sector's turn. The machine volume lowers again.*)

LITTLE RED: I'm going to try to get away.

PENNY: How?

LITTLE RED: I'll run.

PENNY *and* DOODLE-DOO *laugh.*

PENNY: We're chickens.

LITTLE RED: Then I'll fly.

PENNY: We've been caged our whole lives. In seventy-five square inches, less than a sheet of paper. Even if we knew how to fly, we're too weak.

LITTLE RED: I think I remember how. It comes to me in dreams.

DOODLE-DOO: Dreams aren't enough. If you jump out there and don't make it, you'll make yourself even more of a target.

PENNY: And us.

LITTLE RED: Sometimes I can feel flight in my body.

DOODLE-DOO: Even if you remembered, you've picked up some . . . stature since then.

LITTLE RED: That's the steroids.

DOODLE-DOO: It'd be a lot harder.

LITTLE RED: We've laid how many eggs? For how long? We're strong.

PENNY: Not me.

LITTLE RED: No, you too.

> (*The processing machine kicks up louder.* DOODLE-DOO *spins.* PENNY *takes his hand.*)

PENNY: We mustn't panic. They might not even get to us.

LITTLE RED: That machine isn't supposed to be on today at all. Anything can happen.

DOODLE-DOO: We don't have a lot of choice.

LITTLE RED: There's always a choice.

PENNY: That's crazy talk.

> (LITTLE RED *walks out unsteadily. She tries to run, but waddles.* PENNY *ducks.*)

LITTLE RED: You want to stay, you stay. I eat and it's my destiny to be eaten. But it's crazy to stay and wait for death. Especially when so many are hungry.

PENNY: What's that now?

LITTLE RED: On the way from KFC, Ivan saw humans laying on the sidewalks, without enough strength to lift their heads. What's all this for, if people are still hungry?

> (*Beat. She breathes, tries for lift off, but fails. She starts to weep.*)

PENNY: Well, you tried.

LITTLE RED: Give me a boost. If I don't make it, I'll accept whatever comes. See? Positive.

(DOODLE-DOO *and* PENNY *lock arms and form a 'V' that almost sweeps* LITTLE RED *up. Doodle-Doo* collapses from the effort. PENNY *fans him.*)

LITTLE RED: What if . . .

PENNY: Doodle-doo's hurting.

(DOODLE-DOO *gets up and crows.*)

DOODLE-DOO: There might be some snow on the roof, but there's still fire in the furnace.

LITTLE RED *groans.* DOODLE-DOO *grabs* PENNY's *hand.*

DOODLE-DOO: On my count. One, two . . .

(*They launch* LITTLE RED. *She "flies," but like a chicken.*)

PENNY: She's doing it.

LITTLE RED: I'm doing it. It's glorious.

DOODLE-DOO: Damn girl.

(LITTLE RED *hovers in the air and looks back.*)

LITTLE RED: Come with.

(*The machine kicks back up.*)

DOODLE-DOO: One last quickie for the road?

(PENNY *has a moment of temptation.*)

PENNY: Another time. Come on.

DOODLE-DOO: One, two . . .

ALL: THREE.

(*They take flight behind* LITTLE RED. *Music suggestion: "Flight of the Valkyries."*)

END OF PLAY

SAVE ME, MYRON GLICK!

by Craig Gustafson

Premiered July 26, 2019
Riverfront Playhouse
Fasting Cougars, a night of ten-minute plays by Craig Gustafson.
Aurora, Illinois
Producer, Gary Puckett

Director, Craig Gustafson

MYRON GLICK: Ken Kaden
DOBIE GLICK: Patti Shore Kaden
KOSARACHI: Kiara Wolfe

After years of writing newspaper columns, radio, and children's shows, **Craig Gustafson** was content writing the occasional sketch or song parody ("Not Getting Naked Today," "If I Had a Meltdown") for a local awards show. Early in 2018, a loved one unexpectedly passed away and when resurfacing from grief, Craig's reaction was, "Hmm . . . maybe time isn't infinite," and he began writing his ass off, producing a myriad of ten-minute plays, and entering contests worldwide.

His *Lending a Hand* is published in *The Best Ten-Minute Plays of 2019*. A night of his ten-minute plays, "Fasting Cougars," was staged in Aurora, Illinois, in 2019. Included were *Soul Custody*; *Lending a Hand*; *Whooping Mice*; *Torquay Holiday*; *With a Song in My Holster*; *Save Me, Myron Glick!*; *Wolverton Inn*; and *Bubbles the Home Wrecker*. In late 2019, Craig was accepted for membership in the Dramatists Guild of America. Craig is matrimonially ensconced with the daringly freckled and scandalously redheaded Margie.

CHARACTERS

MYRON GLICK, 40s–60s. Kind-hearted, easy-going. An easy mark for
swindlers, but he doesn't really mind. You can't take it with you.

DOBIE GLICK, 40s–60s. Not really a shrew so much as worried about
money to the point of screaming. She has watched her husband giving
away everything they own.

KOSARACHI, late teens–20s. A beautiful Nigerian Princess. Happy,
grateful, loving, imperious, and lethal.

SETTING

The Glicks' suburban living room, Naperville, Illinois.

TIME

The present. A spring evening, around 10:32 p.m.

• • •

*The Glicks' suburban living room. A couch, table and two chairs. Front door up
center, bedroom off right. MYRON and DOBIE GLICK are seated at the table,
playing Yahtzee. DOBIE is quickly adding up her score.*

MYRON: Do you need the car tomorrow, Dobie?

DOBIE: (*Beat.*) Why are you asking me that?

MYRON: Because I thought you might need the car tomorrow. For
groceries. Or what-not.

DOBIE: Is the car here?

MYRON: (*Thinks.*) No.

DOBIE: Then what's the point of asking? Jiminy Crickets, Myron.

(MYRON *adds up his dice. Writes down his score. It's a slow process.*)

When are we getting the car back, Myron?

MYRON: Ohhhh, any time now, I should think.

DOBIE: Okay, see, my point is that the car should be here. That you maybe
shouldn't have loaned it to Ralph next door.

MYRON: He's our neighbor.

DOBIE: He's lived here two weeks. Or one, really. The past week he's been off somewhere with our car!

MYRON: I'm sure he'll bring it back. He's a nice fella.

DOBIE: Arrrggh! I don't care if he's a nice fella! I want our car!

(*They play in silence for a moment.*)

Do we even have money for groceries?

MYRON: Depends on what you want to buy.

DOBIE: Milk, eggs, bacon, bread, coffee, stamps and SOS pads.

MYRON: (*Thinks.*) No.

DOBIE: What can we buy?

MYRON: (*Thinks.*) Nothing.

DOBIE: Nothing? Nothing? Myron, how are we going to eat? How are we going to live?

MYRON: We'll get by. Have faith. Like them.

DOBIE: Like who?

MYRON: (*Sorry he brought it up.*) Never mind.

DOBIE: Who has faith? What are you talking about?

MYRON: (*Unfolds a sheet of paper.*) This. These people. So much trouble. So much faith.

DOBIE: (*Reads.*) "Friend Myron Glick. I write to you from the country of Nigeria, where my family owns the richest emerald mine in all Africa." Oh, Jesus. No. "Permit me, Friend Glick, to unburden my troubles to you. Our palace rests on the peninsula of Oombobemnya, a beautiful and enchanting land, unfested by pirates." Unfested?

MYRON: English isn't his first language. You should give him a break.

DOBIE: "These terrible and ferocient pirates have invaded our lands, set fire to our crops, stolen our emeralds and made out with my sister."

MYRON: He means, "made off."

DOBIE: You're sure about that?

MYRON: Trust me.

DOBIE: "The hideous but courteous pirates will allow me to ransom my lands and my sister. Help me, Friend Glick. My sister Kosarachi, having been with pirates, is now spoiled goods, but I do desire the return of my emeralds. If you will help me pay the ransom, you may have one-third of my emeralds and all of my sister. I cannot pay this ransom, Friend Glick. It is imperative that some kind-hearted scroll helps me in my minute of need! Are you that kind-hearted scroll, Friend Glick? Save me, Myron Glick!" Come onnnnnnnnn, Myron!

MYRON: Finish the . . .

DOBIE: I'm not gonna finish this furshlugginer crap. How much?

MYRON: (*Gathering dice.*) I beg your pardon?

DOBIE: How much did you send this schmuck?

MYRON: (*Rolls dice.*) Two threes, possible full house . . .

DOBIE: (*Reads.*) "Thirty thousand dollars?!" Tell me you didn't send this guy thirty thousand dollars!

MYRON: Of course not. We only had seventeen thousand dollars.

DOBIE: And you sent him . . .

BOTH: Seventeen thousand dollars.

DOBIE: *Myron!*

MYRON: It's a good investment. And we're helping someone in need.

DOBIE: It's a scam. It's the oldest con game in the world and it's called "The Spanish Prisoner." David Mamet made a whole movie out of it!

MYRON: Yeah, but see, this isn't Spanish, it's Nigerian.

DOBIE: (*Exiting right.*) That's it, Myron. That's it. I'm going home to my mother.

MYRON: Permit me to remind you, your mother is dead.

DOBIE: Compared to this marriage, my mother is dancing a topless polka in Rio de Janeiro! You've been taken, Myron!
(*And she's out.*)

(MYRON *sighs; puts away the Yahtzee game. There is a knock on the door. He goes to open it. A beautiful African girl is in the doorway. She is radiant with happiness.*)

KOSARACHI: (*Against all hope . . .*) Good evening.

MYRON: Good evening. What can I do for you?

KOSARACHI: You are . . . Myron Glick?

MYRON: Yes.

KOSARACHI: (*Screams happily.*) I thought I would never find you, Myron Glick!

MYRON: (*Confused but cheery.*) Well . . . here I am! Won't you come in?

KOSARACHI: I shall come in, Myron Glick. So kind. You are famous for your kindness.

MYRON: Oh, I don't think so.

KOSARACHI: But you are! I know this better than anyone, Myron Glick! For I am Kosarachi!

MYRON: Kosarachi?

KOSARACHI: It means, "Tell it to God."

MYRON: That's swell, but what . . . ?

KOSARACHI: I will give you a hunt.

MYRON: "Hint?"

KOSARACHI: Yes, "hint." Thank you for correcting me. Here is the hunt: "Save me, Myron Glick!"

MYRON: (*Beat.*) Nope. No, that doesn't ring a . . . oh, wait. Oh, my God!

KOSARACHI: I am your Nigerian Princess, Myron Glick!
(*She seizes his ears and kisses him. And he stays kissed. His hands flounder a bit, wondering what to do with themselves, as DOBIE enters*)

with a suitcase. She stares, disbelieving. MYRON *finally puts his hands in his pockets and* KOSARACHI *ends the kiss.*

MYRON: Wow . . . that was . . . Oh. Hi, honey. This is Kissarachi. Uh . . . Kosarachi!

DOBIE: Is it?

KOSARACHI: Kosarachi means, "Tell it to God!"

DOBIE: Does it?

MYRON: This is quite a . . . I don't know . . . surprise.

DOBIE: Is it?

KOSARACHI: My brother has sent me to Myron Glick in gratitude for saving our lands and our emeralds. Thanks to the robust pirates, I am no longer a virgin, and thus of no use to my family. Is that not wonderful? I have been sent to Naperville, America, to marry Myron Glick.

DOBIE: Uh huh. Myron? Your thoughts on this development?

MYRON: Well, gosh, it all kind of just happened . . .

DOBIE: *Myron!*

KOSARACHI: She is very raucous, Myron Glick. How long has she been your servant?

DOBIE: (*Moving on Kosarachi.*) That's it . . .

MYRON: (*Stopping* DOBIE.) I'll handle it, Dobie. (*To* KOSARACHI.) I'm very flattered, Kosarachi. Kosarachi? Did I say that right?

KOSARACHI: (*Nodding blissfully.*) It means, "Tell it to God."

MYRON: Dobie is my wife, Kosarachi. I'm already married.

KOSARACHI: Oh, the more the marriott, Myron Glick. I do not object. Mrs. Dobie can be wife number two.

DOBIE: I'm number two?

KOSARACHI: Well, obviously. I am a princess and you are a slattern.
(*She hugs* MYRON *tightly. He extricates himself gently.*)

MYRON: You see, Kosarachi, in America, everybody can only have one spouse.

KOSARACHI: So . . . you, Myron Glick, are not a Republican legislator?

MYRON: Even if I were, Kosarachi. One spouse each. One husband. One wife. Do you understand?

KOSARACHI: (*Sighs.*) Yes, Myron Glick. I do understand. I shall have to kill Mrs. Dobie.
(*She starts for* DOBIE. MYRON *has to get between them.*)

MYRON: No, no, no! For Pete's sake! Look—won't you sit down? Both of you. Please.

(DOBIE *sits at the table.* KOSARACHI *lies on the couch.*)

KOSARACHI: Give me your babies, Myron Glick. I will bear them gladly!

MYRON: Umm . . . my God, what am I going to do?

KOSARACHI: (*Stands.*) You are asking your God for advice? Give me your goat. I will slaughter it for sacrifice.

MYRON: No, please. Sit down.

(KOSARACHi *sits.*)

DOBIE: What's to decide? I mean, really! What's to decide?!

MYRON: Well, honey . . . Kosarachi has nowhere to go!

KOSARACHI: (*Grabbing his arm.*) Nowhere except to your bed, Myron Glick. The pirates taught me many things.

MYRON: Now, Dobie . . .

KOSARACHI: "Walking the plank." It is not what you think it is.

DOBIE: You actually have to think about it? The hell with you.
(*Heads for the door.*)

MYRON: Dobie, please! I need time!

DOBIE: Kosarachi.

KOSARACHI: Yes, Dobie Glick?

DOBIE: Not you. (*To* MYRON.) Tell it to God.
(*Exits.*)

KOSARACHI: (*Hugging* MYRON.) Our troubles are over, Myron Glick! We shall live happily ever after. I shall not just be a Nigerian princess. I shall be a *Disney* Nigerian Princess! First, we must move to an appropriate house and not this . . . (*Searches for the word.*) . . . shit-box. With servants. Servants are very important. And armed guards, to protect us and our children from pirates. And a Macy's charge account.

MYRON: Well yes, all that would be very nice, but it would take money.

KOSARACHI: Why, yes, of course it would.

MYRON: I don't have any money. I sent all my money to your brother.

KOSARACHI: (*Pauses, smiles.*) You will repeat that please?

MYRON: I have no money.

KOSARACHI: (*Cheerfully.*) Goodbye, Myron Glick.
(*Exits.* MYRON *stands for a moment, looking at the door after* KOSARACHI. *Then looking to Heaven. He tells it to God.*)

MYRON: (*Sighs.*) Kosarachi.

(*The lights fade.*)

END OF PLAY

THE SECOND COMING

by *Gabrielle Fox*

Production History:
2017 workshop directed by Jennifer Gaito Siciliano.

Cast: Anna Fawcett as MARTHA, Sam Joseph as JESUS, Albert Lima as MOHAMMED, Patrick McGuiness as CHARLIE, Michael Patrick Sullivan as JOE.

2020 Dark Planet: Not Your Mother's Valentine's Day presented by Planet Connections Festivity directed by Lu Bellini.

Cast: Konrad Custer as JESUS, Charles Everett as MOHAMMED, Michael Gnat as JOE, Sachi Parker as MARTHA, William Serri as CHARLIE.

Gabrielle Fox is an award-winning playwright. Most recently her play was presented in Playwrights for a Cause 2018. She also won the award for outstanding playwriting, overall production and the Planet Activist Award in the Planet Connections Theatre Festivity. Her play *The Home* was presented in the La MaMa New Playwright Marathon in New York. Gabrielle teaches playwriting for Westchester Community College's Community Education Division and the Young Author's Conference. She coproduces and founded the first women's playwright festival in the Hudson Valley now in its third year. She created the Theatre Revolution, LLC, where local artists go global and is a proud member of The Dramatists Guild. www.gabriellefoxwrites .com, www.theatrerevolution.org.

CHARACTERS

JOE, 40 to 60 something. Middle-American suburban survivalist.
CHARLIE, 40 to 60 something, big hearted neighbor.
JESUS, traditional looking Jesus, 30-ish.
MARTHA, Joe's 40–something housewife.
MOHAMMED, African American gun enthusiast.

SETTING

Joe's survival bunker in America (not the south).

TIME

Now.

• • •

JOE sits alone at a card table in a survival bunker, dressed in army camouflage surrounded by boxes, canned food, flashlights, etc. He looks around self-consciously before kneeling on the floor of the bunker.

JOE: Uh . . . heavenly father. Jesus, especially. Bless this drill. As you always do. And bless my family, my country and protect us and help us to protect you and protect this bunker and protect our food and guns and the flag and Christmas and . . . (*Frustrated.*) And uh . . . I don't know, could ya send me a sign? I mean twenty-five years and no one takes this bunker seriously anymore, Jesus. Back in the day there was a miracle every minute. Would it kill you to . . . you know . . . send a sign or God forbid . . . visit? Aren't you scheduled to do that? At some point? That's too much to ask . . . just. A sign. Ok?

    (*He makes a face as if smelling something foul, waves his hand in front of his face.*)

JOE: (*Yelling to CHARLIE offstage.*) Jesus. Charlie! What the fuck'd ya eat?

    (*He stands, grabs a can of air freshener and sprays it. CHARLIE enters, zipping up his pants.*)

CHARLIE: I shoulda had the Chef Boyardee. That dried food shit doesn't sit right with me.

JOE: Military grade, the best!

CHARLIE: Doesn't feel like the best. Let's go up and get some air.

JOE: Not a chance, Chuck. If we can't handle a drill? We can't handle the real thing.
   (*He pulls out an old-fashioned radio with a crank.*)

CHARLIE: Put that away, I brought my iPhone so I can check up on my kids on Facebook.

JOE: There's no internet, your kids are dead. You're not taking this seriously!

CHARLIE: Hey! Just because my kids chose soccer practice over survival training, doesn't make them dead,

JOE: You're too sensitive for this.

   (*JOE continues to unpack boxes of canned goods. CHARLIE sits, pulls out his smartphone and giggles.*)

CHARLIE: These cats . . . that grumpy cat especially . . . did you see the one where it looks like the pope? They look exactly alike. I swear to . . .

   (*He holds up the phone for JOE to see. JOE smacks the phone out of his hand.*)

JOE: Grumpy cat's dead. It's the apocalypse, asshole! Wireless networks are down!

CHARLIE: The apocalypse is boring.

JOE: Not as boring as death! Make yourself useful, clean some guns or something.

CHARLIE: Let's make it the zombie apocalypse.

JOE: How about something real, like the rapture?

   (*Suddenly, JESUS CHRIST comes crashing through the door with a rifle pointed towards them. JOE and CHARLIE jump back with their hands up.*)

CHARLIE: Holy shit, Joe. (*Laughing.*) You really went all out with the drill.

JESUS: (*Threatening, Eastwood style.*) What are you laughing at, Charlie?

CHARLIE: Jesus, he knows my name! I mean, shit, he knows my name. Carl is that you? Stop foolin' around. (*He reaches for JESUS' beard to tug at it.*)

JESUS: Stop right there, Charlie! Joe, tell 'im. Ain't this what you been prayin for?

(JOE *says nothing.*)

JESUS: Joe . . .

JOE: Well . . . sure . . . kinda

CHARLIE: What the hell'd ya pray for Joe?

JOE: The second coming of . . . You know.

JESUS: (*Like a movie announcer.*) The Prince of Peace is back . . . only this time he's pissed . . .

CHARLIE: (*Softly nudging* Joe.) The prince of pissed. (*He snorts, trying to contain his laughter.*)

JOE: Uhh . . . at . . . at us? You're pissed at us, Jesus . . . sir?

JESUS: Not sure yet . . . just trying to sort it all out . . . a lot's changed since the Romans.

CHARLIE: Oh, we're not Romans. Guess you can just move along now.

(*Loud crash offstage.*)

JOE: (*Startled.*) So . . . uh . . . what's going on up above?

JESUS: The kingdom of God has many castles.

JOE: I think you're misquoting.

JESUS: You gonna fuck with Jesus???
      (*Jabs the rifle in his direction.*)
Christ???

JOE: I meant above the bunker . . . not above.
      (*Pantomimes the heavens.*)

JESUS: The rapture.
      (*A crack of thunder.*)

CHARLIE: Joe just mentioned that! That's when we get sucked up to heaven right? And all the sinners stay . . . Wait a minute, why are we still here?

JOE: I'm not goin'? I mean I get Chuck not goin', but me?

JESUS: Haven't decided yet.

(MARTHA *enters with a tray of sandwiches and cans of beer. She walks right into the middle of all of them.*)

MARTHA: Ok, boys. I've got PB&J, crusts cut off like you like 'em and warm beer because there is nooooooo refrigeration in the apocalypse. (*Noticing* JESUS.) Oh . . . I don't have one for you. I'll go get one.

JOE: Maaaartha, how many times I gotta tell you? No contact during a drill. No sandwiches, nothin'

(CHARLIE *takes a sandwich and starts eating it.*)

MARTHA: I know dear but I thought PB&J would be ok. It's survival food, something you might make if I were dead, when it's not a (*Air quotes.*) "drill."

JESUS: This is not a drill

MARTHA: Well, someone needs a snack.
(*She hands him a PB&J.*)

MARTHA: Since cranky pants here would rather eat spaghettios, you can have this.

(JESUS *takes the PB&J, letting his guard down for a moment.* JOE *grabs the gun from him and points it at* JESUS.)

MARTHA: (*Pushing the gun down.*) Joseph, don't be rude to our guest.

JESUS: He can't kill me, I'm already dead.

CHARLIE: Holy crap, Jesus is a zombie. He rose from the dead. The rapture *is* the zombie apocalypse!

JESUS: (*Takes a bite.*) God this is good. (*He sits at the card table to enjoy his sandwich.*)

MARTHA: Look at this place. The apocalypse is no excuse to be a slob.

JESUS: Rapture.

(*Crack of thunder.*)

CHARLIE: (*Under his breath.*) Zombie rapture.

MARTHA: Rapture shmapture.

JOE: Careful, Martha. Jesus is watching. We don't want to miss our chance. How exactly will you decide who to take . . . Jesus, can I call you Jesus?

(MARTHA *begins straightening up.* MOHAMMED, *a large black man, enters.*)

CHARLIE: Mohammed!

JOE: Who the fuck is this?

CHARLIE: Hey brother, what the hell you 'doin here?

(*They embrace.*)

MOHAMMED: You checked in on Facebook. I thought it was one of those drills you were telling me about . . . wanted to check it out.

JOE: (*To* CHARLIE.) You told him?

CHARLIE: If it were the real thing, wouldn't we be taking people into the bunker?

JOE: NOOOOOOO and certainly not the likes of him!

JESUS: Not very Christian. This is the rapture remember?

(*Crack of thunder.*)

Judgement Day is upon us.

(*He opens a bag of potato chips and a can of beer.* MARTHA *hands him a bowl for the chips.*)

CHARLIE: You should be thanking me. He's got a whole house full of weapons. They'll come in handy when the world ends.

JOE: (*Lifts the rifle.*) Chuck, get the feds on the phone. We got a jihadist on our hands.

MOHAMMED: I'm not Muslim.

MARTHA: Oh, thank God.

JOE: With a name like Mohammed? I'm a survivalist, not stupid.

JESUS: Same thing.

JOE: Chuck! The feds!

(CHARLIE *picks up his smartphone from the floor.*)

CHARLIE: Phone don't work.

JOE: Drill's over, this is serious! Call them.

CHARLIE: Musta broke when you smacked it to the floor.

JOE: Jesus Christ!

JESUS: Where would I keep a phone?

MARTHA: I'll get more sandwiches.

JESUS: No need.

(MARTHA *looks to the tray.*)

MARTHA: I only made two. Look, there are two more.

JESUS: And the cooler is full of beer.

MARTHA: Loaves and fishes. Maybe we were already raptured!

MOHAMMED: I'm just gonna go . . .

JESUS: I decide who goes.

MARTHA: Stay, have a sandwich.
(*She joins* JESUS *at the card table and begins passing out sandwiches.* MOHAMMED *heads to the door.*)

JOE: Stop right there, Obama bin Laden.

CHARLIE: Osama.

JOE: Same thing. Where'd you meet him, Chuck?

CHARLIE: Gun show.

(JOE *is so stunned that he lets the rifle down.*)

JOE: Are you fucking kidding me? That didn't raise a red flag for you?

CHARLIE: He was really helpful. I didn't know half the shit on that list you gave me and he and his partner helped me out.

(MOHAMMED *starts to back towards the door slowly.*)

JOE: His partner?

(*Stunned by this knowledge, he turns back to* MOHAMMED. *It does not register that* MOHAMMED *is trying to escape.*)

JOE: You can't be queer! Jesus. Are you hearing this???

JESUS: I hear everything

JOE: You're a fucking queer? Muslims can't be queer.

MARTHA: He says he's not Muslim, dear.

MOHAMMED: What do ya hate more, Muslims or queers? I'm black. I'll just be black, ok? Can I just leave now? You got nothing against black folk, right?

MARTHA: (*Condescending.*) Isn't the correct term (*Air quotes.*) "African American."

MOHAMMED: Seriously?

MARTHA: (*Sarcastic and self-righteous.*) Ooooooh, pardon me. I'm just trying to do the right thing, don't get all uppity.

MOHAMMED: Woman! You did not just . . .

(JOE *lifts the rifle and presses it against* MOHAMMED's *chest.*)

JOE: Are you going after my wife? Y'all like white women, doncha?

MOHAMMED: I was queer five minutes ago! Jesus! Hey, seriously, you have nothing to say about this?

JESUS: I'm sorry. I stopped listening.

MARTHA: He'd listen more if we allowed prayer in school, I know that much.

(JOE *pushes the rifle harder into* MOHAMMED's *chest.*)

MOHAMMED: Go ahead, shoot. I got a suicide vest on.

JOE: Get outta here.

MOHAMMED: I'm trying!

(JESUS *stands and walks between them.*)

JESUS: Wow, shit just got real, huh?

CHARLIE: Got that right.

(*He sits next to* MARTHA, *who hands him a sandwich.* JESUS *puts his hand on* MOHAMMED's *chest.*)

JESUS: Dude, you're gay? Black, Muslim . . . and gay? Really? I thought they frowned on that.

MOHAMMED: I thought you did.

JESUS: I don't give a shit. People love who they love.

MOHAMMED: All right, baby! Gimme some love!

(*They embrace.*)

JOE: The vest!!
(*He scoots under the card table for cover.*)

MOHAMMED: There's no vest. I just didn't want you to shoot me.

JESUS: Oh, it's not loaded. I'm still the Prince of Peace, trying to rebrand, fit in with the times. Hard to change who you really are.

(JOE *stands and walks towards* MOHAMMED.)

JOE: Gay? Black? Muslim? What is it?

MOHAMMED: American. All you need to know.

MARTHA: African American.

MOHAMMED: Ammerifuckincan!

(MARTHA *picks up the rifle and hands it back to* JESUS.)

MARTHA: Ok, drill's over. Let's all just go home and watch some TV, what do ya say?

JESUS: How many times do I have to tell you it's not a drill? It's the frickin' rapture. Now, who among you is without sin?

(*They all look around and at each other and, slowly, they raise their hands.*)

JESUS: Put your hands down. Don't be ridiculous. God, I'm sorry I came back. You shoulda had your shit together by now. You're all such a . . . disappointment.

CHARLIE: I went too far with the zombie thing right? Crossed a line?

JESUS: I'm leaving now.
  (*He heads to the exit.*)

JOE: But wait! (*Beat.*) What happens now?

JESUS: Exactly what you prayed for.
  (*He exits.*)

  (*Blackout.*)

END OF PLAY

A SLEEP AND A FORGETTING

by James McLindon

Premiere Production:
Nylon Fusion Theatre Company's This Round's On Us: Myth/Reality Festival
June 7 and 8, 2019
Tada! 15 West 28th, 2nd Floor
ADDIE: Brandi Bravo
EVAN: Ben Van Berkum

Director: Lori Kee
Sound: Andy Evan Cohen
Lights: Gilbert Lucky Pearto
Stage Manager: Clarissa Marie Ligon
Produced by Nylon Fusion Theatre Company

James McLindon is a member of the Nylon Fusion Theater Co. in New York. His play, *Salvation,* premiered in New York, Giovanna Sardelli directing, to critical acclaim in *The New York Times* and elsewhere. *Comes a Faery* was developed at the O'Neill National Playwrights Conference, Sean Daniels directing, was a finalist for the Humana Festival, and premiered at the New Ohio Theatre. *Distant Music* has been produced eight times across the country. *Dead and Buried* premiered at the Detroit Repertory Theater, received its second production at the University of Miami, and has been most recently performed by the Apollo Kine Theater in Estonia and Dreamcatcher Rep in New Jersey. Mr. McLindon's plays have been developed and/or produced at theaters such as the O'Neill (selection and six-time semifinalist), PlayPenn, Victory Gardens, Lark, Abingdon, hotINK Festival, Irish Repertory, Samuel French Festival, Edinburgh Fringe Festival, New Rep, Lyric Stage, Boston Playwrights, Local Theatre, Telluride Playwrights Festival, Great Plains Theatre Conference, and Seven Devils. His plays have been published by Dramatic Publishing, Smith & Kraus, and Applause Books and produced all over the world including London, Edinburgh, Ireland, Australia, the Philippines, Luxembourg, India, Dubai, and Estonia.

CHARACTERS

ADDIE, a woman, 20s or 30s, any race or ethnicity.
EVAN, a man about the same age, any race or ethnicity.

NOTE

Race-blind and diverse casting is encouraged.

SETTING

A lifeboat on the open sea. It should feel like the present.

• • •

> *Whither is fled the visionary gleam?*
> *Where is it now, the glory and the dream?*
>
> *Our birth is but a sleep and a forgetting;*
> *The Soul that rises with us, our life's Star,*
> *Hath had elsewhere its setting*
>   *And cometh from afar;*
> *Not in entire forgetfulness,*
> *And not in utter nakedness,*
> *But trailing clouds of glory do we come*
>   *From God, who is our home:*
> *Heaven lies about us in our infancy!*
> William Wordsworth, *Ode on Intimations of*
> *Immortality from Recollections of Early Childhood*

ADDIE *and* EVAN *are unconscious in the bottom of a lifeboat.* (*A boat is not necessary, and perhaps not even preferable.*) *The sail, previously raised, has fallen, covering* EVAN. *We hear waves, wind. and seabirds.* ADDIE *begins to stir. She sits up, a little disoriented. She's dressed in white flowing robes.*

ADDIE: What the fuck? (*Noticing she's at sea, alarmed.*) What the fuck!?

(EVAN *begins to stir under the sail, groaning. He is dressed in the same sort of robes.*)

ADDIE: Hey. Hey. Hello? Are you all right? (*Pulling the sail off him.*) Are you alive?

EVAN: Oooooooh. What happened?

ADDIE: I . . . I don't know.

EVAN: (*Still a little disoriented.*) What the fuck? (*Noticing they're at sea.*) What the fuck!?

ADDIE: I know, that's what I said!

EVAN: We're at sea!

ADDIE: I know! There's no land in any direction.

EVAN: Why are we at sea!?

ADDIE: Wait, *you* don't know?

EVAN: How would I know!? Don't *you* know?

ADDIE: No. I just woke up . . . or came to . . . or something. And here we were. Who are you?

EVAN: I'm the one you drugged and dragged off to sea, apparently.

ADDIE: I didn't drug and drag you off to sea! You must've drugged and dragged me off!

EVAN: Why would I do that?

ADDIE: Because . . . I don't know.

EVAN: You really didn't bring me here.

ADDIE: Do I look like a psychopath!?

EVAN: Well, you're dressed pretty weird.

(ADDIE *notices her robes for the first time.*)

ADDIE: Well . . . so are you!

(EVAN *notices his robes for the first time.*)

EVAN: Oh . . . yeah. (*Pause.*) I mean, one second, I'm minding my own business, just . . . just . . . Okay, I don't remember anything before coming to on this boat.

ADDIE: Neither do I.

(*They are perplexed. They both look out over the sea.*)

EVAN: What do we do?

ADDIE: Wait, I guess.

EVAN: For what?

ADDIE: Help to come.

EVAN: Why would help come?

ADDIE: Someone must be looking for us.

EVAN: We don't know if anyone else even knows we're here.

ADDIE: But . . . we must have come from somewhere. And somewhere must want us back.

EVAN: Unless somewhere was trying to get rid of us.

ADDIE: No, no, this is a lifeboat. That suggests some sort of disaster.

EVAN: Being lost on the ocean in a lifeboat *is* some sort of disaster.

ADDIE: I mean, that's what made someone put us in a lifeboat in the first place. Which means . . . we must have been on a bigger boat.

EVAN: That sunk. Let's look for a name. (*Looking around the boat.*) Ships stencil their name on all their crap.

(*They search the boat.* ADDIE *even hangs over the edge to look at its stern.*)

ADDIE: *Para . . . Paradiso.* It says *Paradiso.*

EVAN: We're from a ship named *Paradiso*!

ADDIE: And therefore, what?

EVAN: And therefore . . . I don't know. You come up with something!

ADDIE: Let's see what we have onboard.

(*They rummage around.*)

EVAN: Cases and cases of bottled water here.

ADDIE: There's a ton of food over here. Wow, gourmet stuff. Artisan breads, cheeses, all kinds of fruit. Oh my God, and wine!

EVAN: Throw me an apple, I'm starved.

ADDIE: (*Reaching for one, then stopping.*) Okay—Oh, wait. It says, "Do not eat."

EVAN: What does?

ADDIE: The bag is labeled, "Do not eat."

EVAN: Who would put food you can't eat in a lifeboat? That's stupid, throw me one.

ADDIE: No.

EVAN: Please throw me one.

ADDIE: No!

EVAN: C'mon . . .

ADDIE: What if they're contaminated!? Do you see a radio or an emergency beacon or flares?

EVAN: No.

ADDIE: You didn't even look. Look!

EVAN: (*Looking.*) I don't see anything like that. What if no one comes? How are we going to get home?

ADDIE: Then . . . we're kind of screwed, I guess.

EVAN: Well, I'm not giving up that easily.

ADDIE: I'm not giving up. But we don't know where we are or how we got here. We have no way to contact whoever might be out there. Drifting is all we can do. We can stay calm and drift or we can go batshit crazy and drift, but all we can do is drift.

(*A pause.* ADDIE *sits down.* EVAN *follows her lead reluctantly after a moment. They drift.*)

EVAN: Somebody's probably just messing with us. I heard this story about these guys whose buddy was getting married, so two days before the wedding, they threw him this awesome bachelor party, and you know, did the obligatory strip club.

ADDIE: Oh, strip clubs are obligatory?

EVAN: That's not important. What is, is that they got the groom shitfaced and two of them took him on a plane. To Poland, where they drove him into the countryside, took his wallet, passport. and clothes, left him there naked, and flew home.

ADDIE: Men are depraved.

EVAN: No, no, see, it was funny 'cause he didn't speak a word of Polish and when he went to this farmhouse naked, the farmer called the police—You've never been to a bachelor party, have you?

ADDIE: Yeah, I've missed so much.

EVAN: C'mon, can I have an apple?

ADDIE: No. Maybe whoever put us here did it because they cared about us. Maybe something apocalyptic happened at home. Maybe it was nuclear. Or terrorism. Or something. Something so horrible that whoever put us on this boat gave us some drug to make us forget . . . whatever we had seen.

EVAN: They had time to bring us to a doctor, administer an amnesiac, and get us a supply of apples that we can't eat, but not get us a radio? Or a GPS?

ADDIE: I don't know.

EVAN: (*Grabbing the bag of apples.*) I'm taking an apple!

(ADDIE *grabs the other end of the bag.*)

ADDIE: Look at all this other food! Eat something else!

EVAN: I don't want something else! Why would they have packed them? (*He pulls the bag free.*)

ADDIE: I don't know, maybe they're just for us to plant.

EVAN: On our boat.

ADDIE: Wherever we wash up. Look, probably no theory is going to make perfect sense because something very weird must have happened. Something beyond our understanding.

(EVAN *looks at the bag, then puts it down.*)

EVAN: Maybe we're just fucked. So, in the meantime, what do you want to do . . . y'know, to pass the time?

(*A pause. Suddenly,* EVAN's *eyes do a quick scan up and down over* ADDIE's *body.*)

ADDIE: Oh my God! It took you all of five minutes to get there.

EVAN: No, no, sorry, I didn't mean that. (*Pause*) Well, I mean, unless you want to. 'Cause it could be a long time. (*Smiling charmingly.*) C'mon, women tell me I'm not unattractive.

ADDIE: But they were bachelor party strippers working for tips. I can't believe it: Hashtag MeToo. In a fucking lifeboat.

EVAN: Okay, I'm sorry, I'm sorry. I'm kind of freaking out here. God, what if we die in this boat?

ADDIE: I don't think we will.

EVAN: Says the woman who thinks some catastrophe destroyed the world.

ADDIE: Someone must be out there. Or they wouldn't have bothered to put us in a boat.

EVAN: Yeah. Maybe. (*Taking an apple out of the bag.*) Have one with me. We can't figure this out if we're hypoglycemic.

ADDIE: If you eat one and get sick, then I've got to take care of you. If you die, I'm all alone. C'mon, we really need to not fight.

EVAN: Fighting makes a lot of sense. We're going to be in competition for the same scarce resources. (*Pause.*) I'm kidding.
(*He smiles.* ADDIE *is not amused.*)

ADDIE: If we cooperate, maybe we can figure out how to catch fish. We can take turns sleeping so someone is always awake if a ship or a plane goes by. There's really only one downside.

EVAN: What?

ADDIE: If we bond doing all that, it'll be harder to kill and eat you when the time comes. (*Deadpan pause;* EVAN *is a little unnerved; Finally,* ADDIE *smiles.*)

Kidding.

EVAN: You don't make cannibal jokes in a lifeboat! You just don't!

ADDIE: Sorry.

EVAN: My name is Evan. Okay? Now you know my name, so that'll make it harder for you to eat me.

ADDIE: Evan (*Pause.*) Sounds delicious. (*Offering her hand.*) I'm Addie.

> (EVAN *shakes it. Both sit.* EVAN *contemplates the apple.* ADDIE *leans back and looks up at the sky behind the boat.*)

ADDIE: It really is kind of beautiful out here.

EVAN: It's just water. Endless water.

ADDIE: No, no, look up. Those clouds trailing behind us. They're just . . . glorious.

> (EVAN *looks up for the first time.*)

EVAN: Wow. Wow! They really are.

ADDIE: At least we have that then. While we wait. For whatever.

EVAN: Yeah. (*Suddenly gently appreciating.*) Yeah. It is beautiful. You're right, at least we have that.

> (*They stare at the clouds. They wait.* EVAN *looks at his apple again. He starts to take a bite, then pauses. Then he decides and takes a bite. Distant thunder rumbles quietly.* ADDIE *looks around at the sky, then at* EVAN, *alarmed.*)

ADDIE: Evan? (*Seeing what he's done.*) Evan!

> (EVAN *freezes guiltily with his mouth full. More thunder, closer and louder.*)

> (*Blackout.*)

END OF PLAY

THREE MEN WITH GUNS

by Monica Bauer

Premiered Off-Off-Broadway as part of "Dark Planet: Not Your Mother's Valentine's Day" evening of short plays, presented by Planet Connections Theatre Festivity, February 6–21, 2020, at the Theater at the 14th Street Y, 344 E. 14th Street, New York City, directed by Lucia Bellini.

Original Cast:
DEVON: Russell Jordan
PACO: Randall Rodriguez
MIKEY: John Fico

Monica Bauer has had many short and full-length plays produced Off-Broadway, Off-Off Broadway, regionally, and internationally. She is an alumna of Boston University's graduate program in playwriting. Monica has won many awards, including Emerging Playwright Award, Urban Stages; winner, Tiny Plays for Ireland and America, presented at the Kennedy Center by Fishamble Theatre of Dublin. Full-length plays include *Made for Each Other*; Edinburgh Fringe, Orlando Fringe, Boulder Fringe Festival, Hollywood Fringe (Best Solo Show). *Chosen Child* premiered at Boston Playwrights' Theatre, and was nominated for an IRNE (Independent Reviewers of New England) award for Best New Play. *The Maternal Instinct* was a finalist for New South Writing Prize at the Brighton (UK) Fringe Festival. *Anne Frank in the Gaza Strip* won for Best New Comedy at the Planet Connections Theater Festivity Off-Off-Broadway, and *Vivian's Music, 1969* was a five-star hit at the 2018 Edinburgh Fringe Festival, followed by a run Off-Broadway at 59E59 Theaters, and is available from Original Works Publishing. Several plays are available from Brooklyn Press and Heuer. She is a proud member of the Dramatists Guild. Full production history, awards, and publications at www.monicabauer.com.

CHARACTERS

DEVON, mid 40s to early 50s, African American, very Alpha Male, carrying a messenger bag full of money, and a gun.

PACO, late 30s, very fit personal fitness instructor with a secret dream, carrying an empty gym bag with the name of his gym on it, and a gun, which he does not know how to use.

MIKEY, mid 40s, male, gay, carrying an empty Petco shopping bag, a gun, and a smartphone.

PLACE

A not-yet-gentrified part of the Bronx. In a dark alley.

TIME

Present day. Summer. Late night, after midnight.

• • •

Enter DEVON. *He is very aware of his surroundings, looking for someone, hand in his pocket. He sits on an old abandoned chair, maybe an old stained and abandoned recliner. Waits.*

Enter PACO. *Not so aware of his surroundings. Unsure of himself. Glances over at* DEVON, *tries to catch his eye without being obvious.* PACO *is trying very hard to look cool, and is not succeeding. Finally, he gets up the nerve to speak to* DEVON.

PACO: (*Nervous.*) Hey. Hi. Do you have the time, by any chance?

DEVON: No. Now if you don't mind, I'm meeting somebody here. So . . .

PACO: Maybe I'm the guy you're supposed to meet!

DEVON: (*Taking the full measure of a very nervous* PACO.) I don't think so.

PACO: Appearances can be deceiving. Right? I mean, you never know.

DEVON: It's my business to know. So, I am asking you nicely, since you're such a polite guy and all, to move along here.

PACO: (*Nervously pulling out a gun.*) Give me the money.

DEVON: (*Laughing.*) Really? I'm here for the guy who works for Benny. So, I am politely suggesting you get the hell out of here, before the right guy shows up.

PACO: But I have a *gun*.

DEVON: Look, I am not playing games with your unprofessional ass.

PACO: Unprofessional? Unprofessional? I have a *gun*.

DEVON: Oh, please. If you're a professional I'm a fucking Muppet. I'm fucking Elmo. Look at you! You've never held a gun before in your life! Chances are, you couldn't hit me if I stood still and smiled pretty. All I have to do is roll to the left or the right, you won't know which way to aim, and you'll end up shooting the hell out of that garbage can behind me. Whereas, I am a professional.
   (*He pulls his gun.*)
That means I can drop you at fifty feet, even if you're running like a fucking prize-ass Greyhound in pursuit of the mechanical rabbit. Do you understand? Nod if you understand.

   (*While PACO nods, MIKEY enters; DEVON and PACO immediately put their guns away before MIKEY can see them.*)

MIKEY: Benny sent me. I thought there was only supposed to be one of you.

DEVON: (*To MIKEY:*) Yeah, well. This is a friend of mine. He was just leaving.

MIKEY: Who brings a friend to a drug deal?

DEVON: Yeah, well. I do. Isn't that right, Taco?

PACO: Taco?

DEVON: An affectionate nickname based on his favorite meal. He was just leaving. See you later, Taco.
   (*PACO does not leave. DEVON pulls his gun again, points it at PACO.*)
Jesus, Taco, I was trying to do you a favor here. Give you a chance to walk away.
   (*DEVON speaks to MIKEY, taking his eyes off PACO.*)
This guy here, he's not really a friend. He's just some idiot who thinks he can rob me.

(PACO *realizes* DEVON *is no longer looking at him, so* PACO *pulls his gun and aims it at* DEVON.)

PACO: Apparently, I have to rob both of you now.

(MIKEY *pulls out a gun from his pocket.*)

MIKEY: Actually, I guess I have to rob both of you. You can both help me buy my farm.

DEVON: I take it you are not working for Benny. You want to buy a fucking *farm*?

MIKEY: Not a real farm, more like land, in a rural area. So I can raise puppies. The man at the bank said I ought to go rob a bank, but I don't know how to rob a bank. I *do* know how to do *this*.

DEVON: The hell you do, Mister Puppy Guy.

PACO: I think he knows how to do this. Look at him, his hand's not shaking at all.

MIKEY: What, because I'm gay you think I don't know how to do this? My ex-boyfriend works for Benny. He told me this goes down, every Thursday night.

PACO: Is his name Stanley?

MIKEY: Fuck me. You know Stan? How do you know Stan?

PACO: I'm his personal trainer. That's how I knew to come down here, Thursday night and all.

MIKEY: He wouldn't tell just any old personal trainer about . . .
(*He points his gun again at* PACO.)
Are you sleeping with my ex?

DEVON: Sweet Jesus, will you two take this somewhere else! Gay guy, and Hispanic gay guy?

PACO: I think maybe the two of us gay guys, we both got guns, even if one of us missed, the other would kill you, right? So maybe what this gay guy should do, is team up with the other gay guy, and we split the money. Then you, straight guy, you, like, run away.

MIKEY: Why would I split the money with you? You slept with my ex!

PACO: So what? He's your ex! He dumped you! That's what he told me!

MIKEY: What else did he tell you?

DEVON: (*Nobody is paying attention to him; he speaks almost to himself.*)
You're both dead if you don't get outta here before Benny's guy shows up.

> (MIKEY *puts his gun away.*)

MIKEY: So, let's decide this right now. Fair and square. Like those reality
shows, where the person with the best story gets the prize. I need the money
to buy a puppy farm. See, I got a beautiful Schnoodle from a place in
Pennsylvania.
> (*He flashes a photo he has of the dog on his phone, obviously his*
> *screensaver.*)
I named her Beyonce. She had a sparkle. But she also had advanced kidney
disease, on account of the way they treated her at that puppy mill! I spent all
of my life savings, and I couldn't save her. So. This isn't just for me. This is
for Beyonce. If you love animals, I suggest you both leave right now and give
that dirty drug money to me.

PACO: Yeah, but my story's even better. I need the money to start my own
gym. I can save *lives*. I am a trained *lifesaver*. But every gym that hires me,
every single boss, it's the same story, nobody's there for the right reasons!
People are dying of heart disease and diabetes, the boss tells me I gotta be
nice instead of giving these poor out of shape people the hard work and
discipline that can save their fucking lives!

> (DEVON *slowly and quietly starts to edge away from them to run away*
> *with the money.* MIKEY *notices* DEVON *trying to casually back away.*
> MIKEY *pivots and turns his gun on* DEVON.)

MIKEY: YOU! You aren't going anywhere until we settle this!

> (PACO, *startled by* MIKEY, *fumbles his gun, drops it, picks it up, and*
> *shakily aims it at* DEVON.)

DEVON: I'm the only one here who deserves the money. Because it's not for
me. Unlike the two of you, I'm not a criminal. (*Carefully looks around and*
lowers his voice.) I am an undercover cop. I got some racist Trump-loving
son of a bitch Lieutenant who gives me all these dangerous undercover
assignments, because he's hoping to get me killed! I've had to take this racist
bullshit for the last nineteen years, eleven months, and twenty-nine days.

I've got two days. TWO DAYS LEFT. I can retire on full pension when I get my twenty! And you know what I'm gonna do when I get my full pension? I'm going to go back to college and finish my degree in Black Studies. Then I'm going on to get my Masters and my Ph.D., and then I'm going to teach young people all about racism! If you let me continue with my operation, I am gonna follow Benny's bag man, and then we can arrest the whole crew. But if either of you idiots takes the money, then Benny himself is gonna come after me. I will end up dead, and Benny the criminal will keep right on being a criminal, and all those young people that I was going to teach about racism, they will never get to take a class in Black Studies. There is a shortage out there, people! I am fulfilling a cultural need.

PACO: But you called me Taco. Nobody who wants to teach about racism would call me that.

MIKEY: And you called me a name, too.

DEVON: What name did I call you?

MIKEY: You called me "gay guy." And you called him "Hispanic gay guy."

DEVON: (*In desperation.*) That's what undercover cops do, we play a part. Like a persona. Call people "Taco" and shit. I don't normally call people racial slurs. I apologize to you, sir. And to you; although strictly speaking, I don't think "gay guy" is a slur.

PACO: (*To MIKEY.*) And I should apologize to you for sleeping with your boyfriend, and getting him to tell me about his criminal activities. Honest, I don't usually poach. I don't even know your name.

MIKEY: It's Michael. But that sounds too serious. And "Mike" sounds like a straight guy from Wisconsin. So . . . Mikey. What's your name?

PACO: Paco. Which is disturbingly close to "Taco." Bullies used to call me "Paco the Taco." That's when I started working out. You wanna feel this bicep? I've got guns, you know what I mean?

DEVON: (*Sits down, heavily.*) Maybe it would be best if you both just shot me now.

> (*A beat:* MIKEY *looks long and hard at* DEVON, *seeing him perhaps for the first time.*)

MIKEY: But there's something bigger here, Paco. Something even bigger than real gyms to make people actually work out, and real puppy farms to raise healthier Schnoodles. There's this man, here.

PACO: That guy?

MIKEY: Yes, that guy. That beautiful proud black man. Reparations.

PACO: What now?

MIKEY: For slavery. African Americans, they ought to get some payback, for all those years, all those generations their families worked so hard to build this country up, and they didn't get paid. And after slavery, they still couldn't buy their own farms. They were forced to do share-cropping, and all the profit went to the one percent at the top. And then there was Jim Crow, and the Klan, and they didn't get the actual right to vote until the 1965 Civil Rights Act.

DEVON: I am impressed.

MIKEY: Well, I'm a dog groomer. We have MSNBC on all day long, so you learn a few things.

PACO: He called me Taco! So why not reparations for me?

DEVON: No offense, Paco, but you can kind of pass. In the right light, you got yourself some white privilege going for you. Whereas there's no way anybody's gonna take me for anything other than the beautiful Black man that I am. And that includes the racist Trump-loving, MAGA hat-wearing bastard who keeps sending me out on these things, hoping I'll get killed. But now, tonight . . .

(*He walks over to* MIKEY *and gently puts his hand with the gun still in it, on* MIKEY'*s shoulder.*) . . . some white guy I never met, he sees the entire social justice argument . . . reparations. That's amazing, man. Truly. You get it.

MIKEY: Reparations. It just feels . . . good.
    (*He pulls his phone out and takes a selfie with his new friend* DEVON.)
Like Rachel Maddow would be proud of me. I'm going home. And honestly, Paco, you make a pretty lousy criminal. So why don't you let the police officer here get on with his business?
    (*He starts to leave, tapping on his phone to post his selfie.*)

PACO: Wait! I bet you can get a pretty good workout in, training one of those big dogs. They need their exercise, too.

MIKEY: Have you ever seen a Schnoodle?

PACO: Have you ever considered trying to get in shape?
(Their eyes lock. They put their guns away. They have a moment. They kiss.)

END OF PLAY

TOBY 24/7 GETS LUCKY

by Tom Baum

Produced by Academy of Art University, San Francisco, March 6–7, 2020

TOBY: Tyler Ho
MARCY: Kenzie James

Directed by Tracy Ward

Tom Baum began his writing career as an NBC copywriter and speechwriter. After his first short story was published, in the *Transatlantic Review*, he was given a blind deal by E. L. Doctorow, then an editor at Dial, to write a novel (*Counterparts*). Over the next decades he published several more novels, including *Carny*, the young adult *It Looks Alive to Me!*, the children's book *Hugo the Hippo, Out of Body*, a *People* magazine "Beach Book of the Week," and, most recently, the young adult novel, *We Remember Everything*, and *The Sender*, based on his produced screenplay. While in New York he published several short stories in *Playboy* and *Playgirl*, and wrote three After School Specials. After moving to Los Angles, he worked as a feature and TV writer, alone (*Carny, The Sender*), with Marshall Brickman (*Simon, The Manhattan Project*), and with Wes Craven, as cocreator of the NBC series "Nightmare Café." His TV credits also include *Witness to the Execution* (Writers Guild Best TV Movie award), seven other TV movies, the miniseries *Journey to the Center of the Earth*, and six episodes of HBO's *The Hitchhiker*, one of which, "Made for Each Other," he directed. His produced full-length plays include *Human Services, Front Door Open, Breach, Endangered Species, and Shock Therapy*; produced one-acts: *Wonk Love, The Great Outdoors, Ashley Saves* *the World, Taps for Paps, Dork Love, SchadenFriday, Epicenter, The Out of Body Treatment for Marital Dysfunction, Toby 24/7 Gets Lucky*, and *Free Pass*.

CHARACTERS

TOBY, 20s–30s.
MARCY, 20s–30s.

SETTING

The living room of Toby's apartment, minimally suggested.

TIME

The present.

• • •

Lights up on the front room of TOBY's *apartment, suggested by a couch and a chair.* TOBY *and* MARCY *have just entered.*

TOBY: So, this is me. Can I take your coat?

MARCY: Oh. Yes. Thank you.

(*He hangs his hat and their coats on hooks by the door.*)

TOBY: Can I offer you something to drink?

MARCY: What do you have?

TOBY: Not that much, actually. Beer. Fruit juice. White wine.

MARCY: No tequila?

TOBY: Sorry, no tequila.

MARCY: It's OK. I'm past my limit anyway.

TOBY: Really? I didn't see you drink anything.

MARCY: I had two drinks before you came. And a drink before I left home.

TOBY: Yeah, some people do that.

MARCY: To get in the mood. Even to go to a bar. How pathetic is that?

TOBY: I don't think it's pathetic.

MARCY: Lori brought me there. My co-worker. She insisted.

TOBY: Why did she have to insist?

MARCY: Because I kinda hate crowded places. So, where's this bike you're selling?

TOBY: (*Evasive.*) Oh. Yeah. The bike. It's in my storage cage, downstairs. I don't ride it that much. I don't actually go out that much. Not that great with groups myself.

MARCY: Are you kidding? Everybody seemed to know you. "Hey, Toby 24/7." And asking for selfies. Like you were a famous person.

TOBY: (*Still evasive.*) Yeah, well, I get teased a lot. (*Pause.*) You sure you won't have anything to drink?

MARCY: No really, I'm fine. You must be in some commercial, right?

TOBY: Well ... yeah ... I've been on TV.

MARCY: I knew it! I have a box that skips the commercials, that's why I wouldn't know.

TOBY: Do you ever go online?

MARCY: Not anymore. Why, are you a famous blogger? I wouldn't know. I'm not even on Facebook anymore.

TOBY: Yeah, I used to be. I unfriended myself.

MARCY: It was totally trashing my self-esteem. But going cold turkey sucks, because that means I don't network with anybody except at my job. Not that I'm all that friendly at work. Is it ever worth it? People, right? Mostly, they can't wait to interrupt you, does that happen to you? Like they're totally bored of what you're saying.

TOBY: Like every day's their birthday.

MARCY: That's such a great way of putting it. Lori's like that. I don't think she ever let me finish a sentence.

TOBY: People suck.

MARCY: They all oughta go to N.A.

TOBY: N.A.? Oh wait. Narcissists Anonymous. That's great. I love that. Wow, I am so glad I got up the courage.

MARCY: Yeah, well, you saw me smile at you. And I never do that ever.

TOBY: You have a wonderful smile.

MARCY: Oh gosh. "Careful, Marcy." Oh no, there I go, channeling my mom. "Careful Marcy, you're getting excited." How many times did I hear that? "Don't get excited." Then two hours later, "What are you doing, just sitting there? Act like you're alive."

TOBY: "Do something but don't enjoy it."

MARCY: "Don't fidget so much, people are staring."

TOBY: "Don't call attention to yourself."

MARCY: Totally! We used to live in this apartment? Over this bitchy old lady, she was like 200 years old? She used to pound on the ceiling with a broom whenever I made any noise, not even noise, playing with my tea set or my farm animals, just talking to myself, humming to myself, whatever. I'd hear the broom, I'd feel the broom, right under where I was sitting—freaked me out every time. My mom never told her to stop, never stood up to her, if she saw the lady getting into the elevator, she'd take the stairs.

TOBY: Sounds like my mom.

MARCY: Seriously?

TOBY: OK. We had this ceremony in middle school? About saluting the flag? Each class had an official flag-bearer, and the flag got transferred from one kid to the other, and my mom couldn't come to see me because she was afraid I'd forget the stupid little speech I had to give. So, after that anytime I had to do anything public, like give a book report? I panicked. Like to show myself meant making her miserable.

MARCY: Wow. That is so . . . wow.

TOBY: So, I never raised my hand in class.

MARCY: Oh, me neither. I can't talk to more than one person at a time. And we have conferences all the time at work. I just sit there like a lump.

TOBY: But I'm getting over all that.

MARCY: I know. You seem very secure.

TOBY: Do I? Thank you. That means a lot.

MARCY: So, what's the secret?

TOBY: Well, OK. You have to ask yourself two questions. Who am I? And what am I afraid to be?

MARCY: OK.

TOBY: If you're shy and retiring, that means you really want to show yourself, but it scares you.

MARCY: Makes sense.

TOBY: What you're afraid to be, that's what you really are.

MARCY: If you're afraid of hurting people, you're really a secret sadist?

TOBY: Uh, yeah.

MARCY: If you're a prude about sex, you're really a secret slut?

TOBY: In most cases.

MARCY: The reason I ask . . . my mom said I'd probably die a virgin.

TOBY: My mom wanted me to die a virgin.

MARCY: She goes, "Marcy, If you find an ugly rich man, marry him, 'cause that's your only chance for happiness."

TOBY: "You'd better make a lot of money, Toby, otherwise you'll never find a wife."

MARCY: They really mess you up, don't they?

TOBY: They can't help it. They had parents too.

MARCY: Wow. I am so glad I met you, "Toby 24/7." I never share anything with anybody. And I mean ever. But I feel very safe with you.

TOBY: Safe. OK.

MARCY: No, don't take it like that! I didn't mean . . . like I would never expect you to hit on me, because I think you're gay or asexual or something? Because I don't think that. I mean I sensed a connection right away, that's why I even agreed to leave with you, which I have never done anything like that in my entire life. And it wasn't because people were fussing over you, don't shake your head, they were, you are definitely some kind of celebrity . . .

(TOBY *stops her with a sudden kiss. The kiss lasts until* MARCY'*s phone rings.*)

MARCY: Oh gosh.

TOBY: Who is it?

MARCY: It's Lori. From work. She wants to FaceTime.

TOBY: Is she wondering where you are?

MARCY: Probably. She saw me leaving with you. She's probably worried.

TOBY: You really think you have to talk to her?

MARCY: No. You're right. I don't. She's a total pest. She's probably jealous I left with somebody. She goes to that bar all the time and never hooks up and still she won't lose the weight.

(*Awkward pause.* TOBY *and* MARCY *are about to kiss again when the phone buzzes.*)

MARCY: Maybe I should tell her I'm OK. Otherwise she'll keep calling.

TOBY: If you ignore her, she'll probably get the message.

MARCY: I won't FaceTime, I'll just answer. (*Into phone.*) Hi, Lori.
(*She falls silent, listening. And begins to look alarmed.*)

MARCY: No . . . Ohmigod, I didn't mean to call you a pest, how did you . . . I didn't actually call you fat, oh gosh, this is so weird, what's going on here? (*Glancing around.*) I don't see any, no, are you sure? No . . . Lori . . . please don't do that, don't call my mom, I can take care of myself, goodbye!
(*She ends the call.*)

MARCY: God, I am so stupid! When were you going to tell me?

TOBY: Eventually.

MARCY: Eventually! Ohmigod. You don't have a bike to sell.

TOBY: No.

MARCY: Ohmigod, I can't breathe. Where's my jacket?

TOBY: It's there on the hook. Do you really have to go?

MARCY: Ohmigod, yes, are you kidding me? Where are the cameras?

TOBY: You can't really see the cameras, they're the size of a thumbtack.

MARCY: The whole apartment? Cameras everywhere?

TOBY: Uh-huh.

MARCY: Including the bathroom?

TOBY: Everywhere.

MARCY: You perv! What about in the bar tonight?

TOBY: I have a hat-cam. Basically, I'm known for never going out. But . . . you know . . . the fans . . . they were losing patience with Toby the Hermit.

MARCY: Does your mom know you've been doing this?

TOBY: She says she doesn't watch. She's lying.

MARCY: Like mother, like son. Goodbye, creep.

TOBY: Please don't say that. I don't want you to leave.

MARCY: I don't like the way you said that.

TOBY: How did I say it?

MARCY: Like you were planning to kill me.

TOBY: With all these witnesses?

MARCY: Maybe you want to be caught. Like a terrorist. Or just a regular psycho. No, don't touch me please. How many women have you . . . ? Never mind.

TOBY: How many women have I brought home?

MARCY: Murdered.

TOBY: Marcy . . . please. None. Zero. In fact, you are the first other person to set foot in this apartment . . . not counting the pizza delivery guy, and you couldn't really see him in the doorway. I'm not a terrorist, I'm not a murderer . . . Psycho? . . . There's a lot of debate about that, but I didn't bring you here to kill you. I brought you here because I liked talking to you. In fact, I love talking to you. And I'll say this now in front of all the people watching us, I've never felt so comfortable with anybody in my entire life.

MARCY: You're such a total liar.

TOBY: All right, don't believe me, I'm sorry I said it.

MARCY: How many people are watching?

TOBY: 500.

MARCY: Only 500? That's pathetic.

TOBY: 500 K. When all the hits are tallied, you'll be on a million screens and counting. You said you have trouble talking to more than one person? You're speaking to at least a million.

(MARCY's *phone rings. She freezes as she sees who it is.*)

Is that who—

MARCY: I asked Lori not to call my mom! Ohmigod, I have to take this.
    (*She answers the phone.*)

MARCY: (*Into phone.*) No . . . He's not . . . Because I'd already be dead and bleeding, that's why . . . I had two drinks before I left the house, that's my limit . . . I don't care if it's giving you palpitations, take a Xanax!
    (*She hangs up.*)

MARCY: A million people, seriously?

TOBY: Probably more after tonight.

MARCY: So, you must be monetized.

TOBY: A lot of product placement. There's a chance of an IPO.

MARCY: (*To unseen camera.*) Hear that, Mom? He's rich. (*To* TOBY.) What about your fans?

TOBY: What about them?

MARCY: They all saw me panic. I must look like a total dork.

TOBY: We'll wait for the comments. I'm kidding. I'm sure they'll like you.

MARCY: They weren't expecting a babe.

TOBY: They never said so.

MARCY: I mean nerds and babes, isn't that the trend now? Not that you're a nerd. I didn't mean that. (*To unseen camera.*) Everybody? I didn't mean that. (*To herself.*) Ohmigod, Marcy, you're getting excited.

TOBY: Why shouldn't you get excited. All those people watching, it's exciting.

MARCY: My teeth are chattering!

TOBY: Probably stage fright.

MARCY: You promise I won't die? You're not going to kill me?

TOBY: You will definitely survive the night.

MARCY: What about after?

TOBY: Depends how it goes.
    (*He kisses her. She kisses back, then breaks the kiss.*)

TOBY: Problem?

MARCY: You never turn off the cameras?

TOBY: It's kind of my brand, you know?

MARCY: Yes, well, could you possibly dim the lights?

TOBY: (*Pause.*) Yeah, I can do that.
    (*He picks up a remote, dims the lights. Then turns toward an unseen camera.*)
Mom, do yourself a favor? Turn it off and go to sleep.

    (MARCY *turns toward an unseen camera.*)

MARCY: Mom? Watch this.
    (*She grabs* TOBY *and kisses him passionately. Lights fade on their lovemaking.*)

END OF PLAY

TRUMPETTES ANONYMOUS

Parody of *Mom* (TV series)

by Rex McGregor

Originally produced at Midtown International Play Festival, Short Play Lab, Jewel Box Theatre, New York, New York, July 15–16, 2017.

Cast: Brie Brewer (JEL), Sarah Hewitt (WINDY), Lexie Marceron (CRUSTY), Aimee Thrasher (BONY), Janie Steele (MARGARINE)

Directed by Alice Camarota

Rex McGregor is a New Zealand playwright. His short comedies have been produced on four continents from New York and London to Sydney and Chennai. Rex is a member of the Playwrights Association of New Zealand. He has a master in arts (honors) in languages and literature from the University of Auckland and is currently a senior collections librarian at Auckland Libraries. http://www.rexmcgregor.com.

CHARACTERS

JEL, wealthy socialite, 30s.
WINDY, sensitive nurse, 40s.
CRUSTY, intense law student, 40.
BONY, free spirit, Crusty's mother, 50s.
MARGARINE, kindly retiree, 60s.

SETTING

A meeting room.

TIME

The present.

• • •

WINDY *is arranging five chairs in a circle.* JEL *is applying mascara.*

JEL: You been watchin' *The Crown*?

WINDY: Uh-huh. So romantic.

JEL: Them Brits are lucky. Havin' a strong woman at the top.

WINDY: We had our chance. And we blew it.

JEL: I blame poor people. They cain't be trusted with the vote.

WINDY: You voted for Trump too.

JEL: By accident. My shrink says I got daddy issues.

WINDY: Jel. We have to own what we did.

JEL: I owned up. The next mornin' I felt so dirty I needed a full body chemical peel.

WINDY: I feel terrible every day.

JEL: I'll text you the name of my beautician. She does a dandy hot stone massage.

WINDY: She couldn't rub away my guilt.

JEL: Try cucumber slices on your eyelids. They block out everythin'.

(CRUSTY *and* BONY *come in.* CRUSTY *wears a sweatshirt saying* NOT MY PRESIDENT.)

CRUSTY: Sorry we're late.

BONY: A kid offered Crusty his seat on the subway. Her lecture went on so long we missed our stop.

CRUSTY: I was only warning him of the slippery slope.

JEL: Slope? On a subway train? I always imagine them as kinda flat.

CRUSTY: The boy was on a dangerous path.

JEL: I'd never risk public transport.

BONY: Stage one: manners. Stage two: sexist remarks. Stage three: grabbing women by the hoo-ha.

CRUSTY: I did not say "hoo-ha!"

BONY: No. You said "vagina." Hardly the locker room lingo the kid's used to.

CRUSTY: He needs to learn correct terminology.

BONY: He turned redder than a chimp's ass.

CRUSTY: No need to be crude, Mom.

BONY: What's the Latin term, Windy?

WINDY: Gluteus maximus. For an individual buttock. Or glutei maximi for the whole rump.

BONY: Always handy to have a nurse around.

JEL: Can we get started? I got a new man waitin' at home.

WINDY: Not another father figure, I hope.

JEL: This one's super young. My pool guy. Miguel. Body like a Greek god.

WINDY: Not Cupid, I hope.

JEL: Don't worry. I asked him if he's legal. He said he is.

BONY: Probably referring to his immigration status.

JEL: Omigod! What if he's . . . ?

CRUSTY: Under age?

JEL: Mexican! Trump might deport him!

BONY: Before you've finished using him? I hate it when that happens.

WINDY: Let's begin the session. So Jel can get home and check her young man's status.

JEL: Shoot, I don't care if he's married. If I was that fussy, I'd never fill my monthly quota.

    (*They all sit down.*)

WINDY: Who'd like to start?

CRUSTY: Shouldn't we wait for Margarine?

WINDY: She said to go ahead without her.

BONY: First time she's missed a meeting.

WINDY: She said she had something to do. All very mysterious.

JEL: Maybe she's got a pool guy.

CRUSTY: She's got a husband.

JEL: That never stopped me.

BONY: We know, Jel. You even had Margarine's husband, didn't you?

JEL: Before they got hitched. I don't hookup with a friend's current squeeze.

BONY: I'm relieved to hear it.

JEL: Keep an eye on your fella, Bony. You and me ain't that close.

WINDY: I'll start. My name's Windy. And I voted for Donald Trump.

BONY, CRUSTY and JEL: Hi, Windy.

WINDY: I have no excuse. I wasn't happy with some aspects of Obamacare. I thought a small protest vote would stop Hillary from getting too cocky when she became President. She was miles ahead in the polls. It wasn't supposed to end like this. I'm so sorry! I'm so sorry!
    (*She whimpers.*)

BONY, CRUSTY and JEL: Thanks, Windy.

CRUSTY: Hi, I'm Crusty. I voted for the asshole too.

JEL: Hi, Crusty.

BONY: Shouldn't that be "cavity of the glutinous maxi-whatever?"

CRUSTY: Mom! No crosstalk!

BONY: Maternal instincts override meeting rules.

CRUSTY: I've been clean for [nine] weeks, four days and one and a half hours. My addiction is totally under control. I haven't touched a single erotic novel. Or had a single masochistic fantasy. I've successfully managed a tough regime of strict self-denial.

BONY: She always was a glutton for punishment.

CRUSTY: My law studies are going well. Currently focused on censorship legislation. I'm confident we'll soon be able to ban the entire *Fifty Shades* series.

BONY: My daughter the liberal.

CRUSTY: It's a starter drug, Mom! First you get hooked on toy handcuffs and light spanking. And before long you're in a voting booth ticking the name of a self-confessed sexual predator!
   (*She folds her arms high over her chest, covering the "NOT." BONY notices and nudges* JEL.)

JEL: Should we tell her?

BONY: Against the rules.

CRUSTY: What? . . . Windy?

WINDY: Your arms. They're covering the "not."

   (CRUSTY *furiously takes off her sweatshirt and scribbles out the word "President." She tries to rip the shirt. But when she fails, she jumps up and down on it and kicks it away.*)

BONY: All done?

CRUSTY: Totally!

JEL and WINDY: Thanks, Crusty.

BONY: My turn. Bony here. I voted against Hillary.

JEL and WINDY: Hi, Bony.

BONY: Special treat today. I'm finally gonna confess my motive. You all know me as a sophisticated pansexual. But believe it or not, I was once an innocent young thing. A rose not yet plucked.

(CRUSTY *stifles a guffaw.*)

CRUSTY: Sorry.

BONY: I met this wonderful guy . . . '75.

JEL: Seventy-five! You got granddaddy issues?

BONY: It was 1975. I fell hard. But Hillary landed him. When someone steals my man, there's no statute of limitations on my revenge.

JEL: Good to know.

CRUSTY: Mom? Did Bill *BLEEP-bleep* pluck you?

BONY: Let's just say, when I told you who your father was . . . there was no paternity test.

CRUSTY: You mean . . . ?

BONY: If you want to check his DNA, ask *Bleep-bleep-bleep Bleep-BLEEP-bleep.* She might still have that dress.

CRUSTY: Honestly, Mom!

JEL: Don't freak out, Crusty. It ain't like Bony slept with Donald *Bleep.*

BONY: Well, actually . . . after I lost my first crush my libido was in a very vulnerable place.

(CRUSTY *gasps.* MARGARINE *comes in.*)

WINDY: Margarine. You made it.

MARGARINE: I've just popped by to say I won't be coming to these meetings anymore.

WINDY: Why not?

MARGARINE: My country needs me.

BONY: What's all this?

MARGARINE: I voted for Trump out of empathy with the underdog. I assumed he was about to suffer a humiliating defeat. I made a big mistake.

WINDY: We all did.

MARGARINE: We feel regret. But millions of women are celebrating. They're thrilled to have that man in the White House. They heard how he treated women. And they forgive him. They heard from his victims. And they ignore them. Their blind adoration smacks of Stockholm Syndrome. They're victims too. So, this afternoon I joined the Republican Party.

CRUSTY: Have you lost your mind?

MARGARINE: I'll do whatever it takes to help women in need. Tonight, I'm off to my first meeting for genuine Trumpettes.

JEL: Margarine. It's real nice how you emphasize with folks. But you cain't solve everythin' with emphysema.

MARGARINE: I don't expect you to understand, Jel.

BONY: That'd be asking way too much.

MARGARINE: My meeting's at eight. Must dash.
　　(*She starts to leave. But* CRUSTY *restrains her.*)

CRUSTY: You're not going anywhere!

MARGARINE: What the blazes!

CRUSTY: Not till we've talked sense into you.

WINDY: Crusty! Remember. "No fixing. No advice giving."

CRUSTY: She didn't sit down. The rules don't apply.

MARGARINE: Let go of me!

CRUSTY: Grab my sweatshirt, Jel! We'll use it to tie her up.

JEL: I don't mind some kinky stuff. But I ain't into bondage.

MARGARINE: You're assaulting a woman, Crusty! You're taking after Donald Trump.

CRUSTY: He's not my father!
　　(*She releases* MARGARINE.)

BONY: Relax, honey. I always use protection with sleazeballs.

MARGARINE: Come with me, Crusty. Come with me to the meeting.

CRUSTY: What?

MARGARINE: Let's all go. I bet these Trumpettes have never met the likes of us. Let's shake them up.

CRUSTY: You said you're gonna help them.

MARGARINE: With tough love. God grant me the serendipity to change the things I can't accept. Cunning to change the things I can. And willfulness to make a difference.

WINDY: I'm game. How about you, Bony?

BONY: Always up for a challenge.

WINDY: Jel?

JEL: Them society dames look down their noses at me. I been through too many of their husbands.

MARGARINE: Formal meetings have strict rules ensuring courtesy and respect.

JEL: Wow. Count me in.

MARGARINE: That leaves just you, Crusty.

CRUSTY: Do they let everyone have their say?

MARGARINE: Of course. They may not be Democrats. But they believe in democracy.

CRUSTY: And they're not allowed to heckle?

MARGARINE: Standard meeting protocol frowns on interruptions.

CRUSTY: OK. Lemme at 'em! My systematic reasoning will be irrefutable.

BONY: Not another lecture! I need a drink.

END OF PLAY

YOU ARE HERE

by Nandita Shenoy

You Are Here was originally produced at The Atlantic Acting School in New York City on October 24 and 26, 2019, directed by Zora Howard. The original cast was as follows:

ONE: Raka Dey
TWO: Bintou Cisse
THREE: Cristina Villalobos Ureña
FOUR: Anastasia Martin

Nandita Shenoy is an actor-writer who lives in New York City. When not creating theater or supporting her fellow theater artists, Nandita enjoys cooking with bacon, eating chocolate, and writing about shirtless men. As an actor, Nandita was most recently seen in the Off-Off-Broadway production of Adam Szymkowicz's play, *Marian, or the True tale of Robin Hood,* at the New Ohio Theater produced by Flux Theatre Ensemble. Prior to that, she starred in the Off-Broadway Production of her own play, *Washer/Dryer.* She has also been a part of the World Premier casts of *Trouble Cometh* by Richard Dresser at the San Francisco Playhouse and of *Some Other Kind of Person* by Eric Pfeffinger at Philadelphia's InterAct Theater. Favorite roles include "Amita" in *Sloppy Second Chances* by Mrinalini Kamath at EST, and "Seema" in *The Last Surviving Heir* by Sarovar Banka at Desipina's 7-11 Theater. She was a member of the Repertory Company of the Alabama Shakespeare Festival for a season where she played the roles of "Ursula" in *Much Ado About Nothing*, "Miss Poppenghul" in *Moonlight and Magnolias*, and "Lucius" in

Julius Caesar. She can also be seen in national commercials for IBM, GoDaddy, and HP. Nandita's latest full-length play, *Satisfaction*, was presented as part of the "Main Stage Live" program at the American Academy of Dramatic Arts after readings at the Ma-Yi Writers' Lab Labfest and the Philadelphia Women's Theatre Festival in 2016. Her play, *Washer/Dryer*, had its Off-Broadway premier at Theatre Row in February 2016, produced by Ma-Yi Theater. *Washer/Dryer* received its World Premiere at EastWest Players in February 2015 as a part of their 50th Anniversary Season. Washer/Dryer was also seen in Chicago as part of Rasaka Theatre's residency at Victory Gardens in October 2015. Another full length play, *Lyme Park: An Austonian Romance of an Indian Nature* was produced by the Hegira at the Round House Theater in Silver Spring, Maryland. Her one-acts *Marrying Nandini, By Popular Demand, Rules of Engagement*, and *A More Perfect Date* have received full productions in New York City from Green Light Productions, New Perspectives Theater, New Ground Collective, and Eating Theater, respectively. She is also the recipient of the 2014 Father Hamblin One Act Commission Prize from the Abingdon Theater. Nandita's plays have been read at the Kennedy Center, the Asian American Writers' Workshop, Second Generation, Salaam Theater, the Bleecker Street Theater, The Lark Play Development Center, and by the Red Harlem Readers. In addition to creating theater, Nandita is an advocate for diversity in the theater and sits on the Steering Committee of the Asian American Performers Action Coalition and is a member of the advisory board of the Bingham Camp Theatre Retreat, a development space for musical theater. She has also been a participant of the South Asian Theater Arts Movement. Nandita holds a BA from Yale University in English literature with a distinction in the major. She is a member of the Ma-Yi Writers' Lab, the Dramatists Guild, and the Lincoln Center Directors Lab. She is a proud member of AEA and SAG-AFTRA.

CHARACTERS

ONE, female, 20s, woman of color; the natural leader of the room, likes
    order.
TWO, female, 20s, woman of color; the most contrary of the residents,
    questions everything.
THREE, female, 20s, woman of color; the most laid back of the group,
    happy to go with the flow, enjoys The Room.
FOUR, female, 20s, woman of color: the newest addition to The Room,
    naïve, curious.

A NOTE ON CASTING

While the women are not specifically ethnically identified, all of them should be women of color so that the utopia that the four of them have fallen into is one for them, a space both free from racism and sexism, in theory.

• • •

Lights up on a soft space with a strong decorative style. This can mean what you want it to mean: a white space with lots of pillows, primary colors and bean bags, pastels and chaise lounges. Whatever the décor is, it should reflect a sense of softness and tranquility. Maybe like the waiting room of a spa. Three women are lounging languidly when a fourth falls into the room screaming.

FOUR: Aaaaaaaaaaaaah!

ONE: Did we know another one was coming?

TWO: No.

THREE: Three is a difficult number.

TWO: Is it a difficult number?

THREE: I find it troubling.

TWO: Okay.

FOUR: What's happened? Where am I?

ONE: You are Here!

FOUR: Where?

TWO: Does it matter?

THREE: It really doesn't.

FOUR: I'd like to know.

ONE: All will be revealed.

TWO: Will it?

ONE: Yes.

THREE: Sure.

TWO: You are?

THREE: So contrary today.

TWO: I'm not.

THREE: You are.

TWO: Okay.

FOUR: WHERE AM I?

ONE: Listen, honey. It doesn't really matter because now that you're Here, you're not going anywhere else.

TWO: Or you might.

THREE: But probably not for a while. You'll like it; you'll see!

TWO: Or, maybe you won't.

THREE: You'll at least feel grateful.

FOUR: Grateful? For what?

ONE: Well, the bad stuff is over. And you look great. Probably a lot better than when you . . . (*Makes a dying motion.*) So, there's that.

FOUR: When I???

THREE: Yeah, you know. (*Repeats ONE's motion.*) What was yours like? Was it violent? Were you sick?

FOUR: I???

ONE: Yes, you. (*Repeats the motion.*) Don't you remember?

FOUR: No. Wait. Maybe. Yes?

ONE: It's okay. Why don't you take a load off? Over here! Relax! It'll help you remember.

TWO: If you feel like remembering. Some of us don't.

THREE: Fair. That's very fair.

FOUR: I don't know. (*Looks at her own body.*) Wait. Am I young?

ONE: Uh-huh.

FOUR: As young as you?

TWO: Not exactly, but who wants to argue?

ONE: But only your body. You are however old you are. How old are you?

FOUR: 83?

ONE: Damn!

THREE: The oldest!

TWO: Don't forget Anna was 84.

THREE: Well, Anna's not here, is she?

FOUR: Where's Anna?

ONE: She's moved on. From Here.

FOUR: Why?

THREE: We don't know.

TWO: Does one ever know? Why we go anywhere?

THREE: This behavior does not suit you.

TWO: I know. But what to do?

THREE: Try!

TWO: But isn't that the beauty of Here? We don't have to try?

FOUR: So, I'm?
    (*Makes motion.*)

ONE: Mmm-hmmm.

FOUR: And now I'm here?

ONE: Here.

FOUR: But my body is young?

ONE: Mmm-hmmm.

FOUR: But I'm still old.

ONE: Mmm-hmmm!

THREE: That's the dream! Your older mind with your younger body. How many times did you say There "if I only knew then"?

ONE/TWO/THREE: "what I know now."

TWO: So, there you have it! Tea?

FOUR: Is there a point?

TWO: Of course!

THREE: That's the most positive I have seen you be in eons! I'm so pleased!

FOUR: Eons? You've been here eons?

ONE: Hard to tell.

THREE: Time is strange. And it doesn't really matter so much. Now.

ONE: Because we're Here. We get to relax.

THREE: Be ourselves.

TWO: Do whatever we want, however we want to do it. It's very liberating.

FOUR: It's just the three of you?

THREE: Well, now four including you.

FOUR: Where's everybody else?

TWO: Who cares?

FOUR: And this is okay with you?

TWO: Does it have to be?

THREE: Oh, there she is.

ONE: It's just what it is. We try to enjoy.

THREE: Yes, of course, we do. Give it a try!

TWO: Did you want tea? I'm making some.

FOUR: Sure. I guess. So, you can eat and drink?

THREE: Of course! What would be the point if you couldn't?

ONE: It's part of the reward. Or at least, that's my theory.

FOUR: None of you know why you're here?

TWO: Did you know why you were There?

FOUR: I didn't. But I thought it would be revealed to me, Here, or somewhere.

THREE: Wait a second, were you white back There?

FOUR: No. Were any of you?

ONE/TWO/THREE: No!

THREE: Oh, thank goodness!

ONE: Phylicia! Don't say that!

THREE: I can say what I want. That's the beauty of Here!

TWO: She has a point.

FOUR: Is this heaven? For others?

ONE: Hard to say.

THREE: I believe the kids call it "people of color" now.

TWO: How would you know if it was?

THREE: You are working my last nerve with the questions.

TWO: Okay.   •

FOUR: Is it women only? Where are the men?

TWO: What men?

ONE: There are no men!

TWO: Why would you want men?

ONE: This is an oppression-free space.

THREE: We think it is.

TWO: Mostly.

THREE: Eva!

TWO: What? What?

ONE: We try not to oppress ourselves either. But sometimes that can be hard.
(*Gives a stern look to* TWO *and* THREE.)

It can be hard to unlearn the bad habits of There.

THREE: Yes, very difficult.

FOUR: So now what?

ONE: Whatever!

FOUR: Whatever?

ONE: Well within reason. Here. You do what you want Here until you move on. It's generally very pleasant and not stressful, unlike There which was generally unpleasant and stressful for the likes of us. And I like to think that the reward for surviving it for so long—I mean you! 83 years!—(is Here. No worries, no money, no bother! If you don't like that tea you can always wander back to the champagne fountain.

FOUR: This is a lot to take in.

THREE: It is. But I find it's easier to adjust if you relax into it. Enjoy having a healthy body!
(*She does a cartwheel.*)
I mean, when was the last time you did that?

FOUR: 1973.

THREE: See?

ONE: I could never do that There, but I can Here!
(*She turns a cartwheel, too.*)

TWO: You couldn't do a cartwheel?

ONE: Terrible balance.

FOUR: Hmmm . . .

TWO: You might ask yourself, "What does it mean?" And the answer could be nothing. Or everything. Because what if all the crap you went through in your life, in your career, in your family—what if it led you Here? And you'll think "If I knew that, I wouldn't have done this or that. I wouldn't have cared about the small slights or worried about the money or held on to those toxic relationships that we all had." And maybe that's true. But you don't know because maybe that time you told your friend about the man who made the hairs on your neck stand up, she avoided getting in his car and narrowly missed coming Here many years too soon. And maybe that's why you're Here where you can relax and rest and be who you are without worry even if sometimes you do get on your closest friend's last nerve. Here you can let it all go and recognize that the worry is just a vestige of There that you don't need any more. And maybe that's the point of Here."

THREE: (*Tearing up.*) Am I really your closest friend?

TWO: Aren't you?

(TWO *and* THREE *hug.*)

FOUR: And now I'm Here?

ONE: You are!

FOUR: And I can do anything? Without fear?

TWO: Doesn't it sound grand?

THREE: So different from There!

(*All four women sigh a content sigh.*)

FOUR: I am Here!

END OF PLAY

Ten-Minute Play Producers

Actors Studio of Newport
TASN Short Play Festival
http://www.newburyportacting.org/
Marc Clopton
info@newburyportacting.org

Acts on the Edge (Santa Monica, CA)
mariannesawchuk@hotmail.com

American Globe Theatre Turnip Festival
Gloria Falzer
gfalzer@verizon.net

The Arc Theatre
arciTEXT Ten-Minute Play Festival
Natalie Sallee
natalie@arctheatrechicago.org

Artistic Home Theatre Co.
Cut to the Chase Festival
Kathy Scambiatterra, Artistic Director
artistic.director@theartistichome.org

Artist's Exchange
One Act Play Festival
Jessica Chace, Artistic Director, OAPF
jessica.chace@artists-exchange.org
www.artists-exchange.org

The Arts Center (Carrboro, NC)
10x10 in the Triangle
Jeri Lynn Schulke, Director

theatre@artscenterlive.org
www.artscenterlive.org/performance/opportunities

A-Squared Theatre Workshop
My Asian Mom Festival
Joe Yau
jyauza@hotmail.com

Association for Theatre in Higher Education
New Play Development Workshop
Charlene A. Donaghy
charlene@charleneadonaghy.com
http://www.athe.org/

Auburn Players Community Theatre Short Play Festival
Bourke Kennedy
bourkekennedy@gmail.com

The Barn Theatre
www.thebarnplayers.org/tenminute/

Barrington Stage Company
10X10 New Play Festival
Julianne Boyd, Artistic Director
jboyd@barringtonstageco.org
www.barringtonstageco.org

Belhaven University (Jackson, MS)
One Act Festival
Joseph Frost, Department Chair
theatre@belhaven.edu

Black Box Theatre
FIVES New Play Festival
Nancy Holaday, Producer
(719) 330-1798
nancy@blackboxdrama.com

Blue Slipper Theatre (Livingston, MT)
Marc Beaudin, Festival Director

blueslipper10fest@gmail.com
www.blueslipper.com

Boston Theatre Marathon
Boston Playwrights Theatre
Plays by New England playwrights only
Kate Snodgrass
ksnodgra@bu.edu
www.bostonplaywrights.org

Boulder Life Festival (Boulder, CO)
Dawn Bower, Director of Theatrical Program
dawn@boulderlifefestival.com
www.boulderlifefestival.com

The Box Factory
Judith Sokolowski, President
boxfactory@sbcglobal.net
www.boxfactoryforthearts.org

The Brick Theater's "Tiny Theater Festival"
Michael Gardner, Artistic Director
mgardner@bricktheater.com
www.bricktheater.com

Broken Nose Theatre
Bechdel Fest
Benjamin Brownson, Artistic Director
ben@brokennosetheatre.com
www.brokennosetheatre.com/bechdel-fest-3

The Brooklyn Generator
Erin Mallon
brooklyngenerator@outlook.com
https://www.facebook.com/TheBrooklynGenerator/info

Camino Real Playhouse
Show!Off Playwriting Festival
kathyfischer@cox.net
www.caminorealplayhouse.org

Celebration Theatre
WriteHer Festival
Women Playwrights
Alli Miller
festival@celebrationtheatre.com
www.celebrationtheatre.com

Chalk Repertory Theatre Flash Festival produced by Chalk Repertory Theatre
Ruth McKee
ruthamckee@aol.com
www.chalkrep.com

Chameleon Theater Circle (Burnsville, MN)
jim@chameleontheatre.org
www.chameleontheatre.org

Chagrin Valley Little Theatre
10-10 New Plays Festival
cvlt@cvlt.org
www.cvlt.org

Changing Scene Theatre Northwest
Pavlina Morris
changingscenenorthwest@hotmail.com

Cherry Picking
cherrypickingnyc@gmail.com

Chicago Indie Boots Festival
www.indieboots.org

City Theatre
Susan Westfall
susan@citytheatre.com
www.citytheatre.com

City Theatre of Independence
Annual Playwrights Festival
www.citytheatreofindependence.org

The Collective New York
C10 Play Festival
thecollective9@gmail.com
www.thecollective-ny.org

Colonial Playhouse
Colonial Quickies
colonialplayhousetheater@40yahoo.com
www.colonialplayhouse.net

Company of Angels at the Alexandria
Box 3480
Los Angeles, CA 90078
(213) 489-3703 (main office)
armevan@sbcglobal.net

Core Arts Ensemble
coreartsensemble@gmail.com

Darkhorse Dramatists
darkhorsedramatists@gmail.com
www.darkhorsedramatists.com

Darknight Productions
4 Women Only and 4 Men Only
www.darknightproductions.com

Distilled Theatre Co.
submissions.dtc@gmail.com

Driftwood Players
shortssubmissions@driftwoodplayers.com
tipsproductions@driftwoodplayers.com
www.driftwoodplayers.com

Drilling Company
Hamilton Clancy
drillingcompany@aol.com

Durango Arts Center 10-Minute Play Festival

Theresa Carson

TenMinutePlayDirector@gmail.com

www.durangoarts.org

Eden Prairie Players

www.edenprairieplayers.com

Eastbound Theatre 10 Minute Festival

Themed summer festival

Tom Rushen

ZenRipple@yahoo.com

East Haddam Stage Company

Kandie Carl

Kandie@ehsco.org

Emerging Artists Theatre

New Works Series

https://newworkseries.com/submissions/

www.emergingartiststheatre.org

En Avant Playwrights

Ten Lucky Festival

www.enavantplaywrights.yuku.com/topic/4212/Ten-Tucky-Festival-KY-dead
line-10-1-no-fee#.UE5-nY5ZGQI

Ensemble Theatre of Chattanooga Short Attention Span Theatre Festival

Garry Posey, Artistic Director

garryposey@gmail.com

www.ensembletheatreofchattanooga.com

Fell's Point Corner Theatre 10 x 10 Festival

Richard Dean Stover

rick@fpct.org

www.fpct.org

Fem Noire

Image Theatre

Plays by New England women playwrights

imagetheaterlowell@gmail.com
www.imagetheater.com

Fine Arts Association
Annual One Act Festival-Hot from the Oven Smorgasbord
ahedger@fineartsassociation.org

Firehouse Center for the Arts (Newburyport, MA)
New Works Festival
Limited to New England playwrights
Kimm Wilkinson, Director
www.firehouse.org

Flush Ink Productions
Asphalt Jungle Shorts Festival
www.flushink.net/AJS.html

The Fringe of Marin Festival
Annette Lust
jeanlust@aol.com

Fury Theatre
katie@furytheare.org

Fusion Theatre Co.
info@fusionabq.org
http://www.fusionabq.org

Future Ten
info@futuretenant.org

Gallery Players
Annual Black Box Festival
info@galleryplayers.com

Gaslight Theatre
gaslighttheatre@gmail.com
www.gaslight-theatre.org

GI60
Steve Ansell
screammedia@yahoo.com

The Gift Theater
TEN Festival
Michael Patrick Thornton
www.thegifttheatre.org

Good Works Theatre Festival
Good Acting Studio
www.goodactingstudio.com

The Greenhouse Ensemble
Ten-Minute Play Soiree
www.greenhouseensemble.com

Heartland Theatre Company
Annual Themed 10-Minute Play Festival
Mike Dobbins, Artistic Director
boxoffice@heartlandtheatre.org
www.heartlandtheatre.org

Hella Fresh Fish
freshfish2submit@gmail.com

Hobo Junction Productions
Hobo Robo Festival
Spenser Davis, Literary Manager
hobojunctionsubmissions@gmail.com
www.hobojunctionproductions.com

The Hovey Players (Waltham, MA)
Hovey Summer Shorts
www.hoveyplayers.com

Image Theatre
Naughty Shorts
jbisantz@comcast.net

Island Theatre 10-Minute Play Festival
www.islandtheatre.org

Ixion Ensemble (Lansing, MI)
Jeff Croff, Artistic Director
Ixionensemble@gmail.com

Kings Theatre
www.kingstheatre.ca

Lake Shore Players
Joan Elwell
office@lakeshoreplayers.com
www.lakeshoreplayers.com

Lee Street Theatre (Salisbury, NC)
Original themed 10-minute play festival
Justin Dionne, Managing Artistic Director
info@leestreet.org
www.leestreet.org

Little Black Dress Ink
Tiffany Antone
info@LittleBlackDressINK.org
www.LittleBlackDressINK.org

Little Fish Theatre Co.
www.litlefishtheatre.org

Live Girls Theatre
submissions@lgtheater.org

Little Fish Theatre
Pick of the Vine Festival
holly@littlefishtheatre.org
www.littlefishtheatre.org/wp/participate/submit-a-script/

Luna Theater
New Moon Short Play Festival
lunatheater@gmail.com
www.lunatheater.org

Madlab Theatre
Theatre Roulette
Andy Batt
andy@madlab.net
www.madlab.net/MadLab/Home.html

Magnolia Arts Center (Greenville, NC)
Ten Minute Play Contest
Fee charged
info@magnoliaartscenter.com
www.magnoliaartscenter.com

Manhattan Repertory Theatre (New York, NY)
Ken Wolf
manhattanrep@yahoo.com
www.manhattanrep.com

McLean Drama Co.
Rachel Bail
rachbail@yahoo.com
www.mcleandramacompany.org

Miami 1-Acts Festival (two sessions—Winter (December) and Summer (July)
Submission requirements: no more than 10–15 pages in length; subject is not specific, though plays can reflect life in South Florida and the tropics and the rich culture therein. Area playwrights are encouraged to submit, though the festival is open to national participation. Deadline for the Winter Session is October 15 of each year; deadline for the Summer Session is May 1 of each year.
Steven A. Chambers, Literary Manager
schambers@new-theatre.org
Ricky J. Martinez, Artistic Director
rjmartinez@new-theatre.org
www.new-theatre.org

Milburn Stone One Act Festival
www.milburnstone.org

Mildred's Umbrella
Museum of Dysfunction Festival
info@mildredsumbrella.com
www.mildredsumbrella.com

Mill 6 Collaborative
John Edward O'Brien, Artistic Director
mill6theatre@gmail.com

Monkeyman Productions
The Simian Showcase
submissions@monkeymanproductions.com.
www.monkeymanproductions.com

Naked Angels
151 Bank St.
New York, NY 10014
Jean Marie McKee, Artistic Director
www.nakedangels.com

Napa Valley Players
8 x 10: A Festival of 10 Minute Plays
www.napavalleyplayhouse.org

Newburgh Free Academy
tsandler@necsd.net

New American Theatre
JoeBays44@earthlink.net
www.newamericantheatre.com

New Jersey Rep
Theatre Brut Festival
Annual festival organized around a specified theme
njrep@njrep.org

New Short Play Festival
https://www.newshortplayfestival.com/

New Urban Theatre Laboratory
5 & Dime
Jackie Davis, Artistic Director
jackie.newurbantheatrelab@gmail.com

New Voices Original Short Play Festival
Kurtis Donnelly
kurtis@gvtheatre.org

NFA New Play Festival
Newburgh Free Academy
May not accept electronic submissions
201 Fullerton Ave, Newburgh, NY 12550
Terry Sandler
terrysandle@hotmail.com

North Park Playwright Festival
New short plays (no more than 15 pages, less is fine)
Submissions via mail to:
Jeff Bushnell and Summer Golden
North Park Vaudeville and Candy Shoppe
2031 El Cajon Blvd.
San Diego, CA 92104
jfbushnell@cox.net
zgolden1@cox.net
www.northparkvaudeville.com

North Park Vaudeville and Candy Shoppe
2031 El Cajon Blvd.
San Diego, CA 92104
Summer Golden, Artistic Director
www.northparkvaudeville.com

Northport One-Act Play Festival
Jo Ann Katz
joannkatz@gmail.com
www.northportarts.org

The Now Collective
Sean McGrath
Sean@nowcollective@gmail.com

NYC Playwrights
Play of the Month Project
http://nycp.blogspot.com/p/play-of-month.html

Northwest 10 Festival of 10-Minute Plays
Sponsored by Oregon Contemporary Theatre
NW10Festival@gmail.com
www.octheatre.org/nw10-festival

Nylon Fusion
nylonsubmissions@gmail.com
www.nylonfusioncollective.org

Onion Man Productions Summer Harvest
onionmanproductions@gmail.com

Open Tent Theatre Co.
Ourglass 24 Hour Play Festival
opententtheater@gmail.com

Otherworld Theatre
Paragon Festival
Sci-fi and fantasy plays
Elliott Sowards, literary manager of Otherworld Theatre and curator
of the Paragon Play Festival
elliott@otherworldtheatre.org
www.otherworld.org

Over Our Head Players (Racine, WI)
www.overourheadplayers.org/oohp15

Pan Theater (Oakland, CA)
Anything Can Happen Festival
David Alger
pantheater@comcast.net
http://www.facebook.com/sanfranciscoimprov

Pandora Theatre (Houston, TX)
Vox Feminina
Melissa Mumper, Artistic Director
pandoratheatre@sbcglobal.net

Paw Paw Players One Act Festival
www.ppvp.org/oneacts.htm

Pegasus Theater Company (Sonoma County, CA)
Tapas Short Plays Festival
Lois Pearlman
lois5@sonic.net
www.pegasustheater.com/html/submissions.html

Philadelphia Theatre Company
PTC@Play New Work Festival
Jill Harrison
jillian.harrison@gmail.com
www.philadelphiatheatrecompany.org

PianoFight Productions (Los Angeles, CA)
ShortLivedLA@gmail.com

Piney Fork Press Theater Play Festival
Johnny Culver
submissions@pineyforkpress.com
www.pineyforkpress.com

The Playgroup LLC (Boca Raton, FL)
theplaygroupllc@gmail.com
www.theplaygroupllc.com

Playhouse Creatures
Page to Stage
newplays@playhousecreatures.org

Play on Words Productions
Megan Kosmoski, Producing Artist Director
playonwordsproductions@gmail.com

Playpalooza
Backstage at SPTC (Santa Paula Theatre Co.)
John McKinley, Artistic Director
sptcbackstage@gmail.com

Playwrights' Arena
Flash Theater, LA
Jon Lawrence Rivera
jonlawrencerivera@gmail.com
www.playwrightsarena.org

Playwrights' Round Table (Orlando, FL)
Summer Shorts
Chuck Dent
charlesrdent@hotmail.com
www.theprt.com

Playwrights Studio Theater
5210 W. Wisconsin Ave.
Milwaukee, WI 53208
Michael Neville, Artistic Director

Renegade Theatre Festival
www.renegadetheatre.org

Salem Theatre Co.
Moments of Play
New England playwrights only
mop@salemtheatre.com

Santa Cruz County Actor's Theatre
Eight Tens at Eight
Wilma Chandler, Artistic Director
ronziob@email.com
http://www.sccat.org

Secret Room Theatre
Alex Dremann
alexdremann@me.com
www.secretroomtheatre.com

Secret Rose Theatre
info@secretrose.com
www.secretrose.com

Secret Theatre (Midsummer Night Festival) (Queens, NY)
Odalis Hernandez
odalis.hernandez@gmail.com
www.secrettheatre.com/

She Speaks, Kitchener (Ontario, Canada)
Women playwrights
Paddy Gillard-Bentley
paddy@skyedragon.com

Shelterbelt Theatre (Omaha, NE)
From Shelterbelt with Love
McClain Smouse
associate-artistic@shelterbelt.org
submissions@shelterbelt.org
www.shelterbelt.org

Shepparton Theatre Arts Group
"Ten in 10" is a performance of 10 plays each running for 10 minutes every year
info@stagtheatre.com
www.stagtheatre.com

Short+Sweet
Pete Malicki, Literary Manager
Pete@shortandsweet.org
http://www.shortandsweet.org/shortsweet-theatre/submit-script

Short Play (NYC)
admin@shortplaynyc.com
https://shortplaynyc.com

Silver Spring Stage (Silver Spring, MD)
Jacy D'Aiutolo
oneacts2012.ssstage@gmail.com
www.ssstage.org

Sixth Street Theatre
Snowdance 10-Minute Comedy Festival
Rich Smith
Snowdance318@gmail.com

Source Festival
Southern Repertory Theatre
6x6
Aimee Hayes
literary@southernrep.com
jenny@culturaldc.org
www.southernrep.com/

Stage Door Productions
Original One-Act Play Festival
www.stagedoorproductions.org

Stage Door Repertory Theatre
www.stagedoorrep.org

Stage Q
www.stageq.com

Stillwater Short Play Festival (Stillwater, OK)
Town and Gown Theatre
Debbie Sutton, Producer
snobiz123@aol.com

Stonington Players
HVPanciera@aol.com

Stratton Summer Shorts
Stratton Players
Rachel D'onfro, President
info@strattonplayers.com
www.strattonplayers.com

Subversive Theatre Collective
Kurt Schneiderman, Artistic Director
info@subversivetheatre.org
www.subversivetheatre.org

Ten Tuckey Festival
doug@thebardstown.com

The Theatre Lab
733 8th St., NW
Washington, DC 20001
Buzz Mauro
buzz@theatrelab.org
202-824-0449
https://www.theatrelab.org/

Theatre Odyssey (Sarasota, FL)
Tom Aposporos, Vice President
www.theatreodyssey.org

Theatre One Productions
theatreoneproductions@yahoo.com

Theatre Out (Santa Ana, CA)
Theatre Oxford 10 Minute Play Contest
LGBT plays
David Carnevale
david@theatreout.com
Alice Walker
10minuteplays@gmail.com
http://www.theatreoxford.com

Theatre Roulette Play Festival
Madlab Theatre Co.
andyb@mablab.net

Theatre Three
Jeffrey Sanzel
jeffrey@theatrethree.com
www.theatrethree.com

Theatre Westminster
Ten Minute New (And Nearly New) Play Festival
Terry Dana Jachimiak II
jachimtd@westminster.edu

Williamstown Theatre Festival
10x10 New Play Festival
wtfinfo@wtfestival.org
www.wtfestival.org

Theatre Works 10-Minute Play Festival
https://theatreworks.us/playfestival-event.php

Those Women Productions
www.thosewomenproductions.com

TouchMe Philly Productions
touchmephilly@gmail.com
www.touchmephilly.wordpress.com

Towne Street Theatre Ten-Minute Play Festival
info@townestreet.org

Underground Railway Theatre
Debra Wise, Artistic Director
debra@undergroundrailwaytheatre.org
www.undergroundrailwaytheatre.org

Unrenovated Play Festival
unrenovatedplayfest@gmail.com

Walking Fish Theatre
freshfish2submit@gmail.com

Weathervane Playhouse
8 X 10 Theatrefest
info@weathervaneplayhouse.com

Wide Eyed Productions
playsubmissions@wideeyedproductions.com
www.wideeyedproductions.com

Winston-Salem Writers
Annual 10 Minute Play Contest
info@wswriters.org
www.wswriters.org

Write Act
John Lant
j316tlc@pacbell.net
www.writeactrep.org